Combat I

MW00934113

Pushing Pencils under Fire

By

Nick Stevens

To Kip. All the
best!

For my friends & comrades.

P. M., thank you for giving me the strength to share this.

Thank you, H.H., for reminding me of my promises.

PREFACE

First off, thank you for purchasing Combat Bureaucrat and taking the time to read it. This book is a long-time goal of mine to tell the story of what I experienced as an Army Officer assigned to a remote combat outpost in Afghanistan. I started this project to help deal with some of the lingering PTSD symptoms I was suffering from when I returned from my last combat tour at the end of 2010. At first, this book was just a few isolated stories and notes about some of the more troubling things I experienced over there. After a few months though, I found myself composing an entire narrative. I found the more I got these experiences onto paper, the less they were banging around in my head. The more this deployment to Afghanistan transitioned to a novel, the less of a recurring story it was in my everyday life. In short, it became my own self-directed therapy. Originally I had no intention of sharing this with anyone, but after I had verbally shared some of my war stories and thoughts with my closest friends and loved ones, I received a lot of positive feedback. Almost unanimously, my small sample group wanted me to share my story with a wider audience.

I still wasn't going to do it though. I was too worried, too scared about what people would think about the book; what people would think about me. I was a very angry young man and this was a dark time for me. It wasn't until an Army comrade got nominated for an Oscar that I decided to go for it. I won't get into exactly how it happened here, but you can go to my blog at underwhelmer.com to read the whole story for yourself. Here's the link if you're interested.

http://underwhelmer.com/2016/02/03/on-being-the-impostor/

Long story short, we spoke to each other in Afghanistan about what we wanted to do after the Army. He wanted to make films and I said I wanted to be a writer. His nomination for the Oscar was amazing and I was so proud, but it also showed a key difference between us. He kept his promise to himself, followed through on his dreams, and I didn't. I wasn't writing and, by extension, keeping those promises I made to myself. I had to change that.

So here we are. Newly motivated, I listened to my friends and loved ones and actually finished the book. What follows over the next couple hundred pages is my loosely chronological account of what happened over there. A few house-keeping notes though before we dive in...

First, I am not a military historian. This story is how I remember events unfolding. It is not about specific dates or battles nor does it provide an in-depth analysis of military strategy. This book is about the emotional and personal journey of one guy trying to hold it together over there. I've done my best to make this book easy to understand for those with and without military backgrounds. Also it should be noted that my memory, although pretty good, is not perfect and I'm bound to have messed up some details.

Secondly, I've written this account from my perspective and largely in a vacuum. Meaning, this story is entirely in the first person and I haven't corroborated with everyone mentioned in the book. They may have experienced things differently and are wholly entitled to their versions of what happened.

Thirdly, and feeding into the previous point, I've changed the names and some physical descriptions of the people directly mentioned in the book. This is a point that I went back and forth over for a long time. I wanted to keep the real names in the book for authenticity purposes, but I soon realized that everybody may not like how I represented or remembered them. Also, more importantly, I may have remembered a person (or their actions) incorrectly and I don't want to rake anyone across the coals unjustly. The purpose of this book is not to slander any one person or organization, but to tell my story as I remember it. That being said, I decided not to use the real names of people to give those mentioned a degree of separation from the account that follows.

Lastly, this book is written with as little political and ideological slant as I can manage. I'm not politically charged and, quite frankly, I find our political arena to be a giant circus so you shouldn't expect much bias from me there. I'm no longer in the

Army and I can't use this to further my career as an Officer so you're safe on that front too. It should be noted that Combat Bureaucrat doesn't show anyone (myself included) in a particularly good or bad light. It's just what happened as I remember it; the tears, the blood, the absurdity, the fear, the laughs, the frustrations and the triumphs. Now, what I can't cut out is my sarcasm and dark sense of humor. You're going to have to endure that shit... sorry.

Still on board? Ok then. Let's get started.

PROLOGUE

If ever you found yourself in a valley in Afghanistan, your eyes would eventually wander up toward the mountains that likely surrounded you. Their peaks would be snow-capped year-round even though you'd probably be sweating your ass off in the valley below. In 2010, I found myself encircled by such mountains and sweating appropriately. This particular range, somewhere north of Charkh Valley in Logar Province, stretched impossibly before me into the distance, rising and falling over the horizon. It looked like some giant monster had come here to die and its bones had fossilized.

The sky was oversaturated blue. The clouds were long white wisps. It was August and waves of heat distorted the horizon in the distance. The sun beat down on my neck and my assault rifle was hot to the touch even through my ballistic gloves.

A few kilometers away, I could see twin gray specks trace slow lines across the sky. Those little dots were my F-16 fighter jets, courtesy of the US Air Force. I had pulled some strings and called in a lot of favors to get them dedicated to me for this mission. We often called them *fast movers* but they appeared to be anything but at the moment. They followed each other at what seemed like a relaxed pace from so far away. They were right where I wanted them; kilometers away, out of earshot and almost completely out of sight.

I was acting Commander of Bulldog Troop and this was my operation, my attempt to send our local chapter of the Taliban packing. Our actual commander was out on R&R for about a month and it was up to me, his executive Officer (or XO for short), to take up the torch and lead missions in his absence. As an XO, I was chiefly responsible for keeping our Soldiers fed and supplied and to generally handle all of the logistical concerns so that my commander could focus on leading his Troops in battle. It was a bureaucratic and mundane job that included a lot of lists, highlighters and number-crunching, but it had to be done. Lately, I had been taking care of all the combat missions and all of the logistical concerns simultaneously while the boss was away. Handling two big jobs was beginning to wear on me. I started calling myself a *combat bureaucrat* to keep things light. I sometimes even carried my highlighters and stapler out on patrol with me. My Soldiers would always grin when they saw my bright highlighters poking out of one of my ammo pouches on my ballistic vest. "You never know when good documentation practices might save your life, Soldier." I'd say.

That was usually good for a laugh, but there was little laughing now. I was tired and everything was beginning to ache. My feet were starting to throb. We had been walking for a while and my sixty or so pounds of armor, weapons, radios and ammunition amplified the impact of each step. I slowed my pace and took stock of the seventy American Soldiers and fifty Afghan National Army Soldiers that followed me. We were moving in tactical formation across the brown steppes. We had just wrapped up our mission and were headed back to the outpost. We left a series of orchards and a village behind us and were now entering open ground and headed toward our helicopter extraction point. We had to do nearly everything purely on foot or with helicopters. The terrain was so treacherous that any vehicles we used were constrained to one or two main roads in the valley. These roads, of course, were almost always mined and booby-trapped so we stuck to walking as often as we could.

The men eyed every moving tree branch and I watched some of the Soldiers as they triple checked their weapons. They were anxious, but that was to be expected; we would be fighting for our lives soon. The Platoon in front of me, Red Platoon, had moved its machine gunners to its southwestern flank to better face the mass of trees that would likely hide our future attackers. I took my gaze toward the rear of the formation and saw that the trailing Platoon, Blue Platoon, had done the same. The third and final Platoon, White Platoon, had taken up a good support position on some high ground a few hundred meters away, covering our advance. We wanted to brace as much as we could for the imminent attack without fully showing our hand.

Those last few minutes before our transport helicopters came were always our most vulnerable during any mission. Our Chinook helicopters couldn't land in anything but open ground due to the large air-frame and the wide footprint of their dual-rotor design. The Taliban fighters would be looking for an opportunity to hit us on our way out too; that quick sucker punch while we were busy coordinating with the helicopters and embarking our Troops. Killing US Soldiers was always on the Taliban agenda, but being able to down an American helicopter was likely a promotion and possibly a hefty cash reward for any mid-level enemy commander. It must've looked too good to be true when we left the relative protection of the vineyards and mud-brick walls of the village and crossed into open, vulnerable ground.

A small scooter engine buzzed and whined in the distance. The Taliban used scooters as an early warning system and they had been trailing us the entire day. A single shot suddenly cracked about a kilometer to our south and confirmed my suspicion. They were communicating with each other by firing single AK-47 rounds into the air. The Taliban scouts would ride a single scooter in pairs and place an assault rifle between the rear passenger and the driver so as to appear unarmed. We had to get them to stop them and then get them off the scooter to see if they had a weapon. To counter this, they would simply take one of the dozen or so tiny side trails and avoid all of our checkpoints. Other than killing everyone we saw on a scooter (which admittedly was very tempting at times) there wasn't much we could do to keep from being observed by enemy scouts during every mission.

Normally enemy scouts deeply annoyed me, but today they were doing exactly what I wanted them to do. They had taken the bait and were reporting our movements. Seventy Americans in the open plus the chance to shoot down a helicopter or two was too good an opportunity to pass up. What they didn't know was that my two F-16s were each loaded up with two thousand pound bombs. At a word, they would swoop down and drop their payload right onto the heads of the Taliban fighters that had done their best to kill us these past six months. I was going to turn the tables on their little ambush. Their golden opportunity to kill some Americans would quickly land them in a deadly trap. As the only person with command authority within a ten kilometer radius, I had already given my ground commander's clearance to my Fire Support Officer, Lucas Rollins, to speed up the upcoming close air support mission. I glanced over at Lucas. Despite the heat, the weight of the bulky radio on his back and the imminent fight ahead, he was smiling. He knew there was a good chance that our plan was going to pay off and that in moments we were going to eliminate a significant portion of the Taliban right here in our own back yard. I felt a small grin at the edge of my mouth. It was a bit of a gamble, but it looked like it was going to work.

I pulled my headset a little closer to my mouth and spoke across the radio, addressing all of my Platoon leaders, "Guidons, this is Bulldog 5. Get ready. They're going to hit us any moment now."

"Bulldog 5, this is Red 6. Roger." Lieutenant Woods replied.

"Bulldog 5, this is White 6 Roger." Lieutenant Lynch, quickly thereafter.

"Bulldog 5, this is Blue 6 Roger. We've got you covered." Came Captain Harper's reply.

When we had walked three hundred meters across open ground from the vineyards and mud-brick walls, all hell broke loose. The Taliban opened fire with Cold War era rounds that cracked and hissed through the air. As one, our entire formation went prone to the ground and returned fire. I steadied my weapon and put my scope up to my eye, searching for targets. I saw enemy fire coming from a mud-brick building at the edge of the vineyards. A clump of earth exploded in front of me and sprayed dirt and debris into my face; spoiling my aim. Our machine guns rattled their reply, mortars boomed and Sergeants shouted over the din.

It was time to let the outpost know that we were in a real fight. I pulled the mic close to my face and shouted over the chaos at my headquarters radio station. "Bulldog X-Ray, this is Bulldog 5! Contact! 200 degrees, 400 meters from my last given location! Estimate 20 enemy fighters!"

"Bulldog 5, this is X-Ray. Acknowledged all."

I turned to Lucas, pointing to him. "Do it! Drop the bombs! Commander's initials NAS!"

Lucas began shouting into his radio, bringing the F-16s toward us on an attack vector. We only had a few minutes before the Taliban withdrew. They would hit us as hard as they could and then fade back into the vineyards and villages like they had done countless times before. They did this so they could withdraw before our aircraft and heavy artillery could be brought to bear. Fighting against a modern American Army unit is much like running on a treadmill that increases its incline and speed over time. Given time, it will be nearly impossible to continue as we increase the intensity of the fight with the addition of artillery, aircraft and reinforcements. The Taliban had learned their lesson early in the war. Once they had fired that first shot at us, they knew they were on a timer. They would engage us as long as they could before they had to cut their losses and withdraw. That day, we weren't going to give them the chance to do so. If we could preoccupy and fix these Taliban fighters for a little longer, we could wipe them out. They would not be expecting bombs to be falling on their heads mere seconds into the firefight. It was going to work; it had to work.

Several rounds slammed into the ground next to me. A few others cracked and hissed angrily by my head. The air was rapidly filling up with fast-moving metal. I glanced over my shoulder and saw my Afghan National Army counterpart, Commander Haled, firing an RPK light machine gun from the hip. It was the first time that I noticed that his weapon didn't have a shoulder stock to steady his aim. Part of our mission in Afghanistan was to help train the Afghan National Army units in our area. Most of them were brave, but ill-disciplined and unskilled Soldiers. The contingent with me that day was no exception. Haled's marksmanship was like the expression on his face, wild and uncontrolled. His rounds mostly flew in the general direction of the enemy, but some of them struck mere inches from where I lay prone. As I rolled away from the exploding dirt, screaming obscenities that he couldn't understand without an interpreter, I realized that there now existed the very real possibility that I would be accidentally shot by my own side. I rolled onto my back and shouted at him to stop, but he was too focused on blazing away at the Taliban. I did my best to make myself as small as possible behind a nearby boulder. Fortunately, he ran out of ammunition a moment later and began fumbling with a fresh magazine. I went back to what I was doing and buried my eye back into my scope, searching for targets.

I spotted two Taliban fighters about two hundred meters away, taking shots at us over a mud-brick qalat wall. They would come up, take a shot or two and then duck back down. I settled my red crosshair above one of the fighters, adjusting for the distance. They weren't shifting their positions; just shooting, ducking down and then re-emerging from the same spot. They were being lazy and they paid for it. I gently squeezed two rounds into each fighter; their figures dropping down behind the wall for good. I had always been a good marksman so shooting people felt like the most straight-forward and honest part of my job. There must have been dozens of them because I had just killed or wounded two fighters, but the enemy seemed completely undeterred by the loss. The level of incoming enemy fire intensified. We needed those bombs dropped and we needed them as soon as possible.

I scanned the sky for the F-16s and I was startled to see them screaming overhead, just a few hundred feet above us. I had somehow not heard them approaching over all the chaos and noise. The F-16s zoomed by, seconds away from dropping their deadly payload. The full volume of their engines caught up a split-second behind the jets themselves and momentarily drowned out the sound of our firefight.

Some of the men were cheering as the planes streaked toward their target like wrathful Valkyries. I spared a glance over to Lucas. Something was wrong. Lucas was shouting into his radio. I couldn't hear what he was saying over the aircraft engines. I turned back to the F-16s and, to my horror, watched them pull up from their attack vector.

We were all stunned for a moment. Some of us were kneeling, others in the prone but all of us shared that dumb look of disbelief. Even the Taliban had stopped shooting at us for a moment, no doubt as surprised as we were. Our planes were not going to drop their bombs on the enemy. The enemy was right there, plain as you like and we just let them go. Our one shot, our gamble, just slipped through my fingers. What's worse, we had shown our hand to the enemy. The Taliban had seen that our aircraft were not going to engage them. We were stuck in the open and on our own.

"You get those fucking planes to do their jobs and drop those fucking bombs!" I screamed in near panic at Lucas.

"I did! Saber Command is canceling the airstrike!" He replied, shock and disbelief in his eyes as he pressed the headset to his ear.

"What?!?!? They fucking can't, Lucas! I'm the commander out here and these are my planes!"

My radioman, Sergeant Ingram, was a few feet away. He was tuned in to the command channel so I ripped the radio headset out of his hands and started screaming at Saber Command, "Saber X-Ray, this is Bulldog 5 over!"

I was met with dead air. "Saber X-Ray, this is Bulldog 5, what the *fuck* is going on?!?"

There was more dead air on the line. I turned to Lucas, "Can you get anybody? What the fuck is happening?"

Lucas was about to reply when the Taliban renewed their attack. An enemy mortar round exploded a few dozen feet in front of me, showering Lucas, Ingram and I in dirt and debris. Rocket propelled grenades and recoilless rifle rounds howled by. The Soldiers of Bulldog Troop replied with their own withering barrage of fire. The firefight went back and forth for a few moments; each side attempting to shower the other with hot metal. When it became clear to the Taliban that we weren't easy prey, they began to melt back into the vineyards and villages.

There was a tense moment where we were all waiting for the

shooting to pick back up again. A single M4 carbine shot rang out next to me and I saw a dog topple over in the distance, toward where our Taliban attackers had been in the mud-brick building only moments before.

"Fuck your fucking dog, hadji fuckers." Sergeant Ingram grunted through clenched teeth, smoke coiling out of his weapon. He had shot the dog out of pure spite and anger.

I knew I should have scolded him for shooting some Afghan's dog. We weren't mindless killers and this wasn't what we did. At that moment though, I wanted to burn down the entire valley along with everyone in it. So yes, fuck you and your fucking dog. Ingram was only guilty of feeling what we were all feeling; the unbridled frustration that was our constant companion during this dirty little war.

"Sir! We have a clear path down this wadi! We can follow it about three hundred meters and then flank them!" Woods' voice came across the radio. I could see the lip of the wadi in front of his Platoon.

"No Woods. Hold what you've got. They're already gone." I responded. The trees were completely still then.

Woods didn't reply because he knew that there was a good chance that I was right and the enemy had already melted away. Scooter engines whined and buzzed in the distance, no doubt whisking away some of the enemy dead and wounded. Unless they were cornered or caught in the open, pursuing Taliban fighters as they withdrew was almost always a bad idea. Best case scenario, they would simply outpace our cumbersome and heavily armed Soldiers in the dense terrain and we would spend hours finding nothing. Worst case scenario, they would lead us directly into a string of prepared ambushes and concealed IEDs and booby-traps. I wasn't going to press my luck that day.

"Guidons, this is Bulldog 5. Give me personnel, ammo and equipment reports ASAP. Unless anybody's got any serious casualties, we're moving in 2 minutes." I sounded over the radio network. After all the "affirmatives" came back over the radio, I moved closer to Lucas so only he and I could hear each other. I had a few minutes to figure out what happened before we had to move again.

"What the fuck was that, Lucas?" I asked.

"Fucking Saber Command. They must've called up the F-16's controlling unit, Pyramid Air, and then told them there was an unmanned drone below the F-16s. It stopped the airstrike dead in its tracks." He replied, unable to hide the disappointment in his face.

Saber Command was our direct command, our boss out here twenty four hours a day, seven days a week. Saber Command referred to our Squadron Commander (or SCO) and or his direct Staff Officers that spoke with his authority. My experience with them, during this deployment, was so overwhelmingly negative that I couldn't keep the disdain out of my voice. Just the mental image of our SCO's face was enough to put me on edge. "Why the fuck would Saber Command do that? We had the enemy dead in our sights."

"I know, Nick. It was going to go through and then..."

I cut him off, "Lucas, do you see a fucking drone anywhere out here?"

"There isn't one, Nick." he replied without having to look at the sky. "They were worried about civilians possibly getting caught in the bombs and just made some shit up to stop the airstrike."

"The only civilians out there are the ones shooting at us." I said, stabbing a finger toward the now smoking mud-brick compound. I continued, "I assessed the risk and made the call. Command is over ten kilometers away and have no fucking idea what's going on out here. *I fucking do!*"

"I know man. You don't have to convince me because I know this is fucking stupid. Command isn't getting shot at. They're miles away, safe on their little base in the middle of nowhere. Hell they can't even see anything out here and somehow they're more worried about some random fucking Afghans than their own Soldiers." Lucas said, trying to calm me down. It was all stuff that we had said to each other before to commiserate, but it wasn't helping my mood.

"Sometimes I think they're not going to be happy until they get us all fucking killed."

"I know, Nick, I know."

Saber Command, had done this type of thing to us two or three times before; interjecting at the last possible moment and delaying or outright canceling time-sensitive airstrikes and artillery barrages against the enemy. This had been done in the past usually out of some type of incompetence or misinterpretation on Saber Command's part which, of course, they would attempt to blame on us once we returned from our mission. This time didn't feel like incompetence though. It felt precise and deliberate. Saber Command just kept dozens of enemy fighters on the board and for what? To preserve a building made out of mud and straw that was filled with hostile fighters? To never have to answer to the higher chain of command on the outside chance there were civilians killed in the airstrike? My mind began to fill with doubt and suspicion. In order to interrupt our airstrike like that, that meant command was quietly monitoring all of our radio transmissions to the F-16s. They had interjected directly to the aircraft's command in Bagram Airfield, dozens of miles away. Who, specifically at Saber Command, was doing this to us? Was it the SCO or one of his minions? Was it *all* of them?

All of this was swimming around in my head when I asked Lucas the question, "Hey Lucas, you were talking directly to the F-16s. How many enemy fighters did the pilots spot anyway?"

"Thirty enemy fighters, probably more that they couldn't see." He replied, settling his heavy radio pack back onto his shoulders.

"We could have stopped the fighting down here for weeks; months possibly." I said.

Lucas looked at the mountains, "Yeah."

When we resumed our march toward the pick-up zone, the mountains seemed even bigger than they were before the firefight; looming over us just a little bit more. The drowned sky hung overhead and I watched the horizon as those two gray specks faded off into the distance, their bombs nestled safely against their bellies.

Chapter 1

The Army Needs Angry Young Men. This is How They're Made.

"So Nick, any thoughts about what you want to do when you're done with school, you know, like for a career?"

The question had come from my half-brother, Alex. His arm was perched atop the steering wheel of the parked SUV. I looked outside from my seat and saw my half-sister, Elizabeth, and her boyfriend walking back from the convenience store. They were smiling and laughing. The windows were up so I couldn't hear what they were saying. I imagined it was happy and light from the easy way my sister swung her arms and hips and the lazy, almost love-drunk, way her boyfriend gaped at her. All three of them were older than me, high school and college-aged, while I was still in middle school. The four of us were on our annual road trip from Mississippi to Florida to see our father's side of the family. We shared a dad, an absentee and eccentric dad, but our biological dad nonetheless. Our dad didn't have custody of any of us and this was the only time of year we would see him. Someone, somewhere within the family decided we should at least see each other annually. My mother thought it was a good idea too and sent me off once a year under the pretense of spending time with my dad. The real reason my mother sent me on this trip each year was to be near my dad's parents. "Be sure to ask them for money. Checks are good too." She'd tell me every time I went off. One year it was for football gear, the next it was for piano lessons. I never did any of these things, mind you. My mom would just pocket the money once I'd returned home. She taught me how to hustle and grift my own grandparents and I'd gotten fairly good at it. This was the only time of the year that I saw my siblings and my dad's portion of my family and I absolutely hated it. The drive down made me feel more anxious and uncomfortable the closer we got to our destination. This year was worse than the others and after several hours in the car listening to how happy and great my siblings' lives were, I'd had enough.

I decided to answer Alex. "I want to join the Army and kill as many people as possible."

I let the words hang in the air for dramatic effect. I was a little surprised at myself for putting it so bluntly. Alex was shocked too. He'd done nothing but try to bond with his little brother and I'd spat it back in his face for seemingly no reason.

Alex was still sitting there with a blank look on his face, no doubt searching his newly college-educated brain for what to say. He paused on the moment, not knowing how to respond to his normally quiet and overly-sensitive half-brother who had just openly declared his intent to murder people. At the time, I felt I had shown him the hate and anger I had quietly felt for years and, more importantly, I had shown him that we were nothing alike. It felt like I had won something somehow even though I wasn't sure what it was yet. He eventually fixed his eyes on the steering wheel and settled on a response.

"That's not right, Nick."

He didn't understand and how could he? They had a different mother than me and that made a world of difference in our upbringing. They both had the good mom. They had very good lives and I had been quietly enduring my own private hell for the past several years. On the outside, our father was the unstable parent (dad was already on ex-wife number three by this point in time) so Alex, Elizabeth and I lived with our biological mothers. Unfortunately, I had a different mother than my two siblings. I was the child from the "other woman". I was the living, breathing proof of how our dad had fucked everything up. It was really set up to fail from the word *go*. I got the mom that was the drug addict. I got the mom who dated her dealers and took her son with her when she went to buy to leverage better prices. From my perspective at the time, I saw my siblings' upbringing as stable and secure and with safety nets ready to catch them if they fell. In short, I thought they were allowed to be normal where, by contrast, all I could do was survive. They had done nothing to me but be normal siblings and I'd hated them for that.

I was thirteen at the time and my mother was getting worse every day. Each night she would pass out in the living room. At first, any kind of interaction with her past 5 PM was a gamble and I couldn't talk to her without inviting a verbal or physical fight. Then it became earlier and earlier. First 4 PM and then 3 PM until eventually she was drunk or high the entire day. Some nights I misjudged my timing with her and she'd fly into a rage. She'd usually get a few good hits in before I was able to lock myself in the bathroom. I'd wait there, quiet and still, until she passed out or gave up trying to get in. Sometimes she would be really determined and wouldn't give up for hours. I don't remember getting any sleep on those nights. I still remember her pounding on the door for hours. It was scary when she yelled or hit me, but what was really unnerving was how quickly she could switch tactics. "Mama loves you, baby. Come out. I'm sorry." I fell for it once and learned never to trust her again. I spent a good portion of that year out on the street or over at friends' houses until I had worn out my welcome. Then I'd move on to the next friend's house, eating their food and sleeping wherever they had room. When my mom stopped buying food, I'd eat condiments that I'd stolen from fast food places. I'd supplement that with anything I could easily shoplift from grocery and convenience stores within walking distance of our apartment complex.

My brother Alex and my sister Elizabeth, like normal young people, were primarily concerned with which college they would be admitted to or what new amplifier they should buy for their fledgling band. I wagered that they had never woken up in the middle of the night with cockroaches in their mouth. They probably never had to steal any of their meals either. And I seriously doubted that they ever had to wake up in a different place each day. They likely didn't have to worry about what version of their mother they would get when they spoke to her either. From what I remember at the time, their mother seemed good and wholesome, like one of those moms in the magazines with her perfect hair and nice smile. I imagined she wore pearls while she vacuumed.

I realized then that Alex was still looking at me, searching for some kind of response. Maybe he thought I needed help? Maybe he thought some part of me was twisted up and bad? I didn't care at that moment because by saying that I wanted to kill as many people as possible I had finally put the ball back in my court. It was a declaration. I wasn't going to just let shit happen to me for the rest of my life. I was going to do the opposite and shit on the world for a change. I was going to take charge. In my teenage, hormone-saturated brain, I was still forming the beginnings of what that meant. I was putting the puzzle pieces together and slowly deciding on my future in the military. I don't know what specifically made me think of this, but I thought of Soldiers as possessing the kind of strength and tenacity I wished I had. I think it was because they were rarely portrayed as being scared. They always knew what to do and they did it, no matter how scary it was. I wanted to be like that. I wanted to stop being scared.

A lot of things happened in the next few years. My mom disappeared one day when I was sixteen. She had disappeared a few times before and I thought this time wasn't anything special. I thought she'd gotten high and took off with some guy like she had done in the past. She had always staggered back to the apartment a few days later once she ran out of whatever she was taking so I wasn't too worried at first. This time was different though and she was gone for over a month. Eventually, I couldn't get into the apartment. I guess they locked it up when the bills weren't paid. I was homeless for a few weeks, but I was still going to school. It wasn't too bad because we lived along the Mississippi Gulf Coast and the weather was pretty mild. I didn't have to worry about freezing to death outside or anything; my biggest concern was finding food and staying dry when it rained hard. I did my best to hide it until one of my teachers noticed that I was losing a lot of weight and wearing the same clothes. I was eventually cornered and asked a lot of questions about what was going on at home. I don't remember too much about what happened during that time. It's like my brain put a bubble around those memories to keep me from probing too deeply and remembering all the details. I remember staying in a state home in Mississippi with other abused and displaced kids for a few weeks while the state contacted my father and legally put me under his custody.

When my dad came to get me, I could tell he this was one of the last things he wanted to do. I was cramping his ridiculous Willie Nelson-inspired outlaw lifestyle. He put on a brave face about it though. "We'll do all sorts of stuff together. Two Stevens men together? Watch out world!" He'd exclaimed as we made the trip back from Mississippi to Florida. Willie Nelson, Hank Williams Jr. and all of his other heroes were outlaw country stars, not stellar father figures so it was pretty easy to see what he would rather be doing despite his act. As the only legal guardian Florida or Mississippi could find, I automatically passed to his care. As soon as I was shown my room at his girlfriend's home, I was immediately left alone. My dad only interacted with me when he had to and it was strained and uncomfortable almost every time. No small part of this was surely due to my severely damaged and almost feral nature.

Living with my father and his girlfriend in Florida was difficult. I later learned that my dad had suffered a serious brain injury from a car accident in the late 1970s and as a result, was very emotionally unstable. That explained why he never had custody of me, Alex or Elizabeth and why he only saw us once a year; it was all he could manage. His girlfriend, Tanya, was no better. Pretentious, cold, calculating and controlling were all kind ways to describe her. She had two standard poodles, named Lennon and Cocoa that she cared about more than most people. I had to walk, clean and feed those dogs every single day. I found myself walking two huge poodles along the golf course that was Tanya's backyard every day after school. The contrast to my previous life in Mississippi with my mom was cartoonish and eerie and I never fully adjusted to it. There wasn't a day that went by where I didn't fantasize about just letting their leashes go during one of their walks and watching them run free towards the highway. For my seventeenth birthday, Tanya gave me two books on etiquette written by Emily Post. "I just think it's something you need to work on." She'd said to me as I was holding the books. I smiled and thanked her and thought some more about letting those leashes slip my hand.

I never got to release Tanya's dogs though. Dad's relationship with Tanya was already strained and my newly acquired financial burden was the straw that broke the camel's back. Since it was her house and she had been paying dad's bills for years, she kicked us both out with little to no fanfare. Dad and I moved into a small apartment a few miles down the road. He resented me for inadvertently ruining his meal-ticket with Tanya and resorted to drinking heavily, breaking about twenty years of sobriety. He was mercurial and moody while sober so drinking made him completely uncontrollable. One night, I remember he had cornered me in the kitchen and was screaming at me about disposing of the trash incorrectly. He refused to pay Waste Management and set up a garbage pickup like everyone else. "I'm not giving those fuckers forty dollars a month to rent a trash can." He'd said to me one day. Every few days, I would have to cart our garbage to the convenience store down the street and sneak it into their dumpster in the middle of the night. This time, I'd gotten caught and it got back to him. I'd been threatened and beaten by a few of my mom's boyfriends over the years and I wasn't going to have it happen again now that I was a little larger and able to defend myself better. The alcohol made him bold and he really pressed the point though. He finally backed down when I grabbed him by the collar and pointed a chef's knife at his eye.

Things with my dad certainly weren't perfect, but they were a marked improvement over living with my mom. I think a lot of it had to do with the fact that I was getting closer to that finish line; turning eighteen. If I could make it to eighteen and become my own legal entity, I could go to college and finally get away from my home. Despite everything that was going on, I was making really good grades and I was on track to get a scholarship or two for an in-state college. I knew I needed to get out of the house if I was going to do well in college and have a life that was pointed in the opposite direction of my mom's or my dad's. My dad unexpectedly underwent open-heart triple-bypass surgery during my senior year of high school so my plans to move out were stalled. I thought about just leaving him at home, but he really had no one to help take care of him. He was a brain-damaged asshole, yes, but he was still my dad so I decided to stay and help him recover. I owed him that much at least for getting me away from my mom.

With my senior year wrapping up, I was approached by a recruiter to join Army Reserve Officer Training Corps. I didn't know exactly what that was, but it was explained to me that I would get a scholarship to go to college, get my degree and receive Officer training. To someone like me who had felt like they'd been dealt a shitty hand in life and hadn't felt safe for more than a few days at a time, this was almost entirely too good to be true. Once my dad had recovered to the point where he was self-sufficient, I moved out, got a small place in the next town over and spent the next four years attending the University of West Florida Army ROTC program. During my summers and my spring breaks, I was sent to US Army Airborne School, Air Assault School and Combatives School where I learned how to fight hand to hand, jump out of planes and work with helicopters. I didn't have any money and, although I had scholarships, I still had to work to pay for anything outside of tuition. That meant working two jobs throughout most of college. In short, college was not a fun time. I was extremely busy and hardly had any spare time to do anything other than work, study and sleep.

It was toward the end of college that I met my wife. Well, that's a bit of a false statement. We had already met in high school. We didn't date back then and she received a scholarship to a different college in Florida for sports. She gave it up after a couple of years and returned home. That's when we bumped into each other again. We were a good fit for each other and it wasn't long before we were spending all of our time together. I had reservations about getting married, but she certainly didn't. I knew that I would be assigned all over the world and I didn't want the woman in my life to be uprooted every four years or so because of my career. Army spouse life wasn't a life that made it easy to be anything other than self-employed or a home-maker and I didn't want to force that upon her.

I also had many reservations and issues about trusting people after what I experienced with my mom and dad. We had both just graduated college in 2007 and I had almost made my mind up to end our relationship when she pointed out that we had practically already been living the married life for the past year or so. "We're already monogamous and we live together." She'd pointed out one day. "Also, aren't you happy with the way things are going now? Don't you want to continue this?" I remember her asking. It made a lot of sense to me and we quickly made plans to get married. It was a quick and simple wedding on the beach in Florida. I had flown down to Florida with a shaved head in-between training, put on a tux, said the words and flew back out and resumed my training, a married man.

Chapter 2

Army Training, Sir!

I held on to a lot of anger and used it as a type of fuel to get me through that time. I guess the only reason I wasn't locked away immediately for being a simmering sociopath was the fact that I was very good at most anything put before me and I was very intelligent. I had good grades and blew all of my military evaluations out of the water. Although I didn't think about it all the time, I was still pretty angry at the world by the time I graduated college and got my Officer commission. This didn't raise too many questions though because my aggression was channeled through the military so it was seen as a useful avenue. To the casual observer, I just seemed committed and driven in my pursuit to become a front-line combat Officer.

Nearly all of 2008 was spent in training where I went from one training camp to the next. I learned how to be an Officer, a tanker, a scout, and finally a Ranger. I remember, one time in particular, where I was finishing armor school in Fort Knox, Kentucky. I was getting my final evaluation as it was our last active mission and I was leading a scout Platoon during the training exercise. These operations were force-on-force operations where trainee-led forces combated other Soldiers with blank rounds in simulated skirmishes. Kills and wins were adjudicated by a cadre of training Sergeants and Officers that prowled the simulated battlefields and critiqued and observed every move we made. This operation was in its last few hours. We had successfully conducted an assault, secured the objective and we were closing the noose around the enemy. It was a straightforward operation and we were slamming the last attack home. One of the things about Army training is that the people running it, usually Sergeants, like to crank up the difficulty if a trainee is doing well. We were doing exceptionally well and had the enemy on the back foot so at this point the instructors started giving the opposing force (or OPFOR) god-like powers. They started by resurrecting dead OPFOR Soldiers and giving them extra ammunition and imbuing them with anti-tank weaponry and so forth and so on. It was at this point that a group of enemy Soldiers that we had just killed were resurrected, directly behind us, and given a rocket launcher which they immediately used to knock out my vehicle. In retrospect, it was a huge compliment that the instructors had to bend all these rules just to knock out my command-and-control vehicle in order to give the enemy a chance to fight back. I didn't take it like that at the time. I was furious inside my high mobility multiple wheeled vehicle, or HMMWV (pronounced hum-vee), in my commander's seat. I threw down the radios and tore off my helmet. I could see the OPFOR Soldier that had just taken me out of the fight. We locked eyes for a moment and he gave me the middle finger. I screamed some wordless obscenity at him and I throttled my fist into the metal dashboard of the HMMWV, bending the metal. As one would expect, my hand split open and blood poured everywhere. I flung the door open, intent on murdering that little shit with my bare hands. I was never a particularly big man. I was the smallest Stevens man at six feet and one hundred ninety pounds, but I possessed that kind of wiry, rage-strength that had caught nearly every opponent in my life off-guard and made any fistfight woefully one-sided. Suddenly, I was pulled back into the vehicle by my instructor. He must've sensed that I was intending to do more than go over there and have a polite discussion with that OPFOR Soldier. I was still seething and actually thought about splintering his teeth and going outside the vehicle anyway. After a moment or two, I calmed down and reason came back to me. He eventually talked me down and I sat stewing in my seat until the exercise was over. The other trainees in my HMMWV barely spoke a word to me for the rest of the operation.

An hour later, at the after action report, one of the training Officers noticed that my hand was wrapped up and bleeding. His name was Captain Navarro and he was a Marine Armor Captain with multiple tours in Iraq.

"What happened to your hand, Stevens?" he asked.

There was no point in lying so I just told the truth. "I got really pissed whenever my vehicle got knocked out so I punched the dashboard."

This got a few chuckles from the rest of the training Staff. He looked at me for a moment and one of my fellow trainees that was seated next to me nodded his head to collaborate the story.

CPT Navarro paused for a moment and said, "Well if the Army doesn't want you, the Marines will sure as hell take you. Somebody who's good and hates to lose and who also comes with an anger problem? You'll fit right in."

Ranger School, ironically, helped calm me down a little. It helped me channel my anger and aggression in a much more focused and, when needed, ruthless manner. I remember one time where they put us in a fighting circle filled with wood chips and had us fight, one on one, for control of a Taser. They treated us like attack dogs and, in short, we were. The level of unwavering aggression and determination that we were expected to employ was almost unheard of and I'd put Ranger School up there as one of the most arduous military training programs in existence. We were trained to deal with anything with uncompromising and efficient violence. I remember one instructor telling me something that stuck with me for years. "The wrong plan, if executed with enough violence, will succeed." He was absolutely right because I got to test that theory quite a bit in the years that followed.

When I was completing scout leader's school, I had another operation that I was put in charge of. All of these trainings are similar in that each of the trainees take turns being in charge. One mission an Officer may just be the driver of a vehicle and the next mission, that same Officer may be the company commander of an entire tank company. Usually on each vehicle, or every other vehicle, there will be a Sergeant or Officer from the training cadre to make sure that we are safe and don't get too far out of line. The particular Sergeant that was assigned to me was Staff Sergeant Burch and he always gave me the toughest missions he could come up with. We had one in particular where the he tried to trip me up on the briefing process where I was given one mission and told to plan for it and, when I was halfway done briefing my men, I was given a FRAGO, or fragmentary order, that was completely different from what we were about to do. The intent of this is to put extra stress on the leader and simulate real life scenarios where missions can change last minute. With no time to conventionally plan, I analyzed the map, the mission and the disposition of the enemy as quickly as I could and then briefed the men over the radio while we were moving out towards our objective. Having been in the area before on a previous training mission, I had an idea of what the terrain would look like and where the enemy was most likely hiding. I got lucky and I was 100% correct and we engaged and destroyed the enemy very quickly. SSG Burch, because things were going well, called artillery on us and then he used his special cadre god-powers to knock out my vehicle because he wanted to see how the others would react without my leadership. Again I was pretty pissed, but this time around I kind of understood that it was a huge compliment.

When we got back to the training facilities and did the after action report, SSG Burch pulled me aside and said that he hadn't seen anyone like me in a long time. I took it as a compliment and I asked him what he meant exactly.

"I haven't seen anyone as naturally gifted as you are at leading other people in a long time."

I didn't really know how to take it because here was a hardened veteran telling me that I had a gift for leading people even though it was just training and I'd never been in combat. To be perfectly honest, it made my heart swell with pride. We concluded the rest of the evaluation and I was leaving the room when he spoke up again.

"How did you know the enemy was going to be there?"

I turned around and said, "Well I just thought about where I would be if I was fighting me."

He said, "Okay." And looked down for a moment when his eyes came up and met mine again, "What if you were wrong?"

"Excuse me?" I asked.

"What if you were wrong? What if it wasn't there and you got all your guys killed?

This rankled me a little, "I wasn't wrong and I didn't get my guys killed."

He looked at me with genuine concern and said, "One day you're going to do everything right and everything will go wrong and someone is going to die. You need to be ready for that."

I nodded and said, "Thank you." I recognized this as heartfelt and well-meaning advice, but I wasn't quite sure how to take it. That angry part of me still couldn't see when people were trying to help me.

Chapter 3

Beef Jerky.

With all of my training done, I got to spend a few short weeks stateside with my wife before we had to move to my first assignment in Schweinfurt, Germany. Fortunately, she was allowed to come with me to Europe. We had been married in summer of 2008, but I barely got to see her with all the training. In December of 2008, I was assigned as a Platoon Leader to Red Platoon, Anvil Troop 1st of the 91st Cavalry Squadron. This Cavalry Squadron was part of the 173rd Airborne Brigade Combat Team, based out of Vicenza, Italy. The Squadron had wanted me to arrive a few weeks later. They suggested that I take Reconnaissance and Surveillance Leaders Course (or RSLC for short) in Fort Benning, Georgia to kill more time stateside as everyone in the unit was still on holiday leave. Having just finished Ranger School (arguably the most arduous military training on the planet) I was thirty pounds lighter than when I started and I was all done with training and politely told them, "Fuck no, I'm done. I'll be going to Germany now."

Red Platoon was a small, airborne scout Platoon; less than twenty scouts and before long we knew each other intimately. We had Soldiers and Sergeants from all walks of life. From former cops to talented artists and musicians, red-neck Arkansas hunters to second generation immigrants serving the country they loved, we had it all. We worked, trained and sweat together for an entire year before we were slated to deploy to Afghanistan. I spent many nights away from my wife and she had to handle a lot of the domestic things while I was swamped at work. She really did a lot, even interfacing with German offices and settling us into two different houses when our initial house had sold, unexpectedly, to a private German buyer while I was away on an extended training mission. There was a time when I was working so much that I didn't know what my house looked like in the daylight. In truth, I was one of the lucky ones. Most other Platoon leaders in the unit weren't given much time with their men prior to shipping out to Afghanistan. Some even had to take over their Platoons while in country. Needless to say, I was fortunate to get an entire year with my team before our orders came down for Afghanistan. My Platoon Sergeant, Stew, and I used every moment of that year to make sure the team was as ready as we could be for whatever awaited us over there.

Most new Platoon leaders are taught to rely on and listen to their Platoon Sergeants (usually the highest ranking and most experienced Soldier in the Platoon) when they are first assigned to their Platoons. I was no different and I listened to Stew all the time. He was an outstanding Platoon Sergeant and, although I was technically in charge, we worked as partners in everything we did. It wasn't long before we were regarded as one of the best Platoons in the entire four thousand person strong Brigade.

I knew I had finally earned the respect of the rest of the Platoon when they jumped me during a training exercise in Grafenwoehr, Germany. Grafenwoehr, or simply Graf, was one of the major pre-deployment training events for Army units stationed in Europe. Everybody going to war had to do a thirty day training exercise in Graf. Grafenwoehr was infamous as a training site because it was chosen by Hitler before WWII for its horrible and unpredictable weather that would hide the training maneuvers of the German Army from Allied spy planes. Hitler was gone, but we joked that his parting gift to the US Army was that we got to enjoy the weather in Graf in the decades that followed. I remember seeing "Thanks a lot for the weather, you Austrian fuck." Scrawled onto the wall of one of the hundreds of portable bathrooms that dotted Graf's landscape.

The Army, at least the combat side of it, has a lot of hazing traditions so I had to basically get "jumped into" my Platoon. That's how you knew you were *in* as a Platoon leader; when they surrounded and beat you and usually striped you naked and taped you to something exposed to the elements. I knew it was coming sometime during Graf, but I had honestly forgotten about it that day and let my guard down. The training maneuvers at Graf were designed to evaluate and, if necessary, retrain units from the Squad all the way up to the company level. My commander at the time, Captain Manion, was really indifferent to the idea of being evaluated during training and was putting a lot of his job on me. "I've already done this shit so many times. I'm putting you in charge for the briefing. You could use the experience." He'd said to me once right before going to take a nap. He was a Captain that was long in the tooth and generally burned out from multiple deployments to Iraq and Afghanistan. I had just done his job and briefed the entire Troop, then I had to do my job and planned and briefed for my Platoon. It was past midnight and had just gotten some cold leftover scraps from the day's mess when I was ambushed by ten of my Soldiers on my cot. "Beef jerky!" They'd yelled as they tackled me. I guess that was their code word. I was so hungry and tired. All I wanted to do was eat and get some sleep, but neither of those things were going to happen now. I realized that when a bit of food was swatted out of my hand and I was pressed to the cot by our largest Sergeant, Sergeant Brandt.

I don't know if it was a combination of fatigue, frustration or the years of repressed rage, but I saw red and began fighting my way out. Sergeant Brandt had me pinned pretty well and I could already hear the duct tape that was securing me to the cot. Apparently they thought I was too much of a risk to be stripped naked before I was taped to anything and they were skipping right to the taping part. They were absolutely right about me being a risk. I screamed something wordless and sank my teeth into Sergeant Brandt's two hundred and twenty pound side. He rolled away in pain just far enough for me to get a hand free. That hand was used to start choking the life out of Sergeant Guerrero, the man taping me to the cot. I felt blows raining down on my body, but I kept my grip on Guerrero's throat and somehow got the other hand free. I rolled Brandt off of me and wrenched a leg free. A few other Soldiers jumped on top of me to replace Brandt, but I was already halfway out. With one leg free, I planted a boot into the chest of another Sergeant, Riggs, who went tumbling into two of the others.

I was running out of steam, but I guess the shock and ferocity of my initial resistance was enough to give them second thoughts. The Platoon, doing their best to hold me down, counted to three and scattered into the night. I got up from my cot, roaring after them. I chased them out into the night beyond the tent, but was unable to find anyone. They had all wisely scattered in different directions. I returned to my cot and found Sergeant Brandt, the obvious ringleader, seated on his cot, grinning up at me. I was still pretty heated.

"What the fuck was that? What are you grinning at me for, Sergeant?"

"That was pretty cool, Sir. I've never seen that before"

"What? No, not cool man, I just want to fucking sleep."

"Think about it Sir. You just fought off ten guys. They've never seen an Officer do anything like that. You're like a legend now. You should be thanking me."

It was then that Stew chimed in from his cot across the tent, "I'm staying out of this, but the man's got a point."

"Huh, I guess so." I said and left it at that.

From that point, my Platoon respected me immensely. As silly as it was, the other Soldiers in the other Platoons got wind of what happened and they started treating me differently too. I was suddenly the tough Lieutenant.

Chapter 4

Three Round Burst.

With the training in Graf wrapped up, we returned back to our garrison in Schweinfurt where we fully expected to receive orders to deploy to Iraq or Afghanistan in the coming weeks. It was still undecided at that point which of the two we would deploy to, but Afghanistan was the more sure bet. We were all expecting to get deployment orders in the summer of 2009, but for whatever reason, the big Army kept us in suspense well into the fall. Our parent unit, the 173rd Airborne Brigade, had been doing year-on/ year-off tours to Afghanistan for the past several years; our allotted year was well past due by that summer in 2009.

Most of the Soldiers were occupied with summer barbecues and doing back to school shopping all the while trying to forget about the other shoe that was going to drop at any minute. When it finally happened and our deployment orders were in writing, we all made preparations to really and truly go to war. Some Soldiers wrote letters to their families, more spent time with their girlfriends and spouses and even more spent all of their cash on getting black-out drunk one last time before we had to abstain from alcohol for an entire year downrange. We all had to do the mandatory pre-deployment training; the Army's giant *check the block* system to get Soldiers ready for war in the shortest time possible. We were all screened for medical, mental, legal and financial conditions that would keep us from deploying. Ears were checked, blood was taken, things were injected, psychological profiles screened, powers of attorney written and teeth were appropriately prodded and tapped.

During once such tooth prodding, the Army dentist leaned over to me and hinted that I should have my wisdom teeth taken out. They hadn't ever bothered me. In fact, I had been scarcely aware that my skull had contained these potentially offending teeth this whole time.

"Why would I want them out?" I asked.

"Well, they could start to give you trouble while you're in Afghanistan. They seem to be done growing, but that could change. When are you scheduled to deploy again?" He asked.

"Next month, but they haven't given me any trouble yet. I think I'll just leave them in since I don't think they'll be moving around any time soon." I said with a hint of sarcasm.

"We need to take them out just to be safe."

"You're kidding, right?"

"Nope." He said, simply.

With that, I spent the next four hours getting teeth pried out of my skull. At about the two hour mark, the dentist felt the need to compliment me on my good genetics.

"Wow, you have very strong teeth. They're really making me work." He said as he grasped a large tool that could best be described as the dental version of a shoe horn.

I thanked him for the compliment, but sadly with all of the numbing agent and hardware in my mouth it didn't come out quite right, "Glahaughbug gur!" or something like that escaped my throat.

He grunted and said, "Wow, very strong." The sickening crunch of a defeated molar corroborated his point.

Initially, I would have much preferred to be unconscious during the procedure, but the Lidocaine injections enabled us to enjoy our intimate time together far more than being under general anesthesia. After all, I wouldn't have been able to enjoy those touching moments where he gently put his knee onto my chest to better leverage his surgically sterile shoe horn into my face.

The way I grew up with my mom and dad gave me one valuable perk. I got really good at not being in the moment. I was able to just *detach* myself from whatever was happening to me and it was a lot like watching a movie about myself. That's what I did in that dentist chair. I just entered the third person and watched this comedy unfold. It was pretty funny to watch him on the table, cranking teeth out of my head.

At the end of it all, I was given a dozen or so biodegradable sutures and a nice, hefty bottle of Percocets. Being raised by a drug addict, I was afraid of becoming dependent on any drugs so I had limited taking anything too strong throughout my life. My head was throbbing so I decided to try the Percocets. I had no tolerance to them and they hit me like most people would experience heroin. The first one was hard to stuff into my swollen and throbbing mouth, but once it took effect the others went down with little to no difficulty. After the first few, I began to devour them like delicious, perception-altering Tic-tacs.

Despite the fact that I was completely blasted out of my skull on Percocets for the next several days, I nevertheless had to attend briefings that would prepare me for all eventualities in Afghanistan. We learned a little Pashto, the primary language in Afghanistan. We learned how to not sexually assault people which I was told this was a systemic problem in the Army even though I never saw a sexual assault case throughout my entire career. We also learned how to set up powers of attorney for our spouses so they could better spend our money while we were away.

We even learned how to guard ourselves against the Army's silent killer, suicide. We were ushered into a theater on the base where our Chaplain had put together a presentation for us.

"Okay everybody. Settle down and take your seats." Came the voice of Chaplain Lowe.

He was a tall, slim man not used to yelling. He was having trouble projecting his voice across the small movie theater which was now packed with about four hundred Soldiers, most of our cavalry Squadron. The Soldiers continued to chatter in their theater seats. Some were swapping dip tins. Others were checking their phones and none of them were giving the Chaplain the time of day. I saw a crease of frustration set into the Chaplain's brow. Curious to see how a man not used to yelling would actually yell, I leaned forward in my seat to see how he would deal with the situation;

dropping one more Percocet to make sure I got the full effect. He puffed his chest with an intake of breath and was about to speak.

"EVERYONE SIT DOWN AND SHUT THE FUCK UP!!!" A random First Sergeant bellowed, cutting the Chaplain off before he even started.

As one, the entire theater fell silent. Some stragglers took their seats and all grab-assery came to a screeching halt. I smiled. Even though the yelling had harshened my buzz a little, I loved this aspect of the Army. There were some instances where reason and sense took a back seat to pure brute force and intimidation. The Chaplain was there, an Officer and clearly an authority figure, trying to reasonably address the Soldiers and it was going about as well as a screen door on a submarine. A random First Sergeant, the terrible task masters of most Army formations, was able to succinctly solve the problem with a little profanity and a lot of volume in about two seconds flat. In a word, it was wondrous.

"Thank you First Sergeant. I'd like to welcome you all here today for our pre-deployment suicide awareness briefing." The Chaplain said.

"Today," he continued, "we're going to look at some of the choices that could potentially set our feet on the path to suicide. This presentation is unique in that we'll have some input as to where the story will go. Like you, I haven't seen this film before so I'll be interested to see what happens. To keep this fun and interactive and to also keep you guys awake, we'll stop the movie and take a vote on what choices to make once we reach a decision point in the story. So let's go ahead and get started."

With that, Chaplain Lowe started the projector and the movie sprang to life.

"This is Private Jones" the narrator began in that vaguely mature and patronizing yet mysteriously neutral tone that all male narrators can somehow produce.

"He has just been deployed to Iraq. He got assigned to the same unit as his best friend, Private Smith." He continued.

Two young actors playing Soldiers were seated in the back of a HMMWV and chatting idly. Generic desert scenery blurred past the windows.

"Privates Jones and Smith enlisted together from the same town. They grew up together and were assigned to the same unit. They were best friends." The narrator went on. "All of this was about to change with today's mission."

The HMMWV followed several other HMMWVs down an appropriately dusty road toward a small, generic Iraqi village. Privates Jones and Smith dismounted their vehicle and followed their Sergeant's orders. Several other actor-Soldiers were doing the same. Jones and Smith were both helping to provide security for a meeting between their Platoon leader and the village elder; a very routine mission.

A single shot suddenly rang out and Private Smith slumped to the ground. Someone yelled, "Sniper!" and the Platoon of actors hunkered down behind cover; keeping a sharp eye out for any signs of the enemy sniper. Instead of fighting back, Private Jones was looking at his friend in disbelief. The movie then did a nice fadeout of the sound of battle and then showed Private Jones riding back to base in the HMMWV alone; his eyes fixed on the now empty seat next to him.

The next scene opened with Private Jones and his Platoon receiving a debriefing from his Sergeant. Jones was mentally checked out and clearly thinking about his friend.

"We'll all miss Private Smith "The Sergeant said, "and we'll have to keep doing our jobs. He would want it that way."

At this point, the narrator chimed back in, "Private Jones went back to his bunk. Some of the other Soldiers were up talking, but Jones wanted to write in his journal. What should he do?"

The film then paused and our Chaplain addressed us, "So, that's up to you guys. What do you think this young man should do after losing his friend?"

A few awkward seconds passed and an anonymous voice in the darkened theater finally spoke up, "He should write in his journal."

"Ok." said the Chaplain and with that, he resumed the film by clicking the "write in your journal option."

"You spend all night writing in your journal" the narrator announced. "You don't get much sleep, but you feel that you've gotten some things off of your chest."

"The following morning" the narrator continued "you're dead tired and hardly ready to go on a patrol."

The grizzled Sergeant eyed Private Jones up and down and asked what his problem was. Jones didn't have a good answer and his Sergeant, disgusted, dismissed Jones from the patrol, telling him to "clear his head a while."

Private Jones then went back to his bunk where he found a letter from his girlfriend that had been delivered earlier that morning. Private Jones read on and discovered that his girlfriend of three years was leaving him for one of his friends back home. She had already emptied his bank account and said that she didn't want to hear from him. Additionally, she had been cheating on him since he deployed to Iraq. A moment later, a few other off duty Soldiers asked Private Jones if he wanted to play basketball.

The narrator posed another question to us, "What should you do? Should you blow off some steam with a game of basketball or should you try to call your girlfriend to salvage the relationship?"

The Chaplain then asked us, "Ok guys, what should Jones do?"

The answer was almost immediate, "Call that girl up!"

To which, someone added from the back of the theater, "Trifling-ass bitch!"

Perhaps it was the Percocets, but I found this to be immensely funny and I struggled to stifle my laughter. The Chaplain nodded and selected the "call the girlfriend" option thereby resuming the video.

"The call does not go well." The narrator said immediately.

Private Jones was shown with a pay phone up to his ear, rubbing his scalp as he tried to comprehend the exact level of heartbreak he should be feeling.

"You feel worse than before. You try writing in your journal but it doesn't feel right," the narrator began "you feel like you should talk to somebody, but you're worried what the other Soldiers might think."

Private Jones was standing outside of the fictional outpost's Chaplain Office when the narrator asked, "What should you do? Do you try to take care of this yourself or do you seek help?"

Chaplain Lowe swept his eyes over the crowd, awaiting a response.

Without pause, the answer came back, "Nah, he's got this. Let him figure this out on his own."

The Chaplain looked around the theater, "You guys know that we're trying to *save* Private Jones, right?"

"Sure. Jones seems like a smart kid. He can figure it out." a voice who I vaguely recognized as a young Sergeant from one of the other Troops replied. Several Soldiers snickered quietly in the background. Like sharks smelling blood in the water, they had figured out what was happening and were excited to make Private Jones suck-start his rifle.

"Um, ok guys." said the Chaplain as he selected the "don't get help" option.

"You've spent the past several days not sleeping." the narrator began "You're starting to wonder if you're worth anything to anyone at all. Late in the night, you decide to take your own life."

A single gunshot sounds outside of Private Jones' bunk. In the theater, several of our Soldiers let out small cheers.

"Only you didn't die." the narrator interjected.

"BOOO!!!" came the anonymous jeering of several Soldiers in the back of the theater.

The narrator continued, "You shot yourself, but you lived. You spent the rest of your life as a vegetable; unable to feed, clean or take care of yourself. Now, was your suicide attempt worth it? Should you have asked for help?"

Chaplain Lowe then stopped the film and cut the lights back on.

"Ok, so we learned a lot from that didn't we?" he asked "Despite you guys rushing this poor private towards suicide as fast as humanly possible, we learned that suicide doesn't always pan out, does it? Now I'm going to ask you all an important question. What could have Private Jones done differently to have this all resolve in a more favorable outcome?"

One of the machine gunners from another Platoon blurted out, "Yeah, he should've put his weapon on three round burst instead of single shot like a dumbass."

The theater burst into uproarious laughter. With this crew, it was going to be an interesting war.

Chapter 5

Welcome to Country.

The days that followed were a blur. I was designated as our Troop's Unit Movement Officer which meant that I was responsible for ensuring that our thirty or so million dollars-worth of equipment was properly accounted for, packed and stowed for shipment to Afghanistan. Our more essential and portable sensitive items like night vision devices, pistols, rifles and machine guns were carried by individual Soldiers. These items would fly into Afghanistan with the end user. The bigger stuff, on the other hand, had to be inspected, packed and loaded onto containers that would make the much slower journey across the oceans and seas into Pakistan and finally overland into Afghanistan.

This would've been difficult under any circumstances, but I was still high on Percocets most of the time and it was a small miracle that all of our equipment passed through customs and we didn't lose anything on the way into Afghanistan. Quite frankly, I was quite surprised I didn't accidentally pack myself into one of those containers. I eventually ran out of pills sometime during our stay at Ramstein Air Base in Germany and reality came crashing down on me with sobering clarity. We were on full lock-down in a small hanger awaiting our flight that would take us directly into Bagram Air Force Base (BAF for short) in Afghanistan. We were on lock-down because it was rumored that one of the Soldiers from another unit had tried to desert, but was caught attempting to flee.

I went outside to get some air and I saw the guards that watched us on the perimeter. They were worried more of us would try to escape. *Holy shit. Was it really that bad over there?* I remembered asking myself. I didn't get to ponder this too long because our plane landed a few short minutes later. We grabbed our gear, did one final equipment count and said goodbye to Germany.

I didn't know what to think when I first touched ground in Afghanistan. Our point of entry into the country, as expected, was through BAF. To call it a base was a bit misleading. Bagram Multi-National Military Township would have been more fitting. The place was enormous. Service members of several countries and all uniform types that I recognized, and some that I didn't, wandered to and fro. Electric powered golf carts whined and hummed down pathways to barracks, mail rooms and Burger Kings.

The architectural limits of what one could do with plywood structures was being challenged everywhere I looked. There was a chapel, a fully operational hospital complete with surgical unit, a public bus system along with several fully furnished dining facilities. There was even a paved, fully functioning main street that had enough vehicles on it to cause the occasional traffic jam. This was certainly not the Spartan conditions that books and movies had portrayed. I was surprised that BAF didn't print its own currency.

"There aren't other places like this, are there?" I asked one of our more seasoned Sergeants.

"Good God, no." He replied, "There's only one BAF."

It all seemed so unlike anything I was expecting to experience in Afghanistan. The word *austere* had no place anywhere on BAF. We arrived to our lodging area rather late that first night. Once we had accounted for our men and equipment and decided who was going to sleep on which cot, we all settled down for a few hours of sleep. I remember lying awake thinking that Afghanistan might not be what I expected at all. Maybe, I thought, there isn't much for us to do over here after all. Maybe most of the fighting is already done.

Movies don't prepare you for how loud explosions really are. The special effects sound technicians isolate and turn down the volume of explosions. They do this for gunfire too. What you hear in a movie is a tiny fraction of the total volume. This is done so that the audience can actually sit through the movie and watch the protagonist pump silver bullets into werewolves without accidently biting off their tongues or shitting their pants.

A really loud blast feels like it's inside of you too. It makes your chest and organs vibrate and your teeth rattle. On open ground, the shockwave from the blast usually hits you a split-second before you hear it. That's what happened to me on that first night; that rumbling vibrating feeling a split-second before the deafening boom of the explosion.

"INCOMING!!!" someone yelled.

Men dove to the ground, looking around for orders. The lights flickered and dust was summoned up to the top of the tent, casting a haze on the interior. Disoriented, I rolled off the cot and grabbed my rifle.

"Get to the bunkers!" I heard my Platoon Sergeant, Stew, yelling.

My men looked at me for a moment.

"You heard him! MOVE!" I yelled.

With that, we hurried to the concrete barricades that were next to our tents. The rotten egg smell of low quality explosives filled the air. We all leaned against the twenty foot tall vertical concrete embankments, unsure which side was the safest. One of the Soldiers chambered a round into his rifle and got into the prone on the ground, looking down the sights for any enemy targets.

"What the fuck are you doing?" Stew asked the Soldier. "That was a Taliban rocket from miles away. There's nobody to shoot at except our own people, you dumbass. Now get up and get back over here so we can huddle against this barrier like a bunch of scared children."

We all laughed. The Soldier got up sheepishly and trotted over to the rest us is.

"If we're lucky" he continued, "The next rocket will land on the other side of this fucking barricade, knock it over and crush us to death so we won't have to go through a full year in this shit-hole country."

I smiled at Stew and said, "You always know the sweetest things to say."

"Damn right and welcome to Afghanistan, Sir." He replied. "For the rest of you, welcome to Afghanistan, fuckers!"

It wasn't the first time Stew had pointed out the absurdity of what we were doing or the danger we were walking into.

I remembered when we were taking the bus from Schweinfurt to Ramstein to wait for our plane into Afghanistan. The bus was packed with the Soldiers and all of their equipment. Some of the Soldiers were noisily complaining about not having enough room.

"Not enough room?" Stew asked. "Don't worry. There's going to be plenty of empty seats on the way back, fuckers."

We all laughed at that one at the time. It didn't seem quite as funny now having just been through a rocket attack within our first few hours in Afghanistan.

The rest of the night passed without further incident and in the morning I was able to get a better look at our immediate surroundings. Our unit, like most new arrivals, was housed on the southern end of the airbase, away from all of BAF's shops and creature comforts. The main aircraft flight line of Bagram offered a buffer zone between BAF proper and our temporary housing area; ostensibly to keep the transient riff-raff out of the main areas of the base. If one wanted to go to central BAF to buy supplies or get a better meal, a bus ride was required due to the distance and still active minefields from the Soviet occupation decades before. We generally didn't like to do this because the BAF people were a bit too uptight for our taste. Captain Alexi, the commander of one of our sister Troops, relayed one story to us about BAF people. Captain Alexi usually had some interesting stories so a small crowd had gathered around him as he began his tale in his trademark southern drawl.

"So there I was walking out of the dining facility" he said, "when all of a sudden these golf carts appear out of nowhere. There were about four of them and they have these little Sirens and lights going and everything. They pulled up onto the sidewalk and all of these Air Force security types get out. There's almost a dozen of them and they surround me and about twenty other guys who had also just finished eating. There was this one guy, real mean looking little fucker with a clipboard, that told us to go up to the clearing barrels and that he was going to do a safety check to ensure that we all knew how to clear our weapons. I thought this was pretty odd because I had never seen anything like this so I put my hand up and asked, 'Hey, do I have to do this?' The little fucker with the clipboard goes, 'Safety doesn't respect rank, Captain.'"

Captain Alexi continued, "Now this was odd, mind you, because I didn't have a weapon on me. It was locked up in our armory because it was being repaired and there wasn't a replacement weapon for me. I wasn't worried because, quite frankly, BAF is about as dangerous as a petting zoo. So there I am, stuck in this line because I have to show this prick with a clipboard how to clear my weapon even though I don't have one. The people in front of me are all non-combat types and they're really fucking up. Some don't know how to handle their weapons at all; like they've been carrying around a rifle-shaped paperweights for months. I could kind of see why they needed to do this. Apparently Air Force types just wander around and accidently shoot each other all the time."

We all chuckled in agreeance.

"When my turn finally came," he went on, "I looked at that little prick and his clipboard and I asked, 'You ready?' He said, 'Go ahead.' I got down into a karate stance in front of the clearing barrel and gave the air in front of me a few palm strikes followed by a leaping roundhouse kick. I stuck the landing real well and then settled back into my karate stance and shouted, 'Time!' All of his security guards were on the ground, dying with laughter. He just looked at me, not cracking a smile at all and told me to leave."

"Moral of the story, some people just don't have a sense of humor... fucking BAFists." He concluded.

And that's how the name stuck. We hadn't even been in BAF for forty eight hours and we'd already come up with a colorfully insulting nickname for our hosts; BAFist. "There goes another BAFist." we'd say. We generally reserved the term for anybody that looked like they had no business in any type of combat situation. Having never been in actual combat, I kept my comments to myself. Some of our Soldiers, however, were not deterred.

"Did you see how their weapons look? All shiny metal and new?" I overheard one of our Soldiers asking his buddy.

"Yeah" the other Soldier replied "Like they've never been fired or cleaned... fucking BAFists."

We were scheduled to ship out in a few days, but for now we were restricted to our tent city on the South side of BAF. The entire Squadron, nearly six hundred of us which were organized into five separate Troops, was crammed into five or six large, open-bay tents. Each Soldier had their own cot where they tried to stave off boredom with books, conversation or cleaning their weapons for the fifteenth time. I, like most of the leadership, had to attend several meetings and briefings in an attempt to put some kind of order to our impending BAF departure. This ultimately proved fruitless as helicopter was the only way out of BAF and into our outpost and the availability of said helicopter was spotty at best. So it was that we left BAF in little random groups.

When my number was up to leave BAF, I left with about six of my Soldiers and we boarded an ex-Soviet contractor helicopter. It looked more like a bulky green locust than a functioning helicopter. We each carried our weapons and a few bloated duffel bags. The little helicopter was cramped and noisy, but I at least had a window seat. With no way to talk, move or think over the din of the helicopter, I decided that I would do my best to really take in the view. When we finally lifted off and began our journey over the Afghan countryside, I saw what I had been expecting this whole time. Gone was the artificial scenery of BAF. Titanic, snow-capped mountains soared into the sky forming large bowls around the vastness of brown steppes and plains in between. Most of the ground was arid and inhospitable, but the areas with water were the exception. Small meandering rivers looked like tiny glass veins at this height. They were sunken into the earth from generations of tiny currents eroding the rocky soil. I was shocked to see the amount of vegetation in these little river valleys. Towns and villages sprang up wherever there was greenery and water. It was early December, but there was much more vegetation than what I was prepared to see.

We rounded a particularly impressive set of mountains and then a wide, open valley came into view. Judging from the amount of time that we had spent in the air, this was our valley. Our little locust took up a landing vector towards our final destination, Combat Outpost Baraki Barak. Before now, it had just been a name on a briefing slide. Now we were actually about to touch down. The pilot guided the little aircraft toward an open area that was serving as a helicopter pad. The Soviet-era helicopter touched down gently enough. We tossed our bags out onto the makeshift gravel helicopter pad. The whirring blades of the helicopter kicked dust in all directions. There was an adobe wall that surrounded the helicopter pad and I saw dozens of Afghan children watching us; their loose clothes fluttering in the helicopter's rotor wash. They were just perched atop the wall, watching us unload our bags with the casual curiosity of a bird watching a beaver build a dam. A small ATV sputtered up to us and there were several Afghan children hanging off the sides, oblivious to the whirring helicopter blades a few feet above their heads. When the ATV got close, the children hopped off and began helping my Soldiers with their bags. I watched as these children, most of them between eight and twelve, hefted bags as large as they were. I felt a tug against my arm and turned to see an Afghan child staring up at me. He had bright, inquisitive eyes that were framed by a shock of black hair protruding from under a dirty Yankees cap. He looked to be no more than nine years old. He yelled something in Pashto and pointed to my bag. If I had spent more time studying and less time eating Percocets during pre-deployment language training, I might have understood him. He repeated himself and reached for one of the duffel bags I had shouldered. I unhooked my lightest bag and offered it to him. He reached out and took it with hands that should have belonged to a fifty year old man. I was staring at this child's hands now. They were worn and massive. His fingernails were broad and flat from years of hard, manual labor. I had seen hands like these before on grown men who had spent decades working the earth with hand tools. He gingerly took my bag and trotted off the helipad toward a pile of bags at the center of the outpost.

The engines of the helicopter started their high-pitched whine, signaling that the pilot was readying for takeoff. We all took our cue and then trotted off the helipad toward the main outpost; dust and wind licking at our backs and necks as the helicopter departed. The entire outpost was about the size and shape of a jagged football field and housed about one hundred fifty people, to include some afghan workers and interpreters. Space was used as efficiently as possible, but everything had the feel of improvised quick fixes and duct tape. I was shown to my quarters where I dropped off my bags. I then met with my commander and received all of the situational updates and debriefings. After several hours of PowerPoint printouts and conjecture, I checked on my Soldiers one last time. Nearly all of them had arrived while I was with the commander and they were now sound asleep. Their weapons were clean and orderly and their equipment had been laid out and inspected. I truly had impeccable subordinate leaders and good Soldiers in my Platoon. Everything was organized and taken care of and the Soldiers were getting what they needed most, some well-deserved rest.

I climbed into my cot, trying to shut my mind down. As I drifted off to sleep, my last thought was of the boy and those impossibly old hands.

Chapter 6

What Are You Doing Here?

My Troop, Anvil Troop, was assigned to Combat Outpost Baraki Barak. Combat Outpost Baraki Barak, or COP BBK, for short, was situated in the heavily populated Baraki Barak district of Logar Province, toward the northwest of our Squadron's area of operations. Several kilometers to the south, Bulldog Troop held a more rural river valley called Charkh District. Many more kilometers to the southeast, Comanche Troop held a sparsely populated area called Kherwar. The Baraki Barak district, although sizable, was easily traversed by vehicle due to the surprising number of improved roads. We had arrived in the winter and although there was much snow, many of the main thoroughfares were still passable. According to the outgoing unit from 10th Mountain Division, the Taliban didn't have much stomach for fighting in the cold and that we would have "free reign" as long as there was snow on the ground.

To our west, there was an observation post that afforded a good view into the bulk of Baraki Barak district to the south and west. This observation post sat upon a large spur formation and was known, unimaginatively, as Observation Post Spur. My commander, Captain Manion, sat down with me and the other two Platoon leaders, Steve Bray and Jake McKenzie, and we outlined a plan that would see us through the next few months. Essentially, we would have two Platoons that were running missions at all times. The third Platoon would be split in half with the first half manning OP Spur and the second half manning the defensive towers at COP Baraki Barak. Of the two mission Platoons, one would be the primary mission Platoon, which would be assigned the more difficult and long range patrols, namely in the historically hostile areas, toward the south and west of Baraki Barak. The second mission Platoon would be the reserve mission Platoon. Its missions would be fairly local and the Platoon would also be on standby for quick reactionary force (QRF) type missions in case the primary mission Platoon got in over its head. It all seemed fairly sound. Given the vague general guidance from Squadron Command, (which equated to something along the lines of, "be nice to the local populace in order to get them to rat out the Taliban to us.") it all seemed to make a degree of sense. We would separate the Taliban from the general populace and get them to see that a life of t-shirts, French fries and democracy was better than the brutal regime under which they currently lived.

Once our equipment and our few remaining Soldiers arrived and the 10th Mountain Division Soldiers began leaving the outpost, our patrols began in earnest. My Platoon, Red Platoon, was assigned to OP Spur first. This proved initially challenging as, in the original plan, we would have to drive several kilometers to the west of COP BBK, drop off half of our guys and then drive our vehicles back through hostile territory with a skeleton crew. I decided this was too risky and petitioned the QRF Platoon to escort us for the OP missions. This provided more security and personnel, but it also managed to turn our small patrol into a large gypsy convoy of vehicles and equipment. We used Mine Resistant Ambush Protected Vehicles (MRAPs for short) as our primary vehicle platform. These things were essentially armored dump trucks designed primarily to withstand mine and IED blasts directed from underneath. This resulted in a massive, top-heavy design that had all the subtlety in combat of a gay pride parade. Our huge, armored vehicles clogged the small Afghan roads and local traffic managed to build up around our patrol at an alarming rate. This was disconcerting as the smallest two person scooter could potentially carry enough explosives to kill or wound a half dozen of my Soldiers. After some vehicle readjusting and threatening pointing of weapons toward the local motorists, we were able to move our convoy along with little to no difficulty. Our vehicles chugged and sputtered along the paved roads without further incident. Once we arrived at the foothills of the spur, it became painfully obvious that the eight Soldiers slated for OP duty were in for one hell of a hike. The OP sat at about seven thousand feet above sea level. That meant a half mile hike up a thirty to fifty degree boulder-choked slope with over a hundred pound load for each Soldier. We kept the vehicles around for extra protection while our Soldiers made the climb and settled in for ten days of sitting on a mountain and observing. We continued to keep this ten day cycle for weeks, as the tempo of our change-outs were dictated by how long a small group of men could stay sane on a bleak mountain top.

Those first couple of months went by quickly. Our early

patrols went along the same pattern of the first OP Spur mission. We would have an initial plan, go out and run into some hiccups and have to refine a bit. There wasn't much that we couldn't contend with. The men were well trained and Stew and I were blessed with a bright group that could think on their feet. We would patrol to distant villages and try to develop rapport with the elders. We would visit a few larger farms to see what they needed to ensure that Baraki Barak produced enough food. We could even visit historically unsupportive villages and discuss projects such as wells and road construction. Those early months were fairly simple. The terrain was open and snowy as the land was still in the throes of winter. As we went on our patrols and met with villagers and discussed projects, one thing stuck out in my mind; the complete and utter absence of the enemy. No fighters, no talk of fighters, no bombs, no IEDs, no caches, nothing. I started to wonder if we were going to be fighting at all during this deployment. Our unit was a fighting unit. Nearly all of our Soldiers were veterans from previous deployments to Iraq and/or Afghanistan. On a personal level, most of my training was geared toward fighting and killing the enemy with everything from pointy sticks to main battle tanks. It seemed like a bit of a waste to have such a well-trained fighting unit relegated to playing nice with the locals.

Over the course of those early patrols, I quickly noticed a pattern with the Afghan civilians. They all wanted something from us. Tiny, sixty person villages would ask for paved roads and state of the art irrigation systems. Children would swarm our patrols and ask for pens and crayons. Farmers would show up at the gates of our compound with sickly livestock, hoping we could provide a cure. At this point in the war, the United States had become a generous step-parent to the entire country of Afghanistan. It was apparent in nearly every interaction with the Afghan populace. For years we, as an occupying force, had tirelessly built roads, hospitals, schools and countless other projects in the areas where the fighting had lessened. All of this was aimed at the goal of separating the culturally entrenched Taliban forces from the local populace by granting them a quality of life that they had been deprived for decades. Most villages were eighty percent illiterate and the oldest man had no idea of his own age. Nearly all villages had no running water and limited electricity. To the Afghans, the idea that we couldn't do something seemed improbable and our technology bordered on sorcery. In the mind of most Afghan village leaders, if we could not provide a well or a road to their village because we weren't able to; it was actually because we didn't *want to*. After all, our technology and resources were relatively limitless. How could we not spare a generator or water desalinization device? As one could imagine, this led to some breaks in communication and built a background level of discontent among the Afghan social leaders in Baraki Barak.

This, of course, made my job extremely frustrating. My Soldiers and I had each separately spent several years of our military training learning to find, fight and subsequently kill a conventional, uniform wearing enemy. Now our enemies were village rivalries and the petty jealousies of the few dozen old, wizened men that presided over said villages. I spent countless hours attending public gatherings, or *shuras*, in which all of the village elders and Afghan government officials would congregate and voice their complaints to us, the American forces. They seemed to have no concept of continuity between the American forces that changed out every year. The elders kept addressing my commander and unit as the previous 10th Mountain Soldiers; constantly referencing things that happened last year or before as if they just occurred yesterday. Any attempt to bring the conversation to the present or future was met with casual indifference followed by a return to the discussion of past events.

I began to think that this would be my reality for the rest of the deployment. I started to come to terms with the idea that most of the fighting in Afghanistan had been done by units that came before us. The unit that we relieved upon arriving at COP Baraki Barak, 10th Mountain, admitted to participating in few firefights and most of their contact with the enemy was in the form of booby traps and IEDs. My attitude changed when I spoke with one shop owner in one of the many nameless settlements in the southern part of Baraki Barak. My interpreter had lingered at the opening of this man's shop and had initiated a conversation with him. I had my Platoon pause for a moment and provide security while I joined the conversation. I learned, through my interpreter, that this shop owner was an old Soldier. The gray haired man before me had fought against the

Soviets as a Mujahedeen fighter during the 1970s.

"What are you doing here?" He asked me.

"We're trying to help put in a well for the village." I stated simply.

"Why would you do that?" he asked.

I was a little surprised at the question and responded, "We're here to make sure that there's enough water for everybody."

"The Taliban will take the well from us and charge us for our own water." He responded, simply.

"We'll do our best to make sure that won't happen." I replied, growing a little annoyed at this point.

"The Taliban is here every day. Will you and your men be in this village every day?" He asked.

I was surprised by his matter-of-fact tone. I had dozens of villages that I patrolled. "No, that's why you have to tell me who they are and where they are." I answered.

"If I do that, they will kill my family." He replied, eyes fixed on me. He continued, "When the mountain passes thaw, the Taliban will come with weapons and they will take everything you have given us. The more you fight and kill them, the more they force our sons into their ranks."

He paused for a moment and looked out over the horizon. I tried to think of something to say; something that they had taught us when we learned about negotiating with Afghans. I could think of nothing.

"The more you come here, the more you bring danger to us." he went on. "So I ask you again, what are you doing here?"

I don't remember the exact answer I gave him, all I recall is that it wasn't a very good one. Honestly, I don't remember much of the rest of that patrol because his words kept bubbling to the top of my mind. "What are you doing here?" It was a simple question so why couldn't I answer it with any real conviction? We were there to talk about a well project as we had done in a dozen other villages. That much I knew. I think it was at that point that I realized that I hadn't actually *seen* any projects in progress. Sure, I had seen wells or roads, but they looked like they had all been completed years ago. I had been talking about projects and meeting with elders for weeks now in dozens of different villages, but I hadn't actually *done* anything yet. No new projects were started, no jobs were created and no cure for cancer was found. I had just made plenty of mission presentations in PowerPoint for my commander and patrolled around a lot, but for what exactly? To fight the enemy? There wasn't any detectable enemy presence anywhere we went; just half-baked rumors about Taliban. To build projects? We hadn't built shit yet. To give the Afghans a better life? If we dumped all of our resources from the outpost into the district we would maybe be able to help ten percent of the population of Baraki Barak. There were tens of thousands of Afghans and just over a hundred of us. My efforts, and by extension our efforts, felt like nothing more than busy work.

"What are you doing here" his words floated to the forefront of my mind. "Fuck if I know, old man." I mused to myself. "Maybe I'll find out."

Chapter 7

A Festivus Miracle.

Life on the outpost went along at a reasonable pace. We busied ourselves with patrols and we were even making what could possibly turn into some meaningful relationships with some of the village leaders. With all of this going on, the holidays came to COP BBK very quickly and took us by surprise. First Sergeant Stockdon, our head non-commissioned Officer and top-ranked enlisted man of the Troop, was a natural pick for Santa. We all took pictures on his lap for the wives and families back home. There was something a little unnerving about posing for a picture on the lap of a man dressed as Santa who was also the same man who spent most of his time screaming at you and cultivating the image that, as he put it, "…kept the Soldiers in line because they were more afraid of me than the enemy." To this day, I think there is a picture of me on Stockdon's lap. What you can't see in that picture is how he was whispering "faggot, faggot, faggot" into my ear or how my hand was sliding up his thigh. We did our best to keep things lively.

Stew and I really weren't into the whole Christmas thing. As big *Seinfeld* fans, we refused to participate in the normal Christmas activities. Instead, we joked that we would be holding a Festivus that year. I didn't expect much to come out of it, but the Soldiers of the outpost had other plans in mind. Eventually, word got around that we were holding a Festivus at COP BBK and we were presented with an unadorned aluminum pole by Lieutenant Ritter, the logistics support Platoon leader, during one of our weekly resupply runs. The Festivus movement gained enough momentum to where Stew and I were pressured to plan events.

For the uninitiated, Festivus is the anti-holiday to Christmas. It was the brain-child of one Daniel O'Keefe, a script-writer, who later wrote down and translated the strange holiday into a *Seinfeld* episode entitled, *The Strike*. Unlike Christmas, Festivus is centered on anti-commercialism. Its symbol, the unadorned aluminum pole is a stark contrast to the tinsel-covered, blinking kaleidoscope that is the Christmas tree. Festivus rituals include, but are not limited to, the airing of grievances, the feats of strength and Festivus miracles.

Stew and I were very busy planning missions and generally

holding things together so we delegated the Festivus planning to Sergeant Brandt. After all, Brandt had planned the coordinated attack on me back in Grafenwoehr a few months earlier so he had good planning skills and a decent sense of humor.

I think it should be important to note, at this point in the story, the type of humor combat paratroopers have. It's a very dark and malicious humor; a type of gallows humor that is simultaneously as cruel as it is creative. When left to their own devices, Soldiers will come up with the most hilarious and cruel things to do to each other. I got off easy by being jumped by ten of my guys. Some of my Soldiers later told me that their initiation into their own Platoons at other units involved being rolled up in a mattress and tossed out of third story barracks windows. One other Officer told me that he was jumped by his Platoon in Afghanistan during the previous deployment. He was stripped naked and taped to a howitzer in the middle of the outpost. It was pretty funny until the outpost started taking enemy rocket fire and they left him out there for a solid thirty minutes or so.

The airing of grievances were pretty much in keeping with the spirit of the holiday. Stew led the proceedings within our converted dining hut. Stew began by letting each person know exactly how they had disappointed them over the past year. We all got a good laugh out of it, but when we moved on to the feats of strength, things got interesting. Space was cleared on the floor and a tarp was rolled out. First Sergeant Stockdon and our Fire Support Officer, Jacob Bordeaux, who we affectionately called *Frenchie* took off their shirts and began wrestling on the tarp.

Somebody yelled, "Wrestle your father, Georgie!" and soon we were all cheering and hooting as two grown men rolled around on the floor.

From there, the night devolved into a series of challenges and contests designed to be more disgusting and disturbing than the last. My personal favorite that Brandt came up with was *The Boot Challenge* wherein teams of two had to mix and drink instant ration dairy shakes from their partner's boot in the fastest time possible.

The sock was left in the boot for added flavor, of course. Another challenge involved ingesting freshly shaved chest hair mixed with sugar water.

I'd had about as much as I could handle and stepped outside just in time to see *The Human Chemical Light Challenge* begin. Soldiers were adorned with chemical glow sticks and lifted off the ground and spun around in circles by their comrades. Points were awarded for the complexity of chem-light arrangement and number of revolutions achieved without touching the ground. Bonus points were awarded if motion-induced vomiting occurred.

I left everyone to the rest of the Festivus activities and made my way back to my bunk. Sure, the Festivus stuff did get a little off the rails, but the Soldiers were having a good time and blowing off some steam together. Nobody got hurt and we all had some good laughs. As I drifted off to sleep, I thought about one final thing. We didn't say anything about Festivus Miracles at the ceremony. I thought about that a little more and came to the conclusion that we were already experiencing a Festivus Miracle. We were over here, in this weird country, acting on orders that didn't quite make sense, but we were making the most of it, together. That's what counted; our little band of misanthropes taking it one day at a time.

Chapter 8

How to Burst into Flames.

The *pop-pop-pop* of distant rifle fire echoed in the background. It sounded like it was about half a kilometer away, but it was hard to be sure because the alleyway distorted the sound. The small, American patrol cautiously made its way through the web of crisscrossing alleys and footpaths. Suddenly, a Taliban fighter broke cover and darted from an open doorway to cross the alleyway. I watched as one of Captain Manion's Soldiers went to one knee behind a crate, sighting his rifle down the narrow alleyway. Captain Manion, my commander, found his own crate and did the same. Smoke and dust curled heavily through the air as both men awaited more enemy movement. The distant patter of small arms fire was the only sound as both men held their breath for an impossibly long moment. Two more Taliban fighters burst from the same doorway, attempting to reach the abandoned building. Both Captain Manion and the Soldier opened fire; their M4 carbine rounds deafening in such a confined space. The first Taliban fighter was too fast and reached the abandoned building safely. The second fighter, however, was not so lucky. Captain Manion's rounds stitched a ragged pattern up the fighter's body starting at the thigh and ending with a final shot just under the jaw. The Taliban fighter flopped to the ground, his face wrap covering the crimson ruin that was surely hidden underneath. His dead hands clasped an AK-47 assault rifle to his chest in a vice-like grip.

Manion was already moving forward; his rifle up to his cheek in the high ready position. His Soldier covered his advance from the alleyway. As he approached the abandoned building, he could see that the Taliban fighters had already shut and likely barricaded the front door. He increased his pace as he approached the doorway. He slammed the full force of his armored body, boot first, into the aqua-blue door. The door burst open, splintering at the frame, revealing a detritus filled room and two half-prepared Taliban fighters. Using his initial momentum, Manion closed the distance to the nearest fighter and bowled him to the floor. He then fired three shots into the fighter's upper chest, where he lay on the ground. He then shifted his sights to the second fighter whose bottom half was concealed by a ruined couch. This Taliban fighter was holding a bulky weapon over his shoulder, its bulbous end fixed on the

Captain. Sighting down his rifle, Manion held his breath and fired. A dull metallic *click* sounded, signaling the end of his current magazine of ammunition. A tight panic filled his chest. Sensing that there was not enough time to reload, Captain Manion dropped his rifle and hurriedly fumbled for the pistol strapped to his thigh. A thunderous *boom* heralded the end as the Taliban fighter fired the shoulder mounted weapon, point blank, at Captain Manion. Everything faded to grey.

The word *Retry?* Floated up to the top of the TV screen.

"This game is total fucking bullshit!" Captain Manion yelled as he tossed the controller onto the dirty plywood floor of the command hut.

"Who the fuck fires an RPG at point blank range inside a building?!?!?" he asked the assembled group on the dusty, stained couch.

"Apparently *that* guy does!" exclaimed Captain Barone, Manion's Executive Officer and second in command of Anvil Troop.

"Yeah Sir, Officers shouldn't be clearing buildings anyway. You should let the men do that work!" prodded First Sergeant Stockdon.

"Ha-ha, very fucking funny, First Sergeant." Captain Manion said in his thick New Jersey accent.

"Alright, let me give this shit a shot." Said Barone as he scooped up the controller.

I cleared my throat, "You called for me Sir?" The trio was scarcely aware that I had been standing in the doorway for the past several minutes.

Video game gunfire echoed in the background as Captain Manion turned around on the sofa and faced me, "Yeah Nick. I want you guys on standby for a mission. Get your guys ready. The Rangers are doing a mission up north and want us on standby for a battle-space handover mission."

"Got it, Sir. Where exactly is this mission taking place and what's the timeframe?" I asked.

Captain Manion let a large glob of Redman-laced dip spit ooze out of his mouth and into a bottle before answering my question, "It's up by Pul-i-Alam. It's going off at about midnight tonight so have your guys ready at about twenty-three-hundred hours."

"Isn't that out of our territory?" I asked, knowing full well that Pul-i-Alam was not part of our Troop's sector and therefore not our responsibility.

"It sure is, but Saber Command pushed it down to us." He added simply. Saber Command was located about 10 kilometers to our east. We were the closest, between all of its subordinate combat Troops, to Pul-i-Alam. Saber Command was in charge of all of us though and if they didn't want to police their own backyard then, it seemed, we were going to be told to do it.

"Don't think too hard, Lieutenant. Just do it." First Sergeant Stockdon chimed in with a smirk. He could already tell that I was spinning the whole concept over in my head and getting agitated. First Sergeant Stockdon always had a knack for reading me.

I ignored the jab and spoke to Captain Manion, "Got it Sir. We'll check in with you when we're ready to go."

"Don't bother," he began "I've been sitting around playing this game all day. I'm fucking tired. I'll be racked out by then."

"I'll be up," Barone said without taking his eyes off the screen "Just check in with me."

"Will do." I responded.

I turned toward Captain Manion and asked, "Anything else, Sir?"

His eyes were glued to the screen now, "No. See you later."

I left the command hut and put my dusty patrol cap back on. The night sky was beautiful; more clear and crisp than anything I had ever seen in the United States. There was no industry here and hence, no pollution. That was the one upside to this part of the world. The mountains, the snow, even the night sky; everything seemed so wild and untouched. It made a lot of the natural scenery back home look processed and packaged by comparison. I was doing my best to not think about Captain Manion. I found that focusing on the scenery around me seemed to calm my nerves.

With ease, Captain Manion had put me on edge. The truth was that his leadership, at the time, left much to be desired. He was a senior Captain, ready to pin on the oak leaves of a Major in the next few weeks. He would be replaced by a younger (and still unnamed) Captain and now he was totally checked out. The signs were there for a while though. I remember the off-again, on-again formations in garrison where he spoke to me and the other Platoon leaders, McKenzie and Bray, so hungover he could barely stand. More often than not, it felt like our Troop was held together by our First Sergeant. As intolerably arrogant and abrasive as First Sergeant Stockdon could be, he was equally competent. He could have easily been a Colonel by now had he gone the Officer route with his career; a thought which probably crossed his mind once or twice given the absolute disdain he held for most Officers.

My mind drifted back to the possible mission out at Pul-i-Alam. Although I was glad that Manion wasn't going to be involved in this one, I didn't feel particularly reassured by the fact that Barone was going to be overseeing us alone and unsupervised. With all of his flaws, Manion was highly intelligent and occasionally showed glimmers of good leadership. Barone, on the other hand, was brash and reactionary and had recently played a hand in nearly getting Sergeant Brandt killed. Just the previous week, Brandt was nearly hit by a faulty illumination round that Barone's mortars fired over my Platoon without my knowledge or permission. The round did not detach or detonate or do any of the things a mortar fired illumination round was supposed to do. It just embedded itself into the ground, mere feet from Brandt, like a steel football plummeting from the heavens. Upon returning to the command hut after the mission, I learned that Barone had ordered the mortars to fire directly over my patrol for no reason other than he wanted to see better. Barone had previously not impressed me on several of our training exercises when we were back in Germany. Recalling one particular exercise, I remembered that he ultimately denied a mission-critical request for fire support because he and I were arguing about the location of my Platoon. This almost cost me the mission and left me conducting an attack directly into the teeth of an enemy ambush without artillery support. I was ultimately in the right and this didn't sit well with me or my persistent feelings of self-righteousness so I painted him in a bad light for the rest of our interactions. Whether it was just or not, I saw him negatively and lumped him in the same category as Manion.

I went back to our Platoon area and put the men on standby. I let them know that we were going out to Pul-i-Alam to help the Rangers with some sort of clandestine snatch-and-grab type mission. Our role in a battle-space handover type mission would be to smooth over relations and hand out damage vouchers should the Rangers have to put bullet holes in everything. This particular Ranger battalion had been attached to our Brigade and would be operating in our battle space for the next few months. The Rangers technically fell under Special Operations Command so we weren't privy to the details of their missions or really much of anything that they did. Most of their compounds were sealed off or fenced in to maintain this level of secrecy. I found this odd because many members of our Troop, to include myself, were Ranger qualified. We had completed the Ranger training school and had the same basic level of leadership and training. Some of us had even served in one of the three Ranger combat battalions. According to the Army's own definition, we were all Rangers. Apparently though, if you put them together in a large enough groups, Rangers suddenly became a Special Operations unit. From what I could gather, the Rangers' primary tasks included night-time raids and other snatch and grab type missions. All of this sounded way more interesting than what we were doing and I wondered how many more Rangers we needed to add to our Platoon before we became Special Operations too. As amusing as it was, I had to put all of my pointless thoughts aside and began making preparations for the mission.

Walking into the tactical operations center (TOC for short) which housed all of our radios and command and control elements, I began getting all of the radio frequencies and call signs that we had on file for the Ranger units in our battle space. I scanned the mIRC chat (the Army's secure version of instant messenger) screen to see what was happening in regards to the Rangers. From what I could piece together, it looked like a force of about forty Rangers were operating to our northeast in hopes that they could snag a few high value targets. The path to Pul-i-Alam was a wide open, paved road that had no IED activity so far this year. Since our mission would take place under the cover of darkness, I felt that taking our Mine Resistant Ambush Protected vehicles (or MRAPs for short) on the road would be the most expedient way to get there. Rangers usually fought without any armored support at all so I figured my four armored vehicles would be a welcomed addition to their battle plan. Since we were going to take the vehicles, I left instructions with Barone to have our wrecker truck on standby in case anything broke down or, God forbid, was disabled by the enemy. With everything in order and the men fully prepared, I did what all Soldiers spend eighty percent of their time doing in combat; I waited for stuff to happen.

When the call finally came for us to assist the Rangers, it was close to midnight. The drive out to Pul-i-Alam took only a few short minutes, our vehicles making it there in record time. As an added bonus, we fell out of radio range from COP Baraki Barak once we rounded a particularly large mountain range; no more of Barone's voice over the radio. I established radio communication with some private manning the radios at Saber Command and continued the mission without Barone. The moon provided good illumination and our night vision and thermal devices were working perfectly. As we approached the rendezvous site, I began hailing the Ranger unit. After a few calls, they replied tersely that I would be signaled in by a lone Ranger on a rooftop. This rooftop Ranger would then illuminate an infrared strobe to show where he wanted our vehicles to park. It didn't take us long to find our man shining a brilliant infrared light out onto the road. My men parked in a tight defensive position, guns facing outward in all directions covering the alleyways and rooftops surrounding us. I heard a banging on my door and looked out the window to see the outline of a Ranger waiting. I opened my pneumatic-assisted steel slab of a door and stepped down to greet the man in front of me. He was several inches taller than me, bordering on six foot, six inches. Even in the dark, I could tell from the chunky outline of his rifle and kit that he was fitted with all of the high-tech gadgetry and do-dads that only a special operations budget could afford. His incredibly expensive (and depth perception providing) twin monocular night vision goggles eyed me up and down briefly.

I stuck my hand out, "Lieutenant Stevens, Red Platoon, Anvil Troop."

He glanced down at my hand as though I had just offered him a fist-full of wriggling dicks. "Leave your guys here and come with me LT." He said simply and began walking away briskly.

I brought my hand back and looked around nervously. My Platoon Sergeant, Stew, was trotting up beside me.

"Hey Stew," I began "put Sergeant Brandt in charge. Looks like we've got to go see what's up."

"Roger that, Sir." He responded then put out a quick order to Sergeant Brandt over the radio.

Stew and I were led by our incredibly tall tour guide toward a small group of Rangers inside a slightly official, at least for afghan standards, looking building. Our guide pointed to one of the Rangers who clearly was the commander.

He glanced up at me and then over to the Ent-sized Ranger that had escorted me to him, "Who is this?" he asked.

Ranger Tree-beard spoke, "He's here for the battle space handover. He brought a Platoon and some trucks."

The commander looked back at me, "Trucks?" he asked. The tone in the word *trucks* was more like he had just said *UFOs* or *DeLoreans*.

"Yeah. Four of them." I replied.

"How many guys?" the commander asked me, brushing past the truck issue.

"Eighteen, plus about twenty Afghan National Army guys in four Ford Rangers." I replied.

"Where are the rest of your guys?" he asked me.

"That's it. There's eighteen of us." I said, "We're a scout Platoon."

"Oh." He replied unable to hide the tinge of disappointment in his voice. "Well," he continued "let's get you up to speed."

We spent the next few minutes going over what had happened before I arrived. This commander and his Rangers had arrived with a simple mission; to raid a suspected enemy office building for information regarding IEDs to be planted in the area. They had called my commander up, fully expecting me to walk twenty kilometers to get there. As a consequence, we had arrived too early. After a few minutes, the Rangers eventually found their target building. Stew and I called up our Platoon to provide an outer cordon, with the vehicles as strongpoints. The Rangers went inside and most of their radio chatter died down as they searched from room to room. Listening to the radio, I pieced together that they had found roughly six military aged males (MAMs for short) and some suspicious documents; no obvious bad guys though.

The Rangers began filing out of the target building and I met with the commander. It was three in the morning and we had about two hours of darkness left.

He pointed his dual monocular night vision devices at me, green dots in the darkness, "They're all yours now. Come with me and I'll show you where we've got them. "

I did as I was told and followed the Ranger commander inside the building. We walked through a couple of barely lit rooms, the miniscule amount of light was amplified to blinding levels through my night vision monocle so I flipped it up, away from my eye. We came to a small, windowless room that looked more like a closet than a living area. Six young Afghan men were huddled together on their knees, their hands zip-cuffed behind their backs. They were all oriented away from the door, facing the far wall. Two Rangers stood guard just outside the doorway, their weapons casually trained on the Afghans.

The Ranger commander gestured toward the men in the closet, "They're all yours LT. Get your guys in here so they can relieve my guards. We're way over mission time and we need to bounce. "

I nodded and put out a quick order over the radio to have my men begin relieving the Rangers. I turned toward the Ranger Captain who was already walking away from me, "Hold on a second," I began, "what just happened? What should I tell these guys?" I asked, gesturing toward the Afghan captives in the closet.

"Them?" the Ranger commander began, "We just took some documents. None of these dudes are the guys we're looking for. We'll see if anything we took gives us any leads. As far as a story goes, tell these guys whatever the fuck you want, LT."

With that the Rangers began filing out of the building and assembling on the road outside. My men came in, taking up defensive positions inside the building. Stew eventually made his way next to me. I glanced outside, the Rangers were already gone; undoubtedly marching through the darkness to some helicopter pick-up zone in the middle of the steppes to our west.

Stew stood next to me and took one look at the half dozen zip-cuffed men crammed into the closet, "What the fuck is this?" He asked. "Why are they all like this?" he continued, "None of these guys are armed and they just put them on their knees and zip-cuffed them facing the wall; execution style."

I knew where Stew was coming from. He had done several tours in Iraq and Afghanistan. Names like *Kunar*, *Fallujah* and *Sadr City* were often brought up in conversation with him. He had fought, killed, lost friends and bled in some of the most difficult actions in the past several years. He was starting to see a cycle in all this. The worse we treated our enemies, the harder they fought us; a pattern of reasoning not shared by everyone in the Army at the time. At that time, I believed in Stew and his way of thinking.

"I know Stew," I began, "The Rangers were thinking they'd have to come in, guns blazing. They treat things like deadly threats until proven otherwise; not the other way around."

"Noted Sir." He replied uncomfortably. Stew depressed the activation button on his radio set, "Hey, Sergeant Brandt, send some guys in here and tell them to bring a case of water. We've got six guys that have been hog-tied for hours for next to no reason."

"Roger that." Came Brandt's static-laced reply over the radio.

"Stew," I ventured, "Once we get some more guys and the interpreter in here, we'll cut these zip-cuffs off."

"Roger that." Stew replied. He looked slightly more relieved, but something was still bothering him.

"What's up Stew?" I asked. It was just the two of us so I didn't refrain from using his first name.

"Nick, it's just that we work so hard to build relationships with these people." He began. "We meet with them for hours, listen to their problems, eat food and drink tea with them, give them medicine and food and do all the things that the generals tell us to do in hopes that the Afghan people will side with us instead of the Taliban. Then, some Special Forces-types, who have no vested interest in this patch of ground because they don't own territory *anywhere* in Afghanistan, come in here and do all the goddamn things that we promised the Afghan people we wouldn't do. Hitting houses in the dead of night, kicking the doors in to half the fucking village until they find the right house, pointing guns in the faces of unarmed people and oh, my personal favorite, zip-cuffing a bunch of Afghans in a fucking closet and facing them against the wall, execution style. That's why this shit has gone on for nearly a decade. This shit right here." He finished, pointing a finger at the six Afghans on their knees.

I had to take it all in for a moment; he was absolutely right. "Stew, I get it." I said, "We're all getting frustrated and pissed off. We can't change what just happened."

"I'm sorry to vent like that, but I've just seen this kind of shit for so long." He said.

"Stew, I…" I began, but was cut off by the arrival of two of our Soldiers.

Specialist Ring came into the room first ensuring that it was clear. He was followed closely by Specialist Grey who was carrying a case of bottled water. Our interpreter, Jesse, came in last. Grey placed the case of water down on the floor and took a few steps back in case he had to use his long M-14 rifle in such close quarters. Ring did the same and Jesse casually strolled up next to me with his hands in his pockets. His helmet, as was often the case, was nowhere to be found. I was tired of telling him to go back and get it out of the truck so I let it go. As far as I was concerned, it was on him if he wanted to have his brains spilled out onto the dust someday and this mission would be over more quickly if I couldn't talk to the locals.

As if on cue, one of the men on the floor looked over his shoulder and saw that there was an Afghan interpreter and immediately began speaking in Pashto. Jesse listened for a moment or two and then turned to me.

"He says they don't know what's going on." Jesse said.

I looked down at the man, motioning for him to make eye contact with me and not my interpreter, "We're not sure either. Those men that just left were from a different unit. They were looking for something but wouldn't tell us what it was. We're sorry this happened to you."

Jesse spoke to the man in rapid Pashto. He was a really good interpreter. I'd help him look for his helmet later; it would be wise to help him keep his brain intact for as long as possible. The man on the ground took everything in for a moment or two before speaking, "Ok, but can we have some water?" He asked.

"Of course," I replied "but you're going to have to promise me that you're going to not run away." I said.

Jesse regurgitated my speech to the man. He nodded to me.

"Ok, let's start with names." I began. "I'm Nick and you are?" I asked.

Some more rapid Pashto from Jesse, "My name is Hassan, nice to meet you."

I turned toward Specialist Ring, "Ring and Grey, give these guys a quick pat-down in case the Rangers missed anything. If they're clean, cut these guys loose and let's get them some water."

Jesse immediately began speaking in Pashto. "Goddamnit Jesse," I interrupted, "Don't translate that part for them."

"Sorry Sir." Jesse said, stopping immediately. He put his hands back in his pockets with the look about him of a scolded puppy.

After a few moments, Grey and Ring had searched all six of the Afghans. I nodded to Ring and they cut them loose. The men then stood up, rubbing their wrists. Even on their dark skin, the zip-cuffs had reddened the flesh. I spoke to the Afghans, through Jesse, about what happened. Basically, they were a road construction crew based out of Pul-i-Alam. They assured me that they had nothing to do with the Taliban which came as no surprise to me; apparently I was the only person in Afghanistan who had ever heard of this mysterious Taliban organization. The main concern, as outlined by

Hassan, was that the Rangers had taken their work maps. Without knowing where their worksites were, they wouldn't be able to work. It was a valid concern. I wouldn't be able to get the maps back from the Rangers. Instead, I promised to speak to my commander about getting them some kind of reconciliation pay for loss of future business. I told Hassan to come to our outpost one week from today to speak with me. This seemed to pacify him to the point where we could leave soon. The truth was, that we had piles of Afghan money (unimaginatively called "afghani") stuffed into safes back at the outpost. The exchange rate was something to the order of forty seven afghani to every one American dollar so it wasn't much of a concern.

After shaking hands and exchanging goodbyes, we parted ways with Hassan and his group. It was about thirty minutes before dawn and I wanted to get the hell out of Pul-i-Alam. This village was much larger than the maps had depicted. In the wasting twilight hours, I could see that this was more of a small city than a village. There must have been thousands of Afghans here. This city fell under Saber Command's direct jurisdiction which meant that it wasn't patrolled regularly as Saber only had two of their own maneuver Platoons. One of those Platoons was always loaned out to other units and the other spent most of its time ferrying around Saber's commander, Lieutenant Colonel Dunn. With no combat Platoons regularly patrolling such a heavily populated area, it began to feel more and more like Indian territory.

"All the more reason to get the fuck out of here." I thought to myself.

I gave the order for the Platoon to mount their vehicles. A few moments later, I called across the radio for all of the vehicles to report their status. All the vehicles reported that they were ready to go. I looked over at Asher, my driver, and gave a nod to get the hell out of here. Asher started the vehicle up, but it died moments later. He scrunched his brow at the dashboard and tried again; same thing. He tried a third time, this time feeding the vehicle some gas and it sputtered out after a few seconds. Asher slowly turned his head to me, the look on his face as if he had accidently stabbed an infant in front of me.

"Are you fucking shitting me?" I asked.

"It won't start Sir." Asher said.

"I can fucking see that, Asher." I replied, trying unsuccessfully to keep the frustration out of my voice.

"What, specifically, is wrong with it?" I asked.

"I think it might be flooding." He said.

"Ok," I began, "what do you need to do to fix it?" I inquired.

Asher replied, "I need to let it sit for about thirty minutes and then try again."

"You have twenty minutes, Asher." I began, "The sun will be up in thirty minutes and hundreds of Afghans will come out, sleepy-eyed, to see why there is an American patrol that just appeared overnight in the middle of their city. Some of those people will be the ones that had their front doors kicked in by the Rangers a few hours ago. How happy do you think they will be with these aforementioned Americans, Asher?" I asked.

Asher's face was solemn as he replied, "Not very, Sir."

"That's right, Asher. Not very. There's eighteen of us and hundreds of them; you have twenty minutes." I replied.

Asher nodded and hopped out of the truck. I saw the front hood flip up as he began investigating the engine compartment. I put out a call over the radio, letting everyone know that we had mechanical problems and would be delayed. With the exception of gunners and drivers, all crew members got out of their vehicles and took up a defensive posture. I too, hopped down from my MRAP. I began thinking of how we were going to get this vehicle out of here in case it wouldn't start. We had the wrecker truck on standby back at the outpost, but we couldn't talk to them directly. I could talk to Saber Command and they could relay to the outpost. I didn't want to risk anything getting lost or twisted in the relayed communication. I decided that I would use our on-board MRAP computers to text back to the outpost. I put out a quick message to the outpost letting them know our situation and that we would potentially need the wrecker soon. I saw that Stew was walking up to me, closing the final few steps.

"We have to get out of here ASAP, Sir." He said.

"I know." I replied.

Stew looked around nervously, "I don't want us to be here when the sun comes up. Especially when they figure out that there's only eighteen of us."

"Yeah." I answered, fully knowing the implications of what he said.

"Hey Sir," Stew began, "Steiner knows a lot about these vehicles too. You want me to have him come up and give Asher a hand?" he asked.

"Roger that." I said.

Within moments, Specialist Steiner was trotting up toward my vehicle. He and Asher began working on the vehicle together. Several dogs barked in the background. It sounded like a pack of them were fucking or fighting or maybe both. I looked around the city of Pul-i-Alam. The first slivers of dawn were coming over the horizon. Some of my Soldiers had already switched off their night vision devices; avoiding the blinding amplification of the ever-increasing ambient light. Children began filtering out of the qalat houses. The young children were always the first to awaken in Afghanistan. They came in ones and twos at first, then in their dozens. They kept a watchful distance from my Soldiers, but they clearly weren't going anywhere. Most of them sat idle on steps or walls, driven on by innocent childish curiosity. It was the others that worried me. Some looked at our patrol and darted back inside their qalats. I thought I could see one mouthing numbers, counting the size of our patrol. We were running out of time.

I stuck my head back into my MRAP to see if the outpost had received my message. The blinking icon at the bottom of the screen indicated my new mail. I opened the message and learned that our wrecker recovery vehicle wouldn't start (oh, the irony), but they were getting the maintenance Sergeant, Sergeant Keith, to work on it immediately. I quickly texted back about Saber Command's wreckers, knowing that they had two. Within seconds, the outpost responded saying that one of Saber's wreckers was dead lined for maintenance and that the other was many miles away, halfway down the road with a supply convoy to Charlie Troop in Kherwar. We weren't getting any wreckers to tow us out of here. We had to solve this on our own.

I looked back at my MRAP truck and began running the possibilities in my head. There was a chance that it would start, but there was, as far as I knew, an equal chance that it wouldn't. The truck was filled with sensitive items, weapons and computer systems that would have to be stripped or destroyed in case we had to leave the vehicle behind. Afghans had developed their scavenging skills to preternatural levels and could find a use for anything. A lot of things left behind by American forces could be turned against us by the Taliban. More than once, discarded lamp wire has been used as command wire for IEDs; scrap metal can become shrapnel, etc. I was loathe to leave behind several tons of steel, rubber, plastic and wire.

My thoughts were interrupted by the healthy roar of an engine; my engine. I looked up to see Steiner grinning from my side of the vehicle. Asher was giving me a thumbs up from behind the steering wheel. Nearly a hundred Afghans had started to file out into the streets, rubbing sleep from their eyes. I gave a terse order over the radio and, within moments, all Soldiers were mounted up and ready to go. I was happy to see the ever-growing and bewildered group of Afghans shrink away in my side mirror.

Once we had gotten the Platoon outside of Pul-i-Alam, I turned toward Asher, "What did you guys do?" I asked.

"Well Sir," he began, "Steiner and I had to Gerry-rig some stuff, but we got it to work." Leaving it deliberately vague.

"Alright, I get it. You don't want to give away all of your trade secrets. I'm just glad you two got us out of there. Great job." I said.

Asher grinned at the compliment, "Me too Sir, me too."

We continued along the paved road for several minutes. The sun was fully up at this point. Several small villages blurred past as we made our way around the mountain range that had blocked us from radio contact with our outpost. I made a brief radio check and, for the first time in hours, the outpost's radio channel crackled to life. I fully updated the outpost's TOC with a situation report.

My Platoon radio channel came to life in my ear, "Red 1 this is Red 4, halt the Platoon." It was Stew's voice.

"Roger that." I replied, "Guidons, this is Red 1, assume short halt position."

I was going to ask Stew what the problem was, but I saw it in my passenger side mirror. The MRAP truck between Stew and I was stopped and sitting at a sloped angle. The gunner on top of the MRAP had slunk down, undoubtedly worried about a potential vehicle rollover. I looked down at the front passenger tire and saw that it was wedged in a concrete drainage ditch on the side of the road.
Sergeant Hoffman's voice came across the radio, "Red 1 this is Red 3, and we're stuck in this ditch back here. No injuries. Fucking driver was half asleep and went off the road."

"Got it." I began, "Red 4, do you want to pull him out from your side or do I need to pull him out?" I asked Stew.

Stew responded immediately, "Red 1, I'll pull him out. His rear tires are free. If we pull from the front we'll suck the both passenger side tires into the ditch."

"Roger that." I replied.

It only took a few minutes to get Stew's vehicle hooked up to Hoffman's. We kept recovery ropes and cables mounted on the front and rear of our MRAPs. We tried to use our spare time as a Platoon as wisely as possible, practicing vehicle recovery drills and similar tasks back at the outpost. Already though, several dozen Afghans had come out of the woodwork to see what the Americans were up to. This was a little unpleasant taste of Deja vu for me and I wanted to get us out of here as quickly as possible. My Platoon had been on edge for hours.

"Alright everybody," I began over the radio, "watch your sectors and we'll be out of this shortly."

A few moments later, Stew's truck lurched backward freeing Hoffman's truck from the ditch. Hoffman's front right wheel was a little warped so we would have to watch our speed. We were only about a dozen kilometers away from the outpost; the last thing I wanted to do was get stuck out here in Indian territory with a three-wheeled MRAP. I gave the order for us to move out and not a minute too soon. The Afghan civilians were out in numbers. Apparently the Afghan coconut-shell powered news network had spread the word down to this area that eighteen Americans in four trucks were out mucking about. By and large, they were completely harmless, but all it took was the one RPG or suicide vest that we couldn't see in the crowd to turn one of our vehicles into a smoking wreck. It was hard not to be a little paranoid.

We were on our way again. We made it a few more kilometers down the road when I radioed to the outpost to let them know that we were moving again and inbound. Suddenly, Hoffman's voice came across the radio.

"Red 1 this is Red 3," he began, "Um, I think you're flaming... yup you're flaming."

"Ha-fucking-ha." I replied, "Very funny."

"Red 1 this is Red 4," Stew chimed in, "You're on fire right now."

"Guys, the gay jokes have gone too far." I said. "We're past most of the bad stuff on this one, but we're not out of the woods yet so I would appreciate it if..."

Stew interrupted me, "YOUR FUCKING VEHICLE IS ON FIRE, SIR! STOP AND GET OUT!"

I looked over at Asher and, without and prompting, he slammed on the brakes. We both bailed out, each with our own miniature fire extinguishers. Asher had the wherewithal to lower the Troop deck on the back of the MRAP. The men seated in the Troop compartment piled out of the back. Jesse the interpreter was among them and immediately threw his scarf across his face to keep the curling black smoke out of his lungs. I rounded the back corner of the MRAP and saw Asher extinguishing some small flames inside the driver side rear wheel-well with his tiny red fire extinguisher. He had completely eradicated the flames before I could bring my extinguisher to bear. The smoke cleared up quickly and it looked like there was very little damage to the MRAP itself. Some plastic had melted, but the metal and, more importantly, the wheel assembly looked fine.

I looked around at the small group, "Everyone OK?" I asked.

"Yes Sir." Came the half-murmured reply of several very exhausted Soldiers.

I made a radio call to the outpost to tell them that we were still experiencing vehicle problems and that this time we had introduced the element of fire. I asked the outpost radio operator to put Barone on the radio. The radio operator couldn't find him. Barone had, no doubt, wandered off or fallen asleep hours ago when he got word that our mission was over and we were headed back. I decided to skip the middle-man and I ordered the radio operator to get the maintenance Sergeant, Sergeant Keith, on the radio to see if he could help remotely diagnose why the fuck my vehicle had just burst into flames. It would take a few minutes for Keith to get to the radio so I gave the order to keep moving down the road.

Within moments, my vehicle was on fire again. The announcement came across the radio with much less fanfare this time.

"Red 1 this is Red 4, you're on fucking fire again." Came Stew's exhausted voice over the radio.

Asher and I pulled over, once again, and lowered the Troop deck; same drill as before. The fire, if anything, was consistent and the same wheel had ignited and was burning lazily within the wheel-well. Instead of wasting a fire extinguisher, I doused a couple of bottles of water on the wheel and the flames went out with a hiss. My radio crackled to life.

"You're getting good at this Sir." Came the voice of Hoffman.

I turned, seeing him grinning from the passenger seat of his MRAP. From about fifteen meters away there would have been no way for Hoffman to mistake the chunky outline of my raised ballistic glove-clad middle finger.

I decided that I'd try the maintenance Sergeant, "Anvil X-Ray this is Red 1. Do you have Wrench 7 with you yet?" I asked over the Troop channel.

"Roger that, Red 1," Came the TOC's reply, "I'll put him on now."

"Red 1 this is Wrench 7," came the thick Texas drawl of Sergeant Keith, "What's the problem?" he asked. It sounded like there was half a can of dip in his mouth. In all likelihood, it was a full can.

"Well, my back left tire keeps catching fire on my MRAP and since I don't like fire, that's a problem." I replied.

"Sounds like your brakes are catching. You're going to have to cage your brakes." Keith said.

I waited for a moment or two for him to explain, "What the fuck does that mean?" I asked.

"You know, cage the brakes." He ventured.

"No. I fucking don't know, Wrench 7." I said.

"Well Sir, you've got to get out and cage the brakes." He said again.

"Let's pretend that I haven't spent years being a mechanic and, instead, I've spent the last several hours on this ridiculous fucking mission that WON'T GODDAMN END. SO PLEASE, FOR THE LOVE OF GOD, STOP SPEAKING IN FUCKING REDNECK RIDDLES AND ANSWER MY GODDAMN QUESTION!!!"

His end of the line was as quiet as the grave when I spoke next. "Now please, I don't have a brake thingy so tell me what I have to do to get this thing back there without catching fire again."

Sergeant Keith then proceeded to explain that the MRAP brake system operated off of compressed air, much like the powered door systems and the Troop hatch. This made sense to me. He then informed me that when there is low air pressure in the brake system, it goes back to its default position, which is completely locked. The only way to unlock them is to apply compressed air from a large, industrial sized air compressor or to use a special key, called a brake cage key. Keith kept our only key on his person. As counterintuitive as all this seemed to me, the peerless engineers at the MRAP wing of the Willy Wonka factory decided that it would be a good idea that if the compressed air system inside the MRAP were to be compromised in any way, the brakes and doors would lock up; effectively stranding you wherever the fuck you were. According to Keith, the only thing I could do was limp back slowly to the outpost and get out every few hundred feet and pour water on the grinding brakes to prevent them from bursting into flames yet again.

I listened to all of this with a quiet stoicism that I didn't know I possessed. When Keith was done talking, I put the hand mic down and faced Asher, "Asher," I began, "when you and Steiner fixed this truck, was there a chance that you might have done something, anything, to the air hydraulic system?" I asked.

Asher looked around nervously, "Maybe Sir. It was dark." He said.

I took a deep breath, "It's ok Asher. You did the best you could. Now, let's limp this heaping pile of shit out of here."

With that, we proceeded to move back to the outpost, a few hundred meters at a time. Stew would call over the radio and tell me that I was on fire with the drained enthusiasm of Liberace at a bikini contest. I'd pull over once more and we'd toss more water onto the back wheel. Eventually, we were moving so slow, that I ordered Soldiers on foot to accompany the vehicle and apply water as needed. Hours later, we finally made our way to the outpost. It must have been right before noon, but I wasn't really sure. I had Asher pull the MRAP into the maintenance bay. While my Soldiers were downloading their gear from the mission, I made my way to the TOC hoping to find Barone or Captain Manion. The TOC was empty except for the lone radio operator, Private Rush, who had been on the other end of the radio all morning. I gave Rush my return to base report, citing that all equipment and personnel had made it back from the patrol. Rush began typing the information into the mIRC chat screen.

I watched the words fill the chat Rush, "Rush, put in the report that my vehicle will be down for maintenance for the foreseeable future."

Rush nodded, "What happened Sir?" he asked.

"I don't want to talk about it right now." I said and left the TOC.

I went around the corner to the command team's private quarters. First Sergeant Stockdon's room was open and he was no doubt working somewhere on the outpost. Captain Manion's door was shut tight and I could hear him snoring behind the door. My blood boiled sleeping in this late while one of his Platoons was stuck in the middle of nowhere. I heard the sound of video game gunfire coming from the other room. I walked in and found Barone, seated on the couch, playing the same video game from the night before.

A glob of dip spit left his mouth and lazily fell into an awaiting Gatorade bottle, "Dude, what took you guys so long?" he asked.

"Go fuck yourself." I said.

Chapter 9

Penis Wars.

The weeks that followed the Pul-i-Alam mission seemed to blur together. It wasn't long before the tedium of endless and identical patrols began to sink in. There definitely was a distinct pattern among the Afghan populace; they didn't seem to know anything.

"Where's the Taliban?" I'd ask in countless villages.

"There is no Taliban here." Was the universal reply.

Apart from that one startlingly perceptive shopkeeper I had encountered a few weeks before, no one seemed willing to talk about the Taliban with me. Mind you, this didn't deter me from doing my job. It just put a nice emphasis on the futility of said job. I'd go to villages with my Platoon and we'd try to figure out who the key leaders were in the area and where the Taliban fighters were. I'd extend the olive branch with blankets for winter or grain if the village had a particularly meager harvest. This was met with appreciation but no real answers to the questions I wanted to know. After all, I wasn't doing anything out of the ordinary for these people. They'd been receiving handouts from us for the better part of a decade. It was almost expected. But where were the enemy fighters? Where were the caches? Where are the things that I knew were lying in wait, ready to kill me and my men?

I'm not sure why the first penis showed up. It just kind of happened. I had come back to the Platoon leadership hut, where all the Platoon leaders and Sergeants bunked, from a particularly long and especially fruitless patrol when I passed by Lieutenant McKenzie's bunk. Jake McKenzie was the Lieutenant in charge of Third or "Blue" Platoon and was everything that I was not. He was a fanatically patriotic young man and card-carrying member of the Mormon persuasion. He spoke with a deep and booming voice. He was a staunch conservative and he was happily married. He even played college football for a year or two. In short, he was the man that they made the Army for. I'm not entirely sure what possessed me to grab a large diameter sharpie and draw a twelve inch long, throbbing penis on the plywood wall outside of his bunk, but I did it just the same. Maybe it was because I hadn't laughed or even grinned in weeks? Perhaps, I mused, it was because I received a perverse pleasure in tormenting McKenzie? As childish as it was, that two dimensional penis did make me smile for a moment.

A few hours later, McKenzie returned to the hut and scowled at the penis on the door.

"Did you do this, Stevens?" he asked me. He always refused to call me by my first name even though we were the same rank.

"Damn straight." I replied, turning from the patrol debriefing that I was typing up.

"Two can play at this game." He replied and stormed into his bunk

With that, the Penis Wars were in full swing. The following morning, I saw that McKenzie had covered up my artwork with a poster. McKenzie began telling the other Platoon leaders and Platoon Sergeants how he was going to get back at me. I waited for a few days, but nothing materialized. I awoke one morning to find that a penis had been drawn on my pillow while I was sleeping. It had been done in such a way to appear that it was half-way down my throat. I walked out of my bunk, holding my pillow, eyes ablaze with accusation. McKenzie was seated on a beat up couch where he had gathered the other Platoon leaders and Platoon Sergeants to witness his triumph.

"Ha! Got you!" he exclaimed, much to the delight of the assembled crowd.

To the casual observer, I took it in good stride and the whole thing would likely conclude in a mature and congenial manner. Nothing could have been further from the truth. Unlike McKenzie, my malicious creativity knew no bounds and I immediately began plotting my revenge. I took a male blow-up doll, wrapped in the American flag, and tucked it into his bed while he was on mission. I stayed up until four in the morning just so I could hear his exasperated sigh and the, "Goddamnit, Stevens" that accompanied it when he uncovered my doing. McKenzie then retaliated with an entire bag of pubic hair that had been sprinkled into my bed; unimaginative, but effective. I spent close to an hour picking hair out of my sleeping bag. Once I had shaken out my sleeping bag for the fourth time, I noticed the feces smeared on my book collection. As a self-proclaimed academic, this was a step too far.

Incensed, I decided to formulate my master-plan. McKenzie was always looking through *Ranger Joe* and *UnderArmor* magazines during his down time. Our entire hut was littered with magazines displaying half-naked, heavily muscled men modeling the latest in military-style clothing accessories. McKenzie also kept a collage of his family photos above his bunk. These photos were inches above his face, ostensibly so the last thing he saw before he drifted off to sleep was his family... sentimental sap. I decided that it was high time to flood his conscious mind with the latent homo-eroticism that he so craved. I began cutting out the particularly alluring male specimens from dozens of magazines and gluing them, individually, over his family photos. I removed the collage and then proceeded to draw, in sharpie, directly onto the wood ceiling a life-size portrait of myself. This portrait was, of course, completely nude and endowed with an engorged sex organ better proportioned on a horse. I did my best to capture Adam's pose from *The Creation of Adam*. I spent hours making sure that every aspect of this portrait was as disturbingly detailed as possible. I ensured that the eyes lined up perfectly to where McKenzie slept; my portrait's unblinking gaze boring holes into McKenzie's skull. After several hours, I deemed that my work was complete and covered it back up with the collage facade. Michelangelo would have been proud... or horrified I wasn't really sure which at the time.

When McKenzie finally returned from his patrol, he groaned and took off his armor. He spent a few minutes rustling around before he made his way into his bunk. There was only a mumble of, "goddamnit Stevens" before he drifted off to sleep. I assumed that he had only seen the homosexual man-collage that I had made for him and not my true masterpiece hidden behind it. McKenzie's shouting the following morning confirmed my speculation. I awoke to find him standing outside his bunk, mouth agape, holding the man collage.

"What the fuck Stevens? What the hell is wrong with you?!?!?" he shouted, stabbing a finger up toward my fresco.

"Do you like it?" I asked, inclining my head as I twisted the corner of my mouth a little.

"It's directly on the wood man... The *wood*." He proclaimed.

"Yup. It's never coming off. It'll be your constant companion for the rest of your time in this shit-hole country." I added.

"What did I ever do to you?" he asked. He was doing a good job of looking innocent.

"Oh, please McKenzie. I thought we were past this?" I asked. "Don't pretend like you had nothing to do with the pubic hair and defiling my books." I stated.

His eyes were filled with confusion. "What the fuck are you talking about?" He inquired. "All I did was draw on your stupid pillow and you've been tormenting me for weeks." He said.

I then noticed Sergeant First Class Moss, the Platoon Sergeant for White Platoon, sitting on the beat up couch. He was wearing a pair of Ranger exercise shorts that were deliberately a size too small. His massive, white legs were stretched out before him. He was trying to stifle his laughter.

"What's so damned funny?" I asked.

"IT WAS ME!!! I'm the one that's been doing this! HAHAHA!!!" Moss exclaimed.

"You son of a bitch!" I shouted back, secretly impressed by his subversion. "I'll get you for this. Just you wait." I added.

Moss was too busy laughing at this point to fear anything that I had to say. I turned back to McKenzie. He was trying to pick off all of the sexy man cut-outs off of his family photos. Some of them were peeling the faces off of his loved ones as he removed them.

"Sorry about that McKenzie." I said.

"You're a dick, Stevens." He said simply and walked back into his bunk.

Moss was grinning from ear to ear with his arms folded and those albino legs crossed at the ankles.

"It was sooo fun to watch you mercilessly attack McKenzie."

"You didn't plan this out, did you?" I asked abruptly.

Moss looked at me, "Do go on, Sir." He said.

"You've got QRF cycle next. I'm on ForcePro. I get to sit here and plot. The first mission you go on, I'm going to fuck your world up." I said, as I crossed my arms defiantly.

Realization dawned on Moss, "Ok, but no poop. That's totally off limits. The stuff I put on your books was chocolate." He added desperately.

"Fair enough. No poop" I said. "But know this, I will get back at you and it will be *glorious*."

It wasn't long before Moss and his Platoon were called up as QRF to go deal with a possible high value target in the area. Based off of how far south it was, it was going to be a longer mission and it afforded me time to put into effect my most nefarious plan ever. In keeping with the penis theme, I was going to show Moss how much of a dick he had been this entire time. This would be achieved by cutting a three foot by six foot window into his wall in the shape of a phallus. The outside would be labeled, "a view to a dick" with an arrow pointing to Moss so all passers-by could look upon him like some kind of carnival freak. His bunk was situated along the outside wall of the hut and winter was still in full swing. Not only would this be hilarious and inventive in a metaphorical way, but it would also be cruel and inconvenient in a very real sense as it would expose him to wind and snow. I ran my plan by First Sergeant Stockdon in order to procure the power tools that I would need. As the manager of all things related to Soldier housing Stockdon, surprisingly, gave me his complete blessing to go forth with my plan. Apparently, my level of childish cruelty was encouraged in some circles in the Army.

I started gathering the tools when I noticed some Soldiers gathering outside the tactical operations center. Something was happening. I kept the battery operated jigsaw that I had found and trotted over to them. Several Soldiers were talking in hushed tones.

"What's going on?" I asked.

"Moss's Platoon hit an IED Sir. Some of the guys might be hurt." One of them responded.

"Yeah, Sir." Another chimed in. "We're trying to figure out if there are any casualties."

"Oh." I replied, dumbfounded. This was the first time that any of our men had been exposed to the enemy.

Looking down, one of the Soldiers noticed the band saw in my hands. "What's that for, Sir?" he asked.

I set it down on the crate next to me. "Nothing. It's for nothing" I replied and then made my way back to my bunk.

When I opened the door to our hut, I looked over at Moss's bunk area that, moments earlier, I was going to cut apart with power tools and I realized how much of a stupid, bored child I had been. I tried to shift my thoughts to something happier, but I could only think of Moss and his Soldiers hurt or bleeding in the dust somewhere. McKenzie and his Platoon were already out the gate, moving to assist Moss and his men. With half of my Platoon on OP Spur and the other half manning the guard towers in the outpost, I did the only thing I could do; I waited and worried.

Chapter 10

No Good Deed Goes Unpunished.

I later learned that only a couple of Soldiers from Moss's Platoon suffered minor injuries in the IED incident; no one needed to be evacuated. They had hit an IED that had been buried for months that was somehow still active. It was most likely a pressure plate, victim operated IED. Regardless of the details, it became abundantly clear to me that no matter how I tried to distract myself from it, I was in a war-zone and people were going to get hurt and killed. Nothing was going to change that. Instead of trying to occupy myself with more penis-antics, I decided to pour everything I could into making the most of the situation. I focused on my work with renewed vigor. I poured over maps and patrol debriefings, trying to make the puzzle pieces fit.

Unfortunately, there isn't much that we were doing that felt like we were making a direct impact. We spent a lot of patrols gathering atmospherics, creating relationships and meeting with this village elder or that village elder. I would write reports, chart relationships and generally try to make sense of the very complicated human terrain. The more I uncovered, the less it all made sense. For instance, Village X was called Village X, but only in Village X. Village Y would call Village X a completely different name altogether. In return, village X would not even recognize that Village Y even existed because someone from Village Y stole a goat from them sixteen years ago. Multiply this by about one hundred twenty villages and then add the layer of complexity that everyone's name is some variation of Abdul or Mohammad and pretty soon things start to run together. I often felt like I was moving in circles and I just couldn't shake the feeling that everything I did was just very dangerous busy work.

The talks, the meetings and the shuras often felt like one step forward and two steps back. The majority of the elders and persons of influence (POIs) were very much looking after themselves. Whenever we'd try to help an entire village, the elder would distill the talk down to himself or his family. Afghan local government members were the same; always with that, "what's in it for me?" attitude. Every talk felt like I was dealing with a sleazy used car salesman. I honestly didn't expect much different from the Afghans.

After all, their country had seen constant decades of brutal conflict; everyone was just in survival mode. Even with this understanding, it certainly didn't make my talks more productive though.

With the mountain passes frozen, there wasn't an enemy to directly fight; not yet anyway. We could feel that it was coming though. Some towns definitely had that "pending hostility" feel to them. Shops would close when we walked by. Children were counting the number of vehicles in our patrol with their hands, silently mouthing the numbers as they went. There was a palpable aura of unease when we were in historically enemy controlled towns. It was the classic "bad feeling" that Soldiers were always talking about.

The first time I walked into Jowgi village, I could have cut the tension with a knife. Villagers eyed us from alleyways as old men ushered the children into houses. The women were nowhere to be found; no colorful burkas anywhere in sight. Low silhouetted shops and stands lined the streets. There were very few qalat walls. This set-up give the town a more open and vulnerable atmosphere. My Soldiers fanned out through Jowgi, providing a bubble of security for me and my command section. The little dirty alleyway that served as the main thoroughfare for Jowgi was lined with improvised shops. Open connexes and shacks were filled with knock-off merchandise. In every single one of these shops, there were little plastic bags that gave off an unsettling "wrongness" that was my constant companion in this part of the world. They were too small and too flimsy; colored pink, purple, brown and other odd colors. Afghanistan couldn't feed its people, kick out violent terrorists, practice basic human rights, but, by Allah, there were going to make fucking sure those little bags would be supplied to every Afghan merchant with two coins to rub together.

Behind me, a human intelligence (HUMINT) analyst, named Munoz, lingered at the opening of a shop. It appeared that she had gotten involved in a conversation with a shopkeeper in one of the nicer looking buildings. Curious, I poked my head in to see what the point of attraction was. The shop itself was utterly unremarkable and half-stocked with dusty supplies, covered in labels that I could only begin to fathom what they read. Munoz, who spoke no foreign languages, was accompanied by a level two interpreter. Level two interpreters were interpreters who held US citizenship and thus, could be trusted slightly more than "normal" level one interpreters who were Afghan civilians working for the US government. Munoz's interpreter, Rafid, was speaking with a middle-aged man who I presumed was the shopkeeper. By his side, a small boy looked around nervously. I couldn't understand what was being said, but the body language and voice inflection tipped me off that the boy was the subject of the conversation. Rafid turned and whispered something to Munoz in English. I waited a moment or two before addressing Munoz.

"What's the deal with the kid?" I asked Munoz bluntly.

"Well Sir," she began, "He's the son of the shopkeeper and I think they want our help."

Rafid chimed in, "It looks like the boy was hurt and they want us to help."

I was automatically skeptical. This was the third time today that I had been approached by an Afghan looking for a hand-out. "Show me." I said simply.

Rafid interpreted into Pashto and the little boy nodded. He lifted up his shirt up, displaying his abdomen. A filthy bandage that looked more at home on a Civil War reenactor covered most of his tiny stomach. The little boy winced as he peeled down one corner of the bandage. A dripping, twisted mass of scar tissue and bowels greeted my eyes. I had to suppress a gag as the boy replaced the bandage. The father said something to the boy and the boy nodded and pulled down his waistband, exposing his left thigh. The unmistakable ragged scar of a gunshot scored a deep, ugly line across his leg.

"That's enough." I said. "Tell me what happened."

I gave the order for Stew to come up with the medic. For the next hour, Munoz, Rafid and Stew and I spoke to the shopkeeper and his son. The boy was named Khalid and he had been shot twice about six months ago. According to the father, Khalid had been walking home from school when the shooting started between the Americans and the Taliban. He didn't know who shot him, but he fell between some rocks where he lay for some time. Despite the severity of his wounds, he remained conscious and called out for help. Eventually some villagers found him and took him back to his father. His father then rushed him to several hospitals, seeking surgeons that could deal with this level of injury, until he finally wound up in an Italian run hospital in Kabul. Khalid had been shot in the left thigh, the bullet tumbling up his leg leaving a ragged, but fortunately, non-fatal wound. The second round had struck him in the intestines and had ruined much of his bowels. The surgeons had cut out the necrotic portion of his bowels and routed his now much shorter healthy intestines directly out of his stomach in a kind of budget colostomy bag. Khalid had, for months, been living with his internal organs open to the environment. Miraculously, his wounds had mostly healed without major infection or sepsis. He had been lucky so far, but this was not guaranteed to last. His surgery was a quick-fix and not a permanent solution. There was a high probability that he would die of infection if he didn't have surgical intervention soon.

Stew looked me dead in the eye, "We have to help this kid Sir."

"Yeah, this is horrible." I said.

Stew continued, "Sir, don't you see? This is the whole reason this village hates us."

"I don't follow." I replied.

"You saw those bullet wounds. They were too small to be rounds from Taliban rifles." Stew said.

It dawned on me, "Holy shit, *we* shot this kid."

"More likely than not." He said, "I bet you it was the 10th Mountain guys before us."

It all suddenly became clear. This was our opportunity to not only do the right thing, but to show the people of Jowgi that the Americans are the good guys. The Taliban hadn't helped Khalid yet, but we would because we were better than that. We could show these people that our way was the better way, the right way. This was what the generals and all of the counterinsurgency theorists were talking about. It didn't matter what actually happened. What mattered was the perception of what happened. At that moment, I was standing in a village that was largely under the impression that this poor child was shot by American forces months ago and nothing had been done. This wasn't something that was as convoluted as trying to get a room full of fifteen elders to agree on where a well should be constructed. This was something that was tangible, fixable and it would yield immediate results. In short, a golden ticket.

With the help of our medic, Farmer, we outlined a plan of treatment. For the first few weeks, Khalid and his father would come to our outpost and we would clean and treat his abdomen and then change his bandages. Simultaneously we would be coordinating with our Brigade command to get Khalid set up with an operation to properly treat his hasty colostomy bag. This would most likely have to happen at a surgical unit in Bagram Airbase or in Kabul. We let Khalid and his dad know what was going on at least with the initial part of the plan, the latter part was still up in the air. I learned early on not to promise or mention things to Afghans that you're not one hundred percent sure I could deliver on. With our plan in place, we said goodbye to Khalid and his father and set upon our way back to the outpost. Walking out of the village, I could feel a change in the atmosphere. The people were still wary of us, but they weren't boring holes into us with hateful stares either.

Several days followed and, as sure as clockwork, Khalid and his dad showed up at our outpost. I had made sure to tell Khalid and his dad to show up on a day where my Platoon was on guard cycle. Stew, Munoz, Farmer, Rafid and I all greeted Khalid. The child seemed a little nervous, no doubt this was his first time around so many foreigners with guns. Khalid's dad looked at Rafid and spoke something in Pashto.

"He says thank you so much." Rafid began, "You can't know how much this means to me."

"It's the right thing to do." Stew responded.

"Our pleasure." I echoed.

Rafid translated and the face of both Khalid and his father lit up immediately. Farmer then took the boy into the hut with his father for his check-up. Munoz and Rafid followed in case there was any translating that needed to be done. Stew and I waited outside patiently. I looked around to make sure it was just the two of us.

"I think this is the best thing we've done so far during this stupid fucking deployment." I said.

"I agree." Stew responded, "This could be the first *win* we've really had."

For the first time in a long time, I felt truly optimistic. After several minutes, Khalid and his father emerged from the medical hut. Khalid looked happy as he bounced over to us. Munoz and Rafid followed along with Khalid's father. Khalid shook all of our hands and gave us his thanks through Rafid. When it was all said and done, we had agreed that Khalid would come back once a week to get his bandages changed and his abdominal wound inspected. Rafid gave Khalid and his father his cell phone number in case they needed to call. Khalid and his father parted ways, waving to us as they walked off the compound.

Once they were completely out of sight, I turned toward Farmer, "So, how did it go?" I asked.

"Well Sir," he responded, "The expedient re-routing of his intestines that they did, although crude, was well performed. Now that most of the healing is done, his greatest enemy is infection."

Barry Farmer was nineteen years old, but had the clinical acumen and cool professionalism of a metropolitan ER surgeon. I was always glad that he was our medic.

I nodded and asked, "So he'll have to get a follow-up surgery in order to be fully out of the woods?"

"Absolutely," came Farmer's immediate reply, "Having his intestines exposed like that is a huge gamble. I'm surprised he's as well as he is."

"Ok then, it's settled," I began, "Good work everybody." I told the assembled group.

I had briefed my proposed plan to Captain Manion who, to my surprise, was very much on board with the idea of going through our Brigade in order to get Khalid the medical attention he needed. I expected Manion would require some convincing to get behind the idea, but I suspected that it was Stew's parallel briefing to First Sergeant Stockdon that took care of this for me. Stockdon had children of his own and had seen several kids caught in crossfires in Iraq. He was sold before we ever started talking.

In the weeks that followed, Khalid and his father would show up and get his bandages changed and cleaned. Each week, Munoz and Rafid would learn a little bit more about Khalid and his father and, by extension, Jowgi village as a whole. Khalid and his dad would ask about the treatment and what was happening. Munoz, Stew and I were always happy to say that we were making progress; indeed we were. Brigade had snatched up the story as a potential victory for Information Operations, or IO for short. IO really was a euphemism for propaganda, but it was something that we needed in this war. Our primary objective was to deny safe havens to terrorists by bringing the populace over to our way of thinking. A lot of this was to be achieved by propaganda and due to the language, racial and cultural barriers, we were woefully behind in our race for the hearts and minds of the Afghan people.

During this time, I coordinated a patrol to the village of Jowgi to test the atmospherics. We walked several kilometers out to the village, in order to maximize the amount of Soldiers we had on the ground; taking vehicles meant that we had to dedicate drivers and gunners that could not leave the vehicles. What we found was remarkable. There was a total reversal in the attitudes of the villagers toward us. Instead of hiding, children ran up to us and began asking for candy and pens like normal Afghan children. Shopkeepers kept their doors open and some even smiled at us. We could even see a few women among the crowd. It was clear that our good deeds with Khalid were paying off. I finally felt like we were making a direct impact.

A few days later, Khalid and his father were overdue for their check in. I approached Rafid, who was speaking into his cell phone in a hushed tone. He was looking down at the ground as he spoke, one arm crossed under the other elbow. His dusty sandals rolled around a large gravel rock as he listened to the speaker on the other end. He nodded and then hung up the phone. He stared off into the distance, possibly drumming up a craving for a cigarette. He barely noticed me before I spoke.

"What's wrong Rafid?" I asked.

He stuffed the cell phone into his baggy track pants. When his hand emerged, it was grasping a slightly bent cigarette. "That was Khalid's dad." He said at last.

"What's up? Where are they?" I asked, growing a little impatient.

"They can't come in today. It's not safe for them to travel. Somebody told the Taliban about them." Rafid struck a rations match against its dull green book as he finished speaking; as if it was a type of punctuation mark.

"So somebody in Jowgi ratted them out?" I inquired, trying to fit the pieces together in my head.

"Yeah. They're going to have to be more careful when they come to see us." He said simply.

"Who exactly..." I began before I was cut off by a voice shouting behind me.

"Sir! Captain Manion needs to see you in the command post." Private Rush was yelling at me from the open doorway of the TOC. No doubt, he didn't have anyone to relieve him on the radio otherwise he wouldn't have been yelling at me halfway across the outpost.

"Got it Rush! Be there in a minute!" I yelled back.

I turned back toward Rafid, "Let me go see what the hell this is." I said. "I want to know more. Try to get Khalid and his dad to come in if whatever this is turns into an overnight trip."

Rafid took a long drag and nodded, "You got it."

I trotted off toward the TOC, trying to get my mind ready for whatever mission or task that Manion had for me. By this point, Manion never spoke to me unless he wanted me to do something. I didn't take it personally, he did this with the other Platoon leaders as well. Try as I might, I couldn't get Khalid and his dad out of my mind. I made my way to Manion's room. His door was open so I just spoke up.

"What's up Sir?" I asked.

He let a long glob of Redman dip spit ooze slowly into a Gatorade bottle before speaking. "Nick, you've got a battle space handover mission with the Rangers again."

Manion was staring at a digitized satellite map on his laptop. His eyes never left the screen as he spoke. "Here," he said, "let me show you where this is going down."

Before he spoke, I could tell from looking at the screen that this mission was in the vicinity of Jowgi village. "Is this near Jowgi village, Sir?" I asked.

"It's in Jowgi village, Nick." He responded.

"What are the Rangers doing, Sir? Do you know?" I asked.

Manion finally turned away from the screen and faced me, "Fuck if I know. Some secret Special Forces shit; probably a snatch and grab on some suspected bad guy. They just asked for our help and since you've worked with them before, I want you on this one." He said, matter-of-fact.

I could already see where this was going. The Rangers were going to go into Jowgi, kick in every door at three in the morning and tear down most of the relationships that I had built up. What's more, is that I would be the one there trying to smooth over relationships when morning came. In one night, Jowgi would be back to where it was weeks ago.

"Sir," I began, "do you think it's a good idea for me to be the one that the people of Jowgi are going to see in the morning?" I asked.

Manion looked puzzled for a moment, "What the fuck are you talking about, Nick?" he asked.

"I've been trying to help out this kid and build relationships in this town. So far it's been working. I don't want to undo it by being associated with a night-time raid." I said.

"Wait a minute." Manion began, "You're worried that they're going to recognize you and think that you had something to do with the Ranger's mission?" he asked.

"Yes." I responded.

Manion looked frustrated with me, "They're fucking *Afghans*, Nick." The word *Afghans* hung in the air like he just said *cunts*. "They think we all look the same. They can't figure out how to stop killing each other and putting their dicks in livestock let alone discern one American from the other."

"I just..." I began.

"You're fucking going on this mission and that's final." Manion said.

I bit my tongue for a moment. "Roger Sir."

I tried to lighten the mood, "Well, I think this time I won't be bringing the trucks. Last time didn't turn out so well."

Manion's mood had already soured; he didn't even crack a smile, "You're going to have to take the trucks, Nick."

"Really?" I asked. The look he gave me offered no room for argument.

With that, Manion and I went over the scant few details of the mission. From what we could piece together, the Rangers were going to search Jowgi for a suspected high value target. We had the HVT's name, but only a silhouette for his picture. Since Afghans had very similar and subtly different names, the intelligence on the name alone was about as useful as an Uzi sub-machine gun at a pie-eating contest. The mission was going to kick off at about midnight and they would need me and my Platoon at about two in the morning, but we were to be on standby at midnight. It was already dusk and I hadn't briefed my men yet.

I gathered Stew and the other Sergeants and we went over the mission. Honestly there wasn't enough for us to go over as we had almost no idea what was happening. With just a time and a location as our only real tangible mission details, it felt a bit like a blind date with automatic weapons. I gave the order to triple check equipment and set out a standard battle drill rehearsal session. We went over vehicle rollover drills and talked about the low plan within the vehicles. We then talked about how we were going to react ambush IED's and other things that were usually universal between missions.

When midnight finally rolled around, we got the green light to go ahead and go on the mission to Jowgi. Seeing as how this is a special operations mission, we were given information surveillance and reconnaissance assets that were with us the entire time. As soon as we left the outpost, an unmanned aerial vehicle drone operator checked on with us. I think is call-sign was Eagle one but I could be mistaken. He eagerly and gingerly pointed out things along our route. Targets like civilians and even groups of dogs as we made our way west of the outpost toward the town. I had to calm down the drone operator because he was clogging up the network he was overly eager and seem to think that he was doing the Lords work with how much vigor he called out every single minute detail of the village we had been to dozens of times before. When we finally got close enough to hail the Rangers over the radio, they told us to leave the vehicles outside the edge of the village. We were to proceed on foot. I left half of the Platoon with the trucks outside the town and the rest of us proceeded on foot. Stew, I and about ten of our Soldiers proceeded to make link up with the Rangers.

Two Rangers stopped Stew and I and asked. "Who is in charge? I stepped forward and identified myself as the Platoon leader. "Come with us." They say.
.

Stew and I followed the Rangers toward the rest of their element. They walked quickly and I had to jog slightly to keep up. After a few moments of light jogging past small groups of Rangers through a twisted maze of qalat walls, we eventually made our way to the Ranger Platoon's commander. He had set up a temporary command post on the flat roof of a mud brick house. The town of Jowgi was still asleep and a few faint lights radiated warmly out of tiny mud-brick windows. The commander's hunched figure was pressing a hand mic to his ear and whisper-yelling to someone on the other end. I caught most of his conversation.

"I'm telling you, it's not fucking here." He hissed into the radio.

"Uh-huh, Uh-huh... nope." He continued. "Well you come out here and you look for it then." He seethed; jamming the hand mic into his radio operator's chest with a thud.

I didn't have to hear the other half of the conversation to know that he was having trouble finding his target building. The maps in Afghanistan were usually decades old and, as a consequence, very rarely correct. Entire villages could be mislabeled, mountain ranges could be incorrectly depicted. One could even find themselves waist-deep in a river that wasn't supposed to exist. It didn't require a stretch of the imagination to believe that a particular building was missing.

"Yeah, the maps suck over here." I ventured, trying to lighten the mood.

The Ranger commander gave me a grunt and went back to what he was doing. He held a flashlight up to the map and then looked around. The Rangers then began to search each house, systematically, in the village. Stew and I kept following the Ranger commander around from one impromptu command post to another for the next hour or so. This culminated in the Ranger commander whisper-shouting into the face of one of his subordinates who had snidely called him, "Moses." I found it funny, but decided to keep it to myself. Apparently Stew did too; I thought I heard him snigger.

The Ranger Platoon leader spared a glance at me and asked, "Did you guys bring any vehicles? I told him that we had been asked where they were; at the edge of town. "Bring them in closer." He said.

I explained that Jowgi village was very small my trucks may not fit – probably leave them where they're at. He didn't like this and ordered me to move them in closer anyway. Seeing as how he was the on the ground commander had no choice but to comply. I grudgingly pulled up my hand mic in order to Sgt. Brandt to the trucks in closer to the village. Stew and I then waited around while the Ranger commander ordered his teams to hit more houses. After a few hours, they didn't turn up with anything. The sun was due up in a couple of hours in the Rangers knew that they had to get out of there before their mission time was over. As the battle space handover Platoon, it was my job to smooth things over and to be there whenever the sun came up. To be sort of like the shining smiling face in the morning for the American force that just tore apart their village. The corporate line was to say that we didn't know anything about what had happened the night previously. We were expected to say that we weren't associated with the special operation Soldiers that came in the middle of the night and searched all their homes. The truth was that we were collaborators in the whole thing and oftentimes helped a special operations unit locate their targets. Normally, this was well worth it to find a cache or a high value target, but tonight they had turned up nothing. To make matters worse, this was a town that Stew and I had been working in for weeks to try and get them to like us. We were absolutely the worst Platoon to be there when the sun came up and these sleepy-eyed villagers wandered out onto the streets and tried to piece together what the hell happened last night.

Stew and I agreed that we needed to get the hell out of there. To hell with what command wanted or what the typical response was supposed to be for an event like this. We weren't going to be caught dead in this village whenever the sun came up. That left us at the very short window, about two hours to get all of our men vehicles out of there. Already the dogs and livestock were stirring. A rooster joined in the chorus and I knew it wasn't long before the first villagers made their way out toward us. I had radioed back to the outpost to let them know what we were doing. As usual at this hour, no one was up except for the radio operator, Rush. Rush was a little hesitant at first whenever I told him that were going to come straight back and not actually smooth things over with the locals like we're supposed to.

"Maybe I should wake up the commander?" Rush eventually asked.

"Don't worry about it." I told him. "He would likely agree with me, plus I don't think he'd appreciate being woken up at four in the morning."

Rush sheepishly agreed and that was that. I set about moving the entire Platoon out of there as quickly as possible. Everything was going great. All eighteen of our Soldiers plus our small Afghan National Army contingent were set to move out on time. Just when I started to feel comfortable with the situation, fate struck. One of the MR AP vehicles was too far into the village and had to do an *Austin Powers* style twenty seven point turn in order to get turned around. The other vehicles had to do this too, but this truck was positioned too far down in a narrow road and, during this maneuver, got one of its wheels stuck in a culvert. It took an additional half hour to tow it out of the culvert and get out of there. As we're doing so, a couple of villagers were making their way out toward us they didn't get close enough to get a good view of us but once again it was a race against the clock. I suddenly had a Deja vu feeling with the mission in Pul-i-Alam a few weeks earlier. I was starting to really not like these Ranger missions that I was called to support. This entire time Eagle, our UAV operator, is checking on with us and letting us know every minor detail of what is happening around us. At one point, he told us that we were surrounded. I asked him to clarify and he told me that we had about 6 to 8 armed individuals on roof tops around our vehicles this of course made my asshole pucker up in fear. I began barking orders over the Platoon command channel to figure out what was going on. My Sergeants reported back that there were no hostiles anywhere around us. I was confused it took me a second or two to realize what was happening.

I called the UAV operator on the radio, "What exactly do these hostiles look like, can you zoom in?

"Wait one." Came his reply. "They look like they're wearing helmets they have assault rifles, camouflage and webbing. They're right next to your vehicles.

"Yeah? Could you give me a 10 digit grid location to one of the fighters?" I asked.

"Wait one." He said again. A moment later he read the grid number back to me and I checked it on my map it was right where we were. One of my fire team had set up on top of a building to over-watch the recovery operation of the vehicle.

I sighed before I depress the hand mic and spoke to the UAV operator, "This is Red One. Yeah, that's us so please make sure you know what you are looking at before you cause me to have a fucking heart attack over here in a war zone. Red One out." With that I had switched off Eagle One. I didn't want to hear any more of his bullshit while we're doing this operation. I turned my attention back to the MRAP that we were trying to tow out of the ditch. Suddenly, with a lurch, the vehicle was pulled free we mounted up our vehicles made our way back to the outpost.

The following morning, I received a small ass chewing from Captain Manion regarding why I had strayed from the mission as outlined.

"You can't just do whatever the hell you want, Nick!" he scolded me.

I knew at this point that I was making black marks on my record with those above me, but I didn't really care. I saw this is my one opportunity to do things right for Khalid and show our guys that there was a purpose to us being over here. Everything else we had done just seemed less important by comparison. I was holding onto the idea of helping this kid not just because it was morally right, but because it was the only thing that really seemed to make sense over here. I knew not to attempt to defend my point to Captain Manion just rather to accept the ass chewing, say Roger, and move on and say I'd never do it again. I knew the real prize lay in getting the village of Jowgi to accept Americans again.

A few days later I was approached by the interpreter, Rafid. I asked him where Khalid was and he told me that he wouldn't be coming anymore.

"What you mean?" I asked.

"He can't come here anymore. It's too dangerous. I just spoke to his father and the Taliban threatened his entire family. They said they would kill him if they came to the outpost one more time."

And, just like that, I never saw Khalid or his father again. Jowgi remained a hostile village for the rest of my time in Anvil Troop. The one, tangible good thing that I tried to do just fell through my fingers like sand.

Chapter 11

All Good Things Must End.

My time as a Platoon leader in the Army was coming to an end. I spent nearly 2 years as a Platoon leader and, quite frankly, I was long in the tooth for the position. The Army usually only gave people about one year to 18 months in a particular position. This was especially emphasized for developmental roles such as a Platoon leader in a combat unit. In truth, I was fortunate to have as much time as I did. But that didn't make it feel any better whenever I was told by Captain Manion that I would be leaving my Platoon right before the start of the fighting season. The plan was that I was to be moved to a completely different Troop, Bulldog Troop, and I would take over as executive Officer there.

I would speak to my wife about once every two weeks, usually through email though sometimes I was even able to even get her on one of the prepaid phones that we had for the outpost. We had about six or eight of these phones for all 150 of us. She was happy with the development because it meant that I would spend less time on the front lines out on patrol. I agreed with her and told her that I would be safe on the outpost and my job would be mainly logistics. The truth was that I had no idea what I would be doing. An executive Officer, or XO for short, was supposed to be the second in command of an entire Troop sized element roughly, some 150 Soldiers. Depending on how the commander wanted to use me, this meant I could see more combat than I did as a Platoon leader. I didn't bring this up to the wife as she seemed happy with the idea of me walking around with a clipboard and counting the number of meals, rations, bullets behind the walls of the outpost. Her idea of the war, much like everyone else back home, was that it was something similar to the wars of our grandfathers. They all thought there was a pre-defined front line. If you weren't on said line, you were relatively safe. Conversely, if you were there on the front line then death was surely staring you in the eyes. Nothing could have been further from the truth, as this war had no front lines. Death waited around every corner and every tree and was buried in every qalat wall and could spring out at you at any time regardless of whether or not you were fighter, a truck driver, an aircraft mechanic or even a logistician.

At this point in my military career this was all that I knew; how to be a Platoon leader and how to lead Troops in combat. I'd only had one Platoon and that was Red Platoon. They were my friends they were my family over here. I was extremely unhappy when I learned all that was about to be taken away from me. The Army moves Officers around to keep them from getting too attached to the Soldiers. This is a practice that's gone on for hundreds of years and understandably so. In older wars, units would suffer horrendous casualties and Officers had to give really tough orders that would likely get a lot of Soldiers killed. It made it psychologically unbearable if the men and the Officers were too close. It seemed archaic and a little backward to me at the time because the level of casualties our forces had received during OIF or OEF were not on Civil War or D-Day levels where entire battalions were massacred in under an hour. To me, keeping the Officer with the Soldiers was exactly what you wanted to happen. You wanted them to get close like I had done. That way the unit and the Officer developed a much better working relationship. At least this is how I tried to rationalize my fear and anger at the news of being replaced.

The first detail I heard about my replacement made me hate him immediately. I learned that he was a general's son. Not some high-ranking Pentagon general, but a one star nonetheless. I'd already decided that he wasn't Red Platoon material. My men deserved the best they needed a leader who wasn't handed things. I hadn't even met this young man and I was already filling in the details of his life in the most negative way possible. As with nearly every change-out in the Army, the transition wasn't handled with any type of subtlety or tact. One day, a resupply patrol from headquarters dropped off a blonde, fresh-faced Lieutenant to replace me.

He plopped his bag down in the Platoon command hut. "I'll be back next week with the rest of my stuff" He began, "Can I keep this here?" He asked, indicating the duffel bag he had put outside my bunk.

I nodded impassively from the ruined couch. I must've looked ridiculous as I sat there cleaning my rifle as I sat under a marquee read, "Think Synergy". I had scrawled it on the wall a few weeks earlier in magic marker. I grunted something to him.

"Okay." He said and left me alone.

After I was sure he was gone, I grabbed his bag and threw it outside into the slush and mud. My men laughed and nobody bothered to move it. It sat there for the entire week. When he finally came back, he plucked his soaked bag out from under the hut without saying a word and took the empty room next to mine. I had just a few short days with him to let him know everything worked and what was happening in our territory. I dumped a ton of information on him and, quite frankly, I don't remember much of it. Looking back, I did him a huge disservice all because I was upset. I couldn't see past the fact he was separating me from the only thing that I cared about that time; my Platoon.

When the time came for me to go, I said one final goodbye to my Platoon. I can't remember exactly what I said but it was something along the lines of how much each of them meant to me. I told them they were the best team that I'd ever worked with. I wanted them to be there for each other and look out for themselves. I started to choke up and then Sgt. Brandt and the others closed in and hugged me for a moment. I knew that they were going to be okay because it takes a strong Soldier to be that compassionate. They were a team and they knew right from wrong. Stew and I had done our best to ensure that. And with that, I boarded the convoy to Squadron Headquarters at Forward Operating Base Altimur where I would await my new Soldiers from Bulldog Troop.

Chapter 12

Welcome to the Shark Tank.

Charkh Valley (pronounced like the word *shark*) sits in the Charkh District on the southern tip of Logar Province, Afghanistan. That's how military people would identify where it was. "It's part of Regional Command East." They'd say. Everyone else would find it by simply locating Iraq, since it was on the news way more at the time, and then looking around a bit for Afghanistan, eventually pointing to Kabul, which is on most maps. They'd then trace their finger down a few kilometers to the south to the part that's inked in a slightly different shade of brown than the rest of the country. That unnamed and unassuming splotch of land would be Charkh District. The Soldiers of Combat Outpost Charkh though didn't care how other people identified their little slice of the world. To them, COP Charkh was simply just *The Shark Tank*. They called it that because nothing was more fitting. Just the name alone implied a place where nothing good was going to happen. The general attitude of the Soldiers there was one of quiet determination. They appeared resigned in understanding that they were going to take on the worst of it during this deployment. Their living conditions were bad compared to what I'd seen in country thus. Snow had covered everything and, with the seasons changing, the ground all along the outpost had been churned into a sloppy, wintery slush. Cold, cramped, wet and muddy were the adjectives I would use to describe conditions upon my arrival.

At first I was put in the transient tents which were a little further up the hill and, although they were just basic Vietnam-era olive green tents, they did keep me relatively dry. I had arrived unnoticed in a small convoy one day from FOB Altimur to COP Charkh. When I woke the next morning and walked outside the tent to take stock of my surroundings, I noticed at once that the entire place felt dreary. HESCO barriers formed crooked lines between mournful guard towers that looked depressingly out into the qalats and vineyards that surrounded the outpost. When I looked out beyond the barriers and towers, I saw why everything seemed so lop-sided and improvised. The outpost was crowded on all sides. There were building, roads and walls all around us. We were crammed onto this little plot of land. This was an outpost that was quickly designed and hastily built.

This outpost belong to Bulldog Troop, my new Troop. Its commander was Captain Weaver, a man I'd only met in passing when we were still back in Germany. I'd heard that he was a good commander with a lot of experience. He was also the only black commander within our unit. I had heard, third hand, that he was very stoic but boasted an impressive combat record from Iraq. I met Commander Weaver my second day there. It was good that he had set time aside time to see me this early because I could tell that the Troop was wary of newcomers. Eventually Commander Weaver showed me around the outpost and things began to make more sense. The outpost's haphazard construction was due largely to the fact that it had been moved from a much more tactically sensible location a few kilometers to the southeast to this current location next to the Charkh district center. Commander Weaver then gestured to the three-story building behind us indicating it as the district center. It seemed our outpost actually encompassed the district center itself and that was the driving reason behind moving the outpost here when 10th Mountain Division had occupied the area. We were also situated next to a school which housed three hundred or so young Afghan children between the ages of four and sixteen, all-male of course.

This, in part, explained the hodge-podge, jigsaw kind of makeup of the outpost. This was an outpost that was born out of necessity no doubt to satisfy the new tactical directive we had received from General McChrystal, the ISAF Commander and our boss here in Afghanistan, a year earlier. The guidance was that we would integrate with the local populace and take more of a Special Forces type approach to how we would separate the insurgent fighters from the general populace. The idea was that if we learned enough about the people around us and got them to like us enough that they would give up the enemy fighters in their midst. It would then be easier to detain, remove, kill these fighters, thereby making them irrelevant in the day-to-day life of the local Afghans. This was a radical departure from all the previous years in Afghanistan where conventional US forces would occupy outposts that emphasized tactical defensibility and were removed from the Afghan populace. Having a defensible base in the middle of nowhere kept Soldiers safe and kept enemies at bay, but it didn't do anything to put us into the hearts and minds of the people we were trying to help.

Captain Weaver continued to show me the rest the outpost and I could tell the tour was winding down. We'd simply run out of things to see. The outpost wasn't that big and if he stood in the middle of it you could see nearly all four sides simultaneously. When we had gotten down to the command and control center Commander Weaver had ended his tour right outside of his bunk area.

He paused for a moment and leaned in with a serious look and said, "Hey XO," he was already calling me XO by this point, "I just got one question for you."

"Go ahead and shoot, Sir. What is it? I asked.

"You're a married man, right?" he asked me. I held up my wedding band between us. He chuckled, "Well this question is all the more important then, isn't it? Who is your forgivable?"

"My what, Sir?"

"You know. Your forgivable. The one woman whom, if you fucked her, your wife would forgive you. Who is it?"

I thought for half a second and blurted out, "Rosario Dawson. I think my wife would understand. She's fucking hot."

Commander Weaver looked at me incredulously and asked, "Are you shitting me?

"No Sir. They don't have words yet for what I would do to that woman."

Captain Weaver let out a belly laugh and said, "Wow that's crazy. She's mine too. I think we're going to get along just fine, XO."

With that he gestured toward some rooms at the end of the hall.

"Take your stuff down there. Staff Sergeants Kramer and Ingram will take care of you from here. I'll be in touch.

I said my thanks and trotted down the hall of the U-shaped building. This was one of the only concrete structures on the outpost. Everything else was made of tents and plywood except for the district center. We weren't allowed in the district center except as guests or to conduct meetings with the Afghan officials. It was technically their soil, much in the same way foreign embassies work. So it was a no-brainer that we put all of our command and control elements inside the U-shaped building. I kept calling it the U-shaped building, waiting to be corrected, until I discovered that's what everyone called it. We weren't always the most creative bunch.

The U-shaped building was actually an annex to the school that was right over the wall and the plan was to hand it back to the Afghans at some point during our year there so the school could teach more children. Commander Weaver had told me that we were going to be receiving more buildings and construction assets that would allow us to move the command and control elements out of the U-shaped and up toward the center of the outpost. He didn't have a timeline for this but it seemed to be a foregone conclusion that it would happen and I would be a big part of the logistics surrounding this. I thought about all this is I walked into the far end of the U-shaped building. I threw my stuff down onto an empty cot. The room was very similar to every other room in the U-shaped building. It was gray, dirty and it leaked water everywhere. It reminded me of everything that I had read about Scottish castles in the Middle-Ages because no matter what the temperature was outside, they always managed to be cold and wet on the inside.

"Your bunk is the top bunk." I heard a voice say behind me. I turned around and I saw a bald man with bright blue eyes lounging on a cot across the room.

I went to him, stuck my hand out in a greeting and said, "Hi, I'm Lieutenant Stevens, the new XO.

The man tossed down his magazine and introduced himself

as Staff Sergeant Kramer. When he moved, he got a little closer to the light and I got a better look at his face. His face was crisscrossed with faint scars that could only be from explosions and shrapnel. His brilliant blue eyes burned into me and there was a fine fuzz of pale blonde hair on top of his closely cropped head.

"I'm the outpost mayor." He said, "We'll be working together a little bit. I mostly manage the Afghan workers that we have here on the outpost. So I'm half yours and I'm half the First Sergeant's."

"Oh yeah that's right," I chimed in, "I haven't met the First Sergeant yet. His name is Steele right?"

"Yet you can't miss him. He's the angry little Irish guy with the unicorn tattoo on his neck."

"Really?" I asked.

"Yeah. Don't' tell him I said that. Don't laugh at the tattoo either, he'll break you the fuck in half." Kramer leaned in conspiratorially and added, "He's a former K-1 fighter."

"Don't worry." I said, "I don't plan on making fun of any tattoos, be they unicorn or otherwise."

With that and smiled and said, "Let me show you some of the other people you'll be working with." He yelled down the hallway, "Hey Ingram! Get the fuck over here!"

There came some unintelligible reply and a few moments later a dark-eyed and dark-haired young man trotted into the room. He was about the same age and build as SSG Kramer, but where Kramer was clean-shaven and more traditional in his appearance, Ingram kept a long-haired and relaxed atmosphere about himself. The Oakley shades that dangled around his neck added to this vibe.

Ingram gave me a firm handshake and said, "Hey, I'm Tyson Ingram and I'm one of the human intelligence guys here."

"Oh, do you know Alexis Munoz?" I asked hoping they knew each other.

Oh yeah, that bitch? She's fucking terrible she's the one up in Anvil Troop, right?

I was taken aback, "Yeah that's her, I guess."

Kramer nodded toward me then looked at Ingram, "So this is our new XO."

Ingram said, "Cool. You can't be any worse than the last one.

"What's that supposed to mean?" I asked.

"Clearly you haven't met Lieutenant Tanner yet." Ingram added, "It'll make sense when you do.

"That good, huh?" I asked.

They exchanged a glance and moved the conversation on to something else.

Ingram turned to Kramer and said, "I heard you having trouble sleeping last night, Kramer."

"Yeah." Kramer said, "Last night was a little rough." He turned toward me, "Hope you don't mind Sir. I sometimes have some bad dreams. It's usually nothing.

"Bullshit." Ingram interjected, "It sounded like you were losing your goddamn mind last night." Ingram turned toward me, "Good luck Sir. He's your bunk mate now. I'm done sleeping near his crazy ass."

I could tell that it was true and that Kramer was a little embarrassed, "I'm honored to sleep above you and have you attempt to kill me in my sleep, Kramer."

They both looked at each other and Kramer spoke up first, "I love him already."

I woke up about three or four times in the middle of the night with Kramer pounding on my bed. He was loudly mumbling something about a fire in a Bradley fighting vehicle and I just let him get it out. I kept having to move around to my bunk to try and find new dry spots as the leaks in the roof moved around and seemed to follow me and find the one open spot where my face was protruding out of my waterproof sleeping bag. I woke with a start once or twice as a new jet of ice cold water found its way into my eyes. The name Shark Tank became more fitting when I realized that shark tanks need to be filled with water. I chuckled to myself and got up to go take a piss. It was still dark outside and I put on my headlamp to find my way to the nearest latrine. I switched my headlamp to the red filter and then stumbled my way across the coarse gravel, pale red light guiding my way. I was wearing thin flip-flops and occasionally a big, sharp piece of gravel would stab into my feet. You could always tell how nice an outpost or base was in Afghanistan by the coarseness of the gravel. I noticed that the really nice places had finally crushed gravel that you could barefoot over. That's where the Colonels and generals stayed, the big bases with the nice, fine gravel. When you got further away from those mega-bases and into the lesser-known forward operating bases the gravel got coarser until eventually you got to the combat outposts, like this, where the gravel was basically just sharpened rocks that you had to walk on. After rolling my ankle a few times, I finally reached the latrines.

As I reached for the door handle I heard a voice call out to me, "Hey crazy, what are you doing?"

I turned around and caught a brief glimpse of a thin, middle-aged man in fatigues. I could barely make out a unicorn tattoo on his neck.

"Don't shine that shit on me. Do you want me to get shot?" He asked.

"Oh sorry." I said and I cut off the head lamp.

"You must be the new XO" he said.

"Guilty as charged"

"Well, be sure to walk around here at night with the white light and not the red one, ok XO?"

"Wait, why's that? I asked, truly confused.

"Only Americans have red lights. The Taliban knows that. If you use the white one, the Taliban will be less likely to shoot at you because they might think that you're possibly one of the Afghan workers here. They've taken a few shots at us at night, but so far no one's gotten hit yet. They seem to shoot less at the white lights"

"I'll keep that in mind."

"Where are my manners?" He asked himself. "I'm First Sergeant Steele and, if no one's told you officially, welcome to The Shark Tank. As he said the words *Shark Tank* the moon caught the pearly white of his toothy grin.

Chapter 13

Highlighters, Property Books and Madness.

I didn't have long before I was expected to settle into my new position. I had accepted the fact that there was little chance I would be leading Soldiers into battle anymore, at least during this deployment. There were just too many fresh-faced new Lieutenants joining the unit. And, let's face it, I was a bit long in the tooth, having been in Platoon command for over a year at this point. This eventuality still managed to sadden me and I felt like my purpose as a combat Officer had been blunted slightly. Nevertheless, I set out to do my new job to the best of my ability. After all, if Executive Officer was a useless position, why were there so many of them around? Also, why were they so overworked? Clearly, they had a purpose. I remember seeing the haggard look of many an XO back in Germany. I remember thinking, "Fuck, I hope I don't have to do that job."

Things, as they often do in the Army, had come full circle and now I was searching for the incumbent XO so he could show me the ropes of my newly assigned position. I felt the parallel to what just happened to me and my replacement Platoon leader back at COP BBK. I asked a few Soldiers where Lieutenant Tanner was and they told me that Jim was over there. This struck me as odd. They didn't call him "Sir" or "Lieutenant", "XO" or even just "Tanner." It was just "Jim." This piqued my curiosity as I continued to look for him. When I finally found Jim, he was hunched over a worn picnic table in a moldy part of the school annex. Water seemed to be everywhere, all the time, giving the entire atmosphere that pervasive wet dog smell. Water pooled on tarps and sat in the low areas, growing stagnant. It even dripped onto the paper that LT Tanner was laboring over, smudging the six or seven highlighter colors into something that looked like a kaleidoscope would regurgitate.

He spared me a glance and then said, "Ugh, just a minute. I'll be with you shortly."

"Yeah man, no sweat." I replied, adjusting my rifle on my shoulder.

I set my weapon down and observed Jim while he continued to stare at his work. He was boring a hole into the paper, searching for something. He was a tall and lanky young man with cornflower blue eyes and a close crop of sandy colored hair. His hands were long and fumbled over the paper. His general appearance reminded me of a puppy that, according to nature's design, had rocketed through one tremendous growth spurt, leaving it awkward and uncoordinated for a good part of its adolescence. I seated myself across from LT Tanner and saw that the notebook was actually about thirty sheets of paper stapled together in a packet of sorts. Each one was a rainbow of highlighter markings. The margins were filled with small novels written in at least three colors of pen. Jim was kneading his scalp now and mumbling something about an item code that didn't match up. He was oblivious to the uncapped highlighter that was being jabbed into his scalp, providing him with an edgy, albeit a little Avant-garde, blue accent. I watched his hair color accents proliferate each time he kneaded his scalp. This went on for another five minutes or so before it became clear that he was not going to get to me anytime soon.

I cleared my throat and said, "If you need me to come back later, I can. It's no problem."

"No, no, no. I'm going to get to you." he replied.

Jim glanced over the edge of the picnic table, "Aha! There it is!"

I watched as he reached over and produced a dirty sheet of paper from the floor. He blew it off and folded it over in his hands. His eyes scanned the paper as if he was a British archaeologist reading hieroglyphics by torch light. His gaze halted over a particular part of the page and his face lit up.

He looked up from the paper, grinning, "There's that serial number. I thought we lost a machine gun for a second there! Anyway, come over here so I can show you how to do this."

For the next several hours, Jim showed me the ins and outs of inventory inspection. This task was to become the majority of my daily functions so I was sure to pay attention. Jim kept referencing the worn document before him. This was the inventory printout of everything that the Troop was responsible for; from fighting vehicles to individual sights on each Soldier's weapon. There were thousands of items, each one tracked by an individual serial number. These items had to be inspected monthly. Anything that was missing would become a grave cause of concern because it would start an official inquiry which would usually end with some poor soul having to forfeit his pay to compensate for the missing item. As the soon to be chief inventory Officer, there was a good chance that it was going to be my paycheck that was to be targeted.

"Now all of this shit is a lot to keep track of," Jim continued, "but it isn't the worst of it. There's this thing called Theater Provided Equipment or TPE for short." When I informed Jim that I had dealt with TPE as a Platoon leader, he scoffed. "Psssshh... please. What you deal with was child's play. A Platoon only has a little bit of TPE. The vast majority of it is actually spread among the headquarters section because the fighting Platoons have little use for this shit. The armorer and head radio technician absorb a lot of this shit and keep track of it, but it's ultimately still the commander's stuff and you are responsible for it."

"So what kind of shit is it?" I asked.

"You know all those big defense contractors that are always trying to get bids with the Army, right?

"Yeah like the Halliburton and those Raytheon guys?" I asked

"Exactly." Jim said, "They push all manner of shit on us that we don't even need. The higher ups get a hard-on about some new contraption and make a decision at the theater-wide level and then push it down to formations like us to have no need for whatsoever."

He pointed to one of the MR AP vehicles. "How much do you think one of those costs?" he asked.

"I think they're about 500,000 right?"

"Yeah that's right. They're about a half million each." He said, "We have 21 of them here on this outpost. All the passes are snowed in and there's only one road in and one road out of this place. And, according to the10th Mountain guys that we replaced, this summer that one road will become so heavily booby-trapped, taking vehicles over it would be a death sentence."

"So what you're telling me," I ventured, "is that we have an entire fleet, roughly $10 million worth of vehicles, completely mothballed?"

He looked at me and nodded, "Yup. But it's not our place to question what we have and why. We have it just to keep track of the shit and I'm going to show you how to do that." With that he tossed the stack of papers in my lap and handed me a highlighter and said, "Come on, follow me. Let me show you where to find the actual serial numbers on these damned things."

For the next three hours Jim showed me where to read the serial numbers on all the various pieces of equipment in our inventory. MR AP vehicles kept their serial numbers on the frames, near the side doors, similar to where you would find the factory sticker inside your Honda back home. Other items weren't so easy. Certain machine gunner sights hid theirs. Jim had to pull back parts of the rubber coating just to see the serial number. There were other things that didn't make much sense either. We had radios whose serial numbers were scratched off entirely and written in with magic marker. I held one up to Jim incredulously and he said, "Don't ask." We even had inflatable boats even though there was no water around us and we had a Jaws of Life system. It was in two giant crates that would require four Soldiers each to lift. That was one of my favorite items. It cost about $200,000 and was used, in theory, to cut Soldiers out of vehicles that rolled over onto their sides. This was clearly an item meant for the Iraqi theater. I was told that Iraq had many canals alongside the roads and, because the canals were often filled with water and the roads were high and shoddily constructed, they would often give way under the weight of the MR AP vehicles. Those vehicles would then rollover down into the canals and the Soldiers inside would be trapped and slowly drowning. Somewhere, somehow a high-ranking official thought it was a good idea to buy some of these things and ship them to us even though we had no use for them whatsoever. Even if we did have a use for them, it would be unlikely that anybody would take this gigantic pneumatic device on patrol with them. There was simply no room in the vehicles. You'd have to sacrifice either Soldiers or ammunition or supplies to put them inside your vehicle and it would take thirty minutes to successfully employ the thing. Thirty minutes in which the Soldiers you're hypothetically supposed to save could've drowned multiple times over.

The list of ridiculous shit kept going though. There was another piece of equipment that we had; some real space-age whiz-bang technology. It was basically a focused heat ray. This, of course, immediately reminded me of something out of *War of the Worlds*, but here was it was. The ray gun was a crowd control device; a less than lethal device designed to be aimed at a crowd and fired whereupon it would produce a burning and heat sensation that was so unenjoyable, the crowd would disperse. I found the whole thing preposterous. I asked the armorer, Sergeant Walsh, if he ever tried the thing.

"That thing? What a piece of shit, Sir" he said. "I haven't been able to get the damn thing to turn on let alone find the types of power supply that it needs."

"Awesome." I said. "Well let's just keep it back here never unpack it again. Just keep track of the serial number.

"Sounds like a fucking plan to me, Sir. One less thing I'll have to fucking worry about."

"How much does this thing cost, Sergeant?" I asked.

"I don't know. I think about four hundred thousand."

I looked in disbelief at the ray gun. I would've gladly returned all of that useless equipment for a full refund that same day were I able to. What we needed was more Soldiers, not some piece of fancy bullshit built upon the empty promise that it would make all of our problems go away with the touch of a button.

The radioman, Mathis, had the same attitude as Walsh. If weapon systems, be they lethal or less than lethal, were hard to keep track of then the radios were a fucking nightmare. Several radios were utterly identical yet some belonged to TPE and others were our organic equipment. Some even had duplicate serial numbers. It was impossible to tell which one was truly which. Of course, these radios were found to be on different pages of the property book and not consolidated in one spot. Anytime I had to go do these inspections with the line Platoons, it would take extra minutes whenever we got to the radios. We all had to stand around in the heat with all the equipment lined up in the middle of the outpost. I counted each and every item, checking its serial number, even the ones that were written in sharpie. The whole thing was completely absurd. I knew it, the leadership knew it and the common Soldiers knew it too. But still, we had to do it. It was part of our ritual; part of the daily grind and I was starting to get that feeling about everything that we did.

Our patrols came to and from the outpost regularly. By this point in the deployment, Bulldog Troop had been in some minor skirmishes, but no real battles. I had missed their earlier scraps with the enemy when I was with Anvil Troop. Most of our patrols were sent to check atmospherics in the villages that surrounded COP Charkh. They looked at things, talked to this person, filled out that form, distributed this information, etc. My actions were symbiotic to theirs. I checked on this equipment I monitored those supplies, etc. Everything I did was rolled up into a concise logistics report that went to Squadron Leadership, Saber Command, at the end of each day. I was getting the hang of things and time was starting to move by more quickly.

I was warned early on before I deployed to Afghanistan by someone who told me, "To make the days count while you're over there and not count the days." I couldn't remember who this person was, but they were clearly fucking mental because I couldn't help but count the days at this point. They were all the same and applying a number to them was the only way to differentiate them. So it was that one day I was approached by the third Platoon leader,

Captain Harper, to go out on patrol. I felt this whole thing was a bit odd. I had been focusing on the administrative part of my job I forgot that I was actually, technically, the second in command of the entire outpost.

I looked at him for a moment, "Where's the commander? You should probably ask him."

"Well XO, he said he's gone for the next few days. Remember, he had to go to that meeting with the SCO at Squadron Headquarters."

"Really?" I asked. I hadn't seen the commander all day. I was embarrassed that this had somehow slipped my notice. I'd been mucking about all day, counting radios.

"Yeah. He's over at FOB Altimur. He didn't tell you?"

"No, he did not." I said.

First Sergeant Steele walk by us and asked, "Hey Top, where the commander?"

He said, "He's at FOB Altimur for two more days" He said this with the kind of casual air that implied *didn't you know*?

I turned to Harper and asked, "Well, what would you like from me?"

"Oh nothing much. I was just looking at the patrol schedule and I wanted to make a change. I want to go behind the radio tower mountain and check out this village that's supposed to be a bad spot. I want to take a good look at it before it gets any warmer in the fighting season really starts."

"Look, I think we should probably just stick to the patrol schedule as is," I said, "at least until Commander Weaver gets back."

Harper seemed a little deflated at that point. "Look XO we been over there a few times before. It's not that big of a deal. I just want to check it out because it's potentially getting worse every single day."

"Look man," I could tell he was trying to convince me, "I just got here and I'm not entirely sure where everything is. I'd be a lot more comfortable with you if you and your guys just stuck to the patrols we already have."

Harper looked at me and said, "We were supposed to go over there and look at these this place. This is our job. This is why we're here. I really need to check out this village. I've got good leads that are pointing me over there."

I finally relinquished, "Ok man. If you really need to go over there, whatever."

Harper seemed happy at this development, "Okay. I'll get my guys ready.

I made my way to the command and control room inside the school annex. I studied the maps and found the village that he was talking about. It was behind the mountain directly south of our outpost. It was an area marked on the map that looked like it had spotty radio communication in the past. Our location within the U-shaped building didn't afford the best radio communication within the valley. We had random dead zones in our area of operations. I believed Harper when he said that it was unlikely that anything was going to happen, but I was a little paranoid. I took White Platoon and put them on standby just in case we needed a quick reactionary force for Harper's Platoon. I began setting up mortar target reference points with our Fires Sergeant, Sergeant Spears, to have all my bases covered in case Blue Platoon got into a big fight. I then poured myself a cup of coffee and waited nervously behind the radios for something to happen.

I didn't have to wait long because it only took about an hour into their patrol before Blue Platoon was in a complex ambush. This is my first time having Soldiers under my command under direct enemy fire. The radio transmissions that came back from Blue Platoon were choppy at best, the mountain was cutting off a lot of the communication and providing a ton of interference. After a few minutes of trying to figure out what the hell was happening, the best I could figure out was that they were under attack from three separate directions by a fairly large enemy force. I couldn't figure out their exact location so all of my fire points and their request for mortar support were useless. I called up to Saber command and asked for air assets to be released, but without a proper location of my own friendly forces, they wouldn't release the assets. I was on my own. I released White Platoon to go and try and make link up with Blue Platoon who, at this point, was in a running engagement and fighting a tactical withdrawal back to the outpost. After a very tense hour, Blue Platoon was able to get back into an area where they had direct radio communication with me. As if they had sensed this, their Taliban attackers broke off their attack and began withdrawing back behind the mountain. Once Blue Platoon had linked up with White Platoon, they were able to come back to the outpost. They expended about half of their ammunition and were shook up and dazed, but otherwise unhurt. I ordered rest and refit for Blue Platoon and I had John come into my office.

"What the fuck just happened?" I asked him.

"We got hit from three sides out there." He said.

"I can't believe I let you guys go out there by yourselves."

How the fuck was I supposed to know?" John asked. Before I could answer, he put in, "Thanks for the timely support, too."

It was a low blow, but he was right. An hour was way too long for him to wait for support. Plus, I couldn't support any of his requests for mortar fire. Communication had killed us on this one and it was my fault. "That'll be all, Harper. Go take care of your guys." I said simply, dismissing him.

Some Soldiers in Blue Platoon never forgave me for that. To this day, some think I deliberately left them high and dry out there with no support and, in a way, they're right. I was too young, too green and I simply didn't know enough about Charkh Valley to make the calls that I did. As I sat there in the Charkh TOC typing up a final report to Saber Command, Staff Sergeant Burch's voice bubbled up from my memory, "One day you're going to do everything right and everything will go wrong and someone is going to die. You need to be ready for that." Those words almost came true with Harper's patrol that day. I cursed myself for being so stupid. That first engagement in Charkh valley haunted me for the rest of the deployment.

Chapter 14

Bayonet 6 Cares.

When Captain Weaver returned from FOB Altimur the following day, he didn't make a big deal out of my blunder with Blue Platoon. I fully expected him to rake me across the coals for recklessly putting one of his combat Platoons in danger while he was away. Especially because I was a newcomer and relative stranger compared to most of the Soldiers under his command.

"What happened, XO?" he'd asked me casually after settling down in his bunk.

"I let Blue Platoon go out on a mission that I shouldn't have."

"I heard."

I fully expected to get destroyed by Captain Weaver at this point. "I'm sorry Sir."

"I don't want you to be sorry. I want you to learn. I deliberately left you with little guidance to see how you would handle things. You're going to have to step in and take the reins now and again. I need you to be ready."

"It could've been a lot worse, Sir." I added sheepishly.

"Well, it wasn't. I hope you learned a lot. There's plenty more work for you to do and I need you focused."

"Got it, Sir."

"Good, now I want you to help First Sergeant Steele get this place in order. We've got some important visitors coming."

With that, Captain Weaver outlined the upcoming visit from our Brigade Commander, Colonel Bailey. Our unit was part of the 173rd Airborne Brigade Combat Team and the Colonel, the big boss, was coming to visit our little slice of heaven. We reported directly to Saber Command, which usually implied the top three within the command structure; our Squadron Commander, Lieutenant Colonel

Dunn, our Command Sergeant Major, Sergeant Major Morales, and the Squadron XO, Major Boyle. Colonel Bailey was their boss. He was everyone's boss as the highest ranking person in the entire Brigade of over four thousand people. What's more, is that the Colonel was bringing his Command Sergeant Major with him, Command Sergeant Major Rolke.

The fact that both of them were visiting was utterly terrifying. One of them would've been enough to get me worried, but both of them wandering around here doubled our chances of something horrible happening. Let me explain… Commanders and Officers at that high of a level don't have much to do in Afghanistan. Counter-insurgency is a type of war that's fought at a much lower level of command than other wars, historically. Colonels and Generals are super important when you're battling another huge Army, but there isn't much for them to do in conflicts where your enemy only bands together in groups of twenty or less. That leaves these big-wig Officers and Sergeants Major out on their super-bases in the middle of nowhere with nothing to do except micro-manage, pick the wings off of flies and come up with good ideas.

Now they were coming here to COP Charkh. We had done our absolute best to improve our outpost every single day, but the place still looked haphazard and disorganized. It was a mess, a functioning mess, but a mess nonetheless. The last thing I wanted was for the Colonel or the Command Sergeant Major to find something on our COP that would become their *pet project*. I wanted them to show up, look around and say some fucking meaningless words, then depart. I wanted our outpost to be so unremarkable that there would be no way they could ever recall it in memory let alone focus their more than ample idle time on it.

I immediately went to First Sergeant Steele and Staff Sergeant Kramer. They shared my feelings of controlled panic and we quickly set upon the task of making the outpost more presentable. We had less than a week to do this and the three of us put in a lot of long hours to ensure that there weren't any sore thumbs sticking out. Kramer and I focused on energizing the Afghan workers and getting outpost organized and compiling all of the materials and resources we had laying around. Steele, on the other hand, had to spend an inordinate amount of time enforcing Soldier discipline standards to ensure that no one was in violation of anything by the time CSM Rolke arrived. Steele' big push was on the CSM's major pet peeves, Soldier eye-protection.

"XO, I'm going to lose my goddamn mind if I catch another Soldier walking around here without eye protection." He said to me in the command hut.

He had been up the ass of every Soldier and Sergeant on the outpost about wearing their ballistic glasses, 24/7, for days now. "That's the CSM's pet peeve, isn't it?" I asked.

"You've got no idea, XO. Let me show you this shit." With that, he gestured me over to his secure laptop and opened an email from the CSM. It was part of his weekly address to all of the First Sergeants within the Brigade. His version of a Roosevelt fireside chat. "Read that." He said, pointing to the most recent email from the CSM.

I genuinely struggled to make it through the email. It was rife with spelling and grammatical errors. It made little sense and I was only able to piece together the gist of what was being said through the repetition of certain words and context of sentence fragments. *Eye protection good. No eye-protection, no good* was the general message, I think. "Very funny, First Sergeant." I said. Where's the real email from the CSM?"
He looked at me with genuine concern for a moment before answering, "No XO, that's the email from him. He wrote it."

I was dumbfounded. "You're fucking shitting me." I said. This was the worst thing I had ever read in the Army and it came from the number one enlisted man in the Brigade. It was so bad, it would've given a copy editor cancer.

"No, I'm not. They're all like that." Steele said as he opened other emails that were equally horrific.

"Holy shit, he's your boss and he's mentally retarded." I concluded.

"That's not nice, Sir." Steele replied.

"I didn't hear you deny it."

"Look, he's the CSM and there's nothing you or I can do about it. He's actually not dumb. He just sucks at writing."

"Well, having read that," I began, "I don't see how you're so worried about him being here. I've got a way to keep him occupied."

"Really, what's that, XO?" Asked First Sergeant Steele.

"As soon as he steps off the helicopter, just hand him a Chinese finger trap. Should keep him busy for seven or eight hours. It might even give me an excuse to finally use those Jaws of Life we have collecting dust in the back."

"You're a fucking dick, XO. That's why I love you."

When the day finally came and the Colonel was on his way, I was saddened to learn that he would be coming alone. The CSM was involved in some task that he couldn't leave unattended. I imagined it involved finger-painting or perhaps a fiendishly difficult child-proof Aspirin bottle somewhere. The Colonel touched down shortly thereafter. He had met Captain Weaver back before we deployed so they spoke only briefly. He was a tall, slim man. His bald head, along with his build, made him look as though someone had stretched out Elmer Fudd on a medieval torture rack. I was briefly introduced to him, but he barely seemed to notice.

His thumbs danced across a BlackBerry as he glanced up to say, "Hello."

What followed was extremely anti-climactic. He was taken all over the outpost by Captain Weaver, receiving a very similar tour to the one I had received weeks earlier. We culminated the visit with a PowerPoint presentation in the command area. The presentation seemed more for us than the Colonel as he refused to put his BlackBerry away. I found myself staring at the device and wondering where the fuck he had gotten it and how it was working in 2010. Maybe he was completely bananas and the BlackBerry was communicating with no one? All of his mannerisms and reactions just seemed... off. Everything was a little strained with him, but in a muted way. He seemed quietly annoyed that he had to be out here with us at all. I was still trying to put it all together when he departed a few hours later. I mean, I was happy that he wasn't digging into our asses about anything and was leaving us alone though. What he did instead wasn't negative, it was just strange. Had we not greeted him on the helicopter pad, I think he would've just sat there on his BlackBerry until his return flight came to pick him up.

I caught Captain Weaver alone a few moments later, "What the hell was that, Sir?" I asked.

"I know, right? That was weird as fuck." He replied instantly.

"I think I have it figured out though." I said, a grin twisting the edge of my mouth.

"Do tell, XO."

"That's not the Colonel."

"Intriguing, go on." Weaver was smiling now.

"It's an alien wearing his skin, like in *Men in Black*. Think about it. All of his reactions were off. He's still trying to figure out human emotions. You're lucky you weren't alone with him anywhere secluded. He would've eaten you, head first, like a fucking praying mantis. The real Colonel is in little bits somewhere in the desert where this thing shit him out like owl pellets."

Captain Weaver did his best to keep a serious look on his face. It lasted about three seconds. "BWAHAHAHAHAHA!!! That's funny as fuck! I think you're right."

And that's how it started. From that point on, our Brigade Command Team consisted of a flesh-eating alien masquerading as a Colonel and, arguably, the highest achieving mentally retarded person in the Army. About a week later, First Sergeant Steele called me into his bunk.

"Come take a look at this, XO." He said. "It's an email from the CSM about our visit last week from the Colonel."

"Oh boy," I said, rubbing my hands together, "I can't wait to read this gem."

"Hardy-har-har, just read the email, you ass."

Again, I made it through the email with some difficulty, but I was able to piece together the gist of what it meant. The theme of this one was *B6 Cares*. B6 was the radio call-sign for the Colonel. What the CSM was trying to say was, "despite how the Colonel behaved, he cares about you guys."

"Who else got this email?" I asked Steele.

"All of the First Sergeants, about fifteen total."

I thought more about that in the days that followed. The Command Sergeant Major sent out a message to most of his subordinates saying that the Colonel cared. This was done because his actions, while at our outpost, showed us the opposite; he didn't care. He was indifferent and treated his time with us like a chore. I think that's why I jumped to the crazy conclusion that he was an alien. I thought I was doing it to be funny at first, but the more I thought about it, the more I realized that I *wanted* to think he was an alien. The alternative was much worse; that he was just a man that didn't give a shit. If he were an alien, it would at least explain why he didn't seem to understand or care about the humans around him. I started to like the CSM a lot more. At least our eyes were going to stay safe during this deployment.

Chapter 15

What's in Your Heart.

It wasn't long before I was the fully fledged XO of Bulldog Troop. A few weeks ago, Jim had left the outpost for good which transitioned all logistical authority to me. I was already discovering that there were a lot of skeletons in the closet regarding our property. It seemed that only about 90% of it was truly accounted for. The remaining 10% hadn't been unpacked since the Troop arrived in Afghanistan some months before.

I was left with my Staff to find the remaining items. My Staff consisted of the armorer, Sergeant Walsh, Staff Sergeant Spears, our indirect fires NCO, Staff Sergeant Ingram, the Intel guy, and Mathis, the communications expert and finally Staff Sergeant Kramer, the COP Mayor. All of these individuals had done a very good job of showing me the ropes. Spears had shown me not to take myself too seriously. He had a very relaxed attitude in his Alabama country drawl would always put me at ease. He was a large and powerful black man and was responsible for all the indirect fires within the Troop as our fires NCO. He introduced me to our mortar Platoon, who called themselves *Ghostbusters*, who would be providing the aforementioned indirect fires. Spears played college football years ago, but had unfortunately blown his back out. As a natural athlete, he eventually found his way into the Army. There was one other Lieutenant in the headquarters section. That was the fires Officer, Lieutenant Lavelle. I recognized him immediately whenever I first saw him. We went through training together whenever we were in ROTC. We spent one month together in the same Squad at Fort Lewis, Washington to attend a 30 day training called *Leadership Development and Assessment Course,* or LDAC for short. LT Lavelle did his best to get others to do his work for him during that training. He was a generally nice and amiable guy, but I often felt like he was working some hidden angle when I interacted with him. I did my best to conduct all of my business through SSG Spears.

As COP Mayor, SSG Kramer was in charge of the interpreters and workers on the outpost. He ran the day to day operations of our little outpost and took orders directly from the First Sergeant. His job was to keep things in order and keep the dozen or so Afghan workers we had living with us happy and productive. This meant that we had to pay them and sometimes bribe them to keep them working. We had several pieces of heavy equipment, to include some excavators and cranes, and these were the only people that knew how to operate them on the outpost. We needed those cranes to load and unload equipment and we were constantly using the excavator to improve our defenses. In short, we had to do anything to keep these skilled workers on our outpost and happy.

Staff Sergeant Ingram dealt primarily with intelligences, route planning and analytics. He also dealt with many of the biometric measures we used to screen the local populace while out on patrol. Our patrols would also carry bomb detecting chemical kits, similar to the ones used in airports, to check civilians while out on patrol. The biometrics equipment worked by scanning the retinas of a suspect and checking the results against a database. This sounded good in practice, but the equipment often simply didn't work or needed to be in perfect lighting conditions to detect that there was a human eye in front of it. Also, the bomb equipment gave us so many false positives that we had to be careful in how we employed it. Considering that most of the IEDs in the valley were constructed from home-made-explosives that meant that anyone who touched many common farming chemicals would come up as "bomb-makers" within the system. We obviously couldn't arrest or screen every single farmer in the valley so had to fall back on our best tool to discern who was a bad guy and who wasn't; our judgement.

Now Sergeant Walsh was a real gem in the group. He showed me many ways organize and streamline the sensitive items checks and inventory lists. My monthly inventory checks would rule my life if I let them. Walsh understood the game and how it was played. The life of the XO and the property management game in general within the Army is a series of juggling acts. There are too many balls and not enough skilled hands to keep them in the air at once. Some of them are going to hit the ground. Some of these balls were lint balls and some were crystal balls. My job was discerning which was which and to ensure the crystal balls never touch the ground. The life of the XO and, ultimately, his success was measured in degrees of failure. All XO's failed, but it was to what extent that they failed that was the *true* measure of their success. Of all the people there in the headquarters Staff, it was SGT Walsh that really embodied the logistical game within the Army. He was organized, efficient and he kept his bases covered. I learned a lot from him. He had informants and people peppered throughout the logistics chain in Afghanistan that would help make our jobs a little bit easier. These were people that were purchased with small favors, very carefully and over time. In short, he was the perfect armorer to have on my side and I wouldn't have been successful without him.

Sensitive items, like rifles and night vision devices were almost untouchable. We didn't dare mess with those. The Army was very black and white about those items and I'd seen good people get locked up for fudging the numbers on these. Beans, bullets and fuel, however, were a little different. I could already tell from where we were situated and through speaking with Captain Weaver that we were in the most active of all the Squadron's areas. This was a place that was going to see a whole lot of combat. Once the ground was soft, the local Taliban fighters could go and dig up all their weapons that they'd cached before the winter. The mountain passes would thaw as well so they would receive fresh shipments of weapons and reinforcements from their allies in Pakistan and Iran. That's when the real fighting would start. The only problem was that our recommended amount of ammunition was so pitifully low that I worried it would be enough for all of our Soldiers in a protracted engagement. I knew that I needed more if we were going to make it through this. So I had no problem whatsoever in creating a surplus in my weapons and stockpiling as much ammunition as I could. Acting alone, I began to alter our usage and inventory reports to Squadron, little by little, to make sure that we gained a little extra ammunition during each resupply run. In pure black and white terms, what I was doing was wrong. This was a war though and I was willing to do whatever it took to keep myself and my Soldiers safe. There's an expression in the Army that I still use in civilian life: *It's better to be judged by twelve than carried by six*.

One evening, I was attempting to find new a new home for some surplus machine gun ammo when I was approached by

Sergeants Kramer and Spears.

Kramer looked at me and then clicked his tongue, "Wow Sir, we've got you all criminalized now. Spears, get a load of this stockpile he's building up."

 I stopped stacking ammo crates and smiled, "Yeah, look at this. I can't believe what you guys got me doing."

It was Spears that spoke next in that Alabama drawl, "Shit Sir. We didn't do nothing. We just showed you what's in your heart."

Chapter 16

Specials.

The specials were operating in our area. That's what we called them, *specials*. It was a catch-all term to describe the myriad Special Forces units that were in Afghanistan. The Rangers that I had worked with earlier in Anvil Troop technically fell under this umbrella too, but we usually just called them Rangers. Specials usually denoted one of the actual US Army Special Forces Groups, the SEALs or something more clandestine.

For the longest time I wanted to be Special Forces. I was on a path that would take me there eventually. My plan was to do my time as a cavalry Officer inside the 173rd Airborne Brigade Combat Team and then transition to the 75th Ranger Regiment because, at the time, they had a mobile gun system Platoon. This meant one slot for a very lucky and highly motivated armor Officer. My plan was that I would somehow get into Ranger Regiment and then do my time there very well and then continue to work my way into Special Forces. I was elated whenever I discovered that the 173rd had a way for Officers to fast-track directly into Special Forces. Essentially, an Officer could drop his packet and participate in Special Forces assessment and selection.

The idea had been implanted in my head by Captain Valentine a few years earlier. I was at Fort Lewis, Washington participating in the Leadership Development and Assessment Course, or LDAC for short. This was the course that all ROTC cadets had to go through to see if they made the grade or not. The bar was set spectacularly low and nearly everyone who attempted passed. The plan was that a cadet would go through the course during their third year of college. Life had other plans for me and I fractured my leg while training for this course and had to push it back until the summer of my senior year. LDAC was the only obstacle between me and putting on my Lieutenant bar. I had received very good training from my ROTC instructors back in Northwest Florida. Several of them were prior Ranger instructors from nearby Camp Rudder, Florida. They weren't easy on us and they did their best prepare us for the rigors of combat. Although their hands were often tied by Cadet Command, they did their best to give us the best training they could. I think that's part of the reason why I did so well out there at LDAC. This caught the attention of Captain Valentine, who was the Officer in charge of our training company. He was a Special Forces Officer and he had taken an interest in me. I, of course, took an interest in him as well, trying to learn all that I could about Special Forces and what it entailed. At the end of camp, we had to do our counseling with the Officer in charge. Valentine spoke very simply to me and told me that I wouldn't be happy anywhere in the Army except Special Forces. He said that I wouldn't feel challenged and I simply wouldn't be allowed to do the things I wanted to do. I took it as a compliment, but it left me feeling uneasy. What exactly did that mean? What was so wrong with the regular Army that I wasn't going to be able to enjoy it? My close friends in college, most of which were fairly artistic and very left-wing, found it almost unbelievable that I was joining the Army in the first place, let alone becoming an Officer. They warned me against it from day one, "They're not going to let you be creative and they're not going to let you do any of the things you want to do." I had dismissed because sometimes during training exercises I was given a degree of latitude and I ran with it. Some of our training missions were very successful and I enjoyed the level of creativity I was allowed to employ.

Over the years though, Captain Valentine's words had wormed their way into my brain and left me with a general feeling of unease. I'd always kept Special Forces as a distant goal on the horizon. Consequently, I also held Special Forces Soldiers in very high regard. I wasn't super thrilled with what I experienced with the Rangers with my time on COP BBK, but I thought most of it had to do with my shitty attitude and less to do with anything they did.

It was early April and nearly all the snow had melted. We had just received our Rapid Aerostat Initial Deployment tower (or RAID tower). The RAID tower was a 100 foot tall tower which mounted an impressive 20x zoom daytime and infrared remote control camera. It quickly became one of our most useful outpost defense tools despite its convoluted and stupid name. It offered us a spectacular vantage point and got rid of a lot of the blind spots around our outpost. In short, the thing was a godsend. One morning, I awoke to the sound of gunfire to our south. I donned my armor, grabbed my weapon, cut my radios on and headed into the tactical operations center. There I found Commander Weaver standing behind First Sergeant Steele. Steele was in a chair operating the control system for the RAID tower. Private Piper, our Troop TOC radio operator, was manning the radios. Radios, which despite the gunfire, were surprisingly silent. The only communication seemed to be a cross talk between our guard towers who were all collectively trying to figure out where the fire was coming from and who was doing the shooting.

I looked at Captain Weaver and asked, "Do we have any patrols out right now?

He answered without taking his eyes off the screen, "No they're all inside the wire. I don't know what this is."

Steele continued to pan the RAID camera around, switching between thermal and live feed, white hot and black hot infrared in an attempt to spot the shooters. After a few moments of scanning, we were able to see some US Soldiers firing at some unseen assailant. These were US Special Forces; their multi-camouflage pattern uniforms, all tan equipment and SCAR heavy rifles all had a very distinct silhouette. The bushy beards and their rolled-up uniform sleeves also gave them away. They looked like cover art for a *Call of Duty* videogame. Commander Weaver was the first to say it that must be the Special Operations group recently assigned to Saber Command a few weeks back. First Sergeant Steele nodded and grunted, affirming the suspicion. I didn't add anything to the conversation as, at the time, I had never seen Special Forces Soldiers in combat before.

"Hey Sir did these guys check into our sector?" Steele asked.

"Nope." Said Weaver, "I have no idea why they're here."

I was thinking about something intelligent to say, some kind of insight to explain what was happening. Before I could get anything out of my mouth, First Sergeant Steele said, "Oh, fuck."

Weaver and I both searched the screen for what Steele was talking about. What I saw there immediately changed my outlook on the war. These elite Soldiers were shooting at civilians. Granted, they weren't hitting them; just shooting around them with harassing fire. This was a small Special Forces team, maybe five to seven of them, and it seemed that they were shooting at unarmed civilians. I listened to the crack of the rifles and they all sounded like US weapons. There was no return fire that I could hear or see, no distinctive AK or RPK sounds, just the sound of our weapons.

Commander Weaver and I both shared confused looks with one another. Steele had a different expression on his face though. His was one of sadness and disappointment so I fielded my question to him, "Why are they doing this?"

"I have no fucking idea, Sir. Maybe that's just how they get their rocks off? Maybe they just want to start a fight?"

"Top," began Weaver, "they probably received some harassing fire from the village and they're just protecting themselves."

"By shooting back at unarmed civilians for a solid then minutes, Sir?" Steele replied. "Fucking no one is shooting at them now. They need to stop. This is wrong and we all know it."

I felt a sinking feeling in my stomach. I was watching my idols do something horrible right in front of me. I watched more carefully and saw that they weren't actually hitting the civilians, but they were shooting around them in their general vicinity. Civilians dove for cover and ran from their fire. I couldn't believe my eyes. It was like watching Superman mug somebody in an alleyway.

"We have to tell somebody." I heard myself saying.

"Tell who, Sir?" Came Steele' reply. "Who's going to believe us? We're just a regular Army unit and it would be our word against theirs."

This left me even more deflated as I watched the screen. The shooting was about a kilometer away so there was a slight delay between the firing on the screen and the actual sound of the weapons. For the next twenty minutes or so, Commander Weaver attempted to raise the Special Forces unit on the radio. Once the shooting had died down, they decided to answer his hails. I didn't need a crystal ball to predict what they were going to say. They claimed that there on a high-priority mission and crossed through our sector. They had come under attack while moving south of our outpost. They returned fire and that was end of that.

Chapter 17

Snipers, RPGs and Taliban, Oh My!

The fighting began once the snow was gone. It was April and I was one of the first people scheduled for R&R leave out of the entire Troop. It was customary for leaders to take either very early or very late R&R, leaving the bulk of our Soldiers to go during the center of our deployment. The idea was that the Officers and senior Sergeants weren't out during the bulk of the fighting. My R&R date was fast approaching, but I was dealing with quite a bit of work as the new XO within the Troop. I kept having to cover combat missions whenever Weaver was out or otherwise disposed of. We would receive sniper fire or a few pot shots and maybe an RPG against the walls. At first, it came in fits and starts. A few shots here and there, then maybe nothing the next day. The following day might add a few rockets to the mix. At this time, we were still receiving aerial resupply and some of our personnel movement was done via helicopter. The level of enemy fire that we received on a daily basis wasn't enough for us to shut down the airfield just yet.

With the snow gone, the trees had really filled in and it was even clearer that this outpost was not put in a very good tactical location. The thick trees and orchards came up almost to the walls. To our immediate southeast, there was a medieval mud brick fortress about 300 feet away. This was a favorite firing point for our daily attackers. Our heaviest rounds couldn't penetrate the thick walls and became kind of a cat and mouse game between our guard towers and our fortress attackers. To our east there wasn't much except a few buildings and sparse vegetation. Our attackers, wisely didn't use this direction too often. To our north there was Hill 337, a barren hill, which loomed over the outpost by a hundred feet or so. This hill provided good sight lines along the only route into and out of our outpost. We'd often occupy this hill whenever we were expecting a resupply convoy into the outpost. The Charkh bazaar was directly to our southwest. That's where the bulk of the enemy fire came from. This was the district market area and the Taliban held it firmly in their control. This was a winding market area filled with many compressed mud brick buildings and choked vineyards, irrigation ditches and narrow alleyways.

In short, most of the area surrounding the outpost was a

congested nightmare and, in some places, we couldn't see more than one hundred feet from the walls. Most of our enemy fire came from the south and southwest and, subsequently, the majority of our heavy weapons were focused in that area. Although we had mortar fire reference points set up all over the area, we couldn't use them. Policy form the Brigade Commander kept us from firing any type of support fires, be it mortar, artillery or a 1000 pound aircraft bombs, within 500 feet of any civilian structure. This, obviously, meant any structures that were physically there, but it also meant any structure that were *supposed* to be there. This meant that if any map showed a structure within 500 feet of where you wanted artillery, you weren't going to get artillery support. As you can imagine, this left us with absolutely none of the indirect fire support tools when we needed them. We could drop bombs, call in air strikes or mortar strikes in open fields and deserts and mountains all day long, but none of the enemies were there. The Taliban knew that all they had to do was engage us within 500 feet of a structure and they were largely safe from our bombs. A fact that they leveraged against us every time they fired a shot at us.

Getting shot at became part of our daily routine. A tower would call up a contact report give us a vague idea of where it was coming from, but the Soldier in the tower had little idea how many people were shooting at him or really what direction it was coming from. With so much vegetation, it was hard to pinpoint where the enemy fire was actually coming from. It took a few minutes during each engagement to figure out where exactly where it was coming from let alone do anything about it.

My job during all this was to ensure that the towers had enough ammunition and supplies to make it through these engagements. I stayed on the radio and would go up to the ammo storage area which, by this time, had been relocated to the airfield. Prior to this, it had been located by the U-shaped building where a lot of our Soldiers and headquarters elements were. I advocated that it be moved up by the airfield and away from the bulk of our Soldiers. I did this because one lucky hit would cause my giant stockpile of ammo to go up like a nuclear warhead and take out nearly all of our men. First Sergeant Steele thought this was a good idea too and ordered Kramer and the workers to start moving things immediately. It didn't take long for us to get all the ammunition up away from the bulk of our Soldiers. The problem with this those it left me running across an open helicopter pad to get to the ammo containers. The Taliban could see me and I would get shot at nearly every single time on my way up to the ammo area. I think the Taliban and knew that I was the ammunition resupply guy and they would try to aim for me as best they could. Fortunately for me though, their aim wasn't particularly good and I was able to do my job with no extra holes.

It was during this operational tempo that my number came up for R&R. As abruptly as all the fighting had started for me, it stopped. The helicopter came for me one morning. I got on it with a couple of other Soldiers and basically did in reverse my deployment to Afghanistan in reverse. I first went to FOB Altimur where I waited around for a few days and then it was off to Brigade HQ at FOB Shank to do some more waiting. The waiting culminated at Bagram Airfield. From Bagram, I went to Kuwait where waited around for a flight for a day or so and I was transported back to Frankfurt, Germany. I spent a couple weeks with my wife and we took a 10 day trip to Greece. I was genuinely happy to see her and I was genuinely happy not being shot at. By this point, I hadn't been in hard combat long enough for it to really mess with my mind. I didn't have to stretch the truth too far with her when she asked about my job. I told her that I was in more of an administrative role and not in a direct combat. The truth was that since taking my new admin job in Bulldog Troop, I'd increased the amount of danger I was in by ten-fold. Bulldog Troop was the Troop that was in the shit, they would be fighting almost every day of this war. The other two line Troops had barely been shot at by this point and we were in steady engagements every single day.

Bulldog Troop had unfairly earned a reputation as the bastard child of the Squadron. Even while in training, I felt that this Troop got the less favorable assignments and caught more flak from the chain of command. We were a Cavalry Squadron yet our Squadron Commander was an Infantryman, his Sergeant Major was an Infantryman and the Squadron XO, despite being an Armor Officer, was the SCO's pet and would go through great lengths to please him. They created a very pro-infantry mentality that favored the one Infantry Troop in our unit. We had one Infantry Troop, Comanche Troop, in our Squadron and the SCO absolutely loved them. He always favored them back in training and would often compare the two cavalry Troops to Comanche Troop. He placed them down south of us in an area that was much more wide and open and away from the civilian population, which meant that it was further away from the enemy. This place was called Kherwar. As my time with Bulldog Troop went by, it became obvious that we were the non-favored Troop. Commander Weaver was not known to back down and was often right and had many disagreements with the SCO. This would've been bad on its own, but Weaver was almost always right. A point that earned him disfavor from the SCO and probably had a lot to do with why we were given such an absolute bitch of a territory to manage.

When my time was up on R&R, I made my way back to Afghanistan. When I finally filtered back to the outpost, I noticed that a change had come over the entire Troop. That day, I learned that one of the Soldiers, a female Soldier, had nearly died during a mission. We were a combat unit and didn't directly have any female Soldiers, but we were given half of an MP Platoon within the Brigade. As a scout unit we were all male but MPs allowed females in their ranks. That left our outpost with about three women on it. Captain Weaver was given a mission from Squadron to clear out the Charkh Bazaar while I was away. He had to lead a large contingent of the Troop out into the market district. I'm sure this wasn't his idea and he was undoubtedly pushed by Squadron to go in there and take control of the Bazaar area. During the patrol, an IED that was buried within in a mud-brick wall, was detonated by the enemy. The blast killed an ANA Soldier and severely wounded this young female Soldier. According to Captain Weaver, she almost died on the spot. He showed me some footage from one of the Soldiers' helmet cams. It showed her being medically evacuated.

They were able to get her out, but what had the mission accomplished? We pushed the Taliban out of the Bazaar for half a day, but without a force to hold it, they moved back in later that evening. We had lost a fighting Soldier for that. Now the question came to the forefront and I could see it on Commander Weaver's face. What was the desired end-state of that mission? It was one thing to patrol around a district and make the days go by. It was another thing entirely to walk into an enemy-held area with no support or real long-term goals and invite huge risk. If we kept doing this type of thing, we were going to lose more people. After a long talk with Captain Weaver, he and I basically came to the same conclusion; we have to look after our own. No one else was going to do it for us and we had few friends within Squadron leadership. We could never directly disobey or ignore orders. We were legally bound to follow orders from our superiors to the letter. With that operation though, Saber Command had shown us that they were willing to put us in extreme danger for little or no strategic gain.

The following day, I awoke to the sound of a much more intense enemy attack. It seemed the ferocity of the attacks had not abated while I was away. In fact, they had gotten worse. Before I left for R&R, we would've attempted to clear our own mortar fires with higher command, but now we just fired our mortars directly at the enemy without their permission. If we weren't going to get assets or support from Squadron, we had to play dirty. We had to do things on our terms to look after our Soldiers because our command sure as hell wasn't.

After one particularly vicious barrage, Captain Weaver looked at me and said, "I heard you have some extra rounds, XO. I think we are going to need them."

I grinned, "I don't think that's going to be much of a problem, Sir." As bad as things were at that point, I still felt hopeful. I knew that Captain Weaver would always do what was needed for our guys.

Chapter 18

We Just Can't Have Nice Things

It was strange being the chief logistician on COP Charkh. Nearly everyone around me was entirely focused on fighting and I wasn't. Instead of a rifle, I found myself, more often than not, armed with a clipboard; a strange feeling when your outpost is under attack nearly every single day. My job was to count munitions, fuel and food and to ensure that serial numbers stayed the same on sensitive items from one month to the next. One of the more useful things about my job was the ability to requisition special equipment. Our Squadron was given a certain amount of discretionary funds that we could use to acquire things that we needed. All we needed to do was make a case for it. The Soldiers at Charkh needed quite a few things when I first got there. There was no way for Soldiers to do laundry and we barely had any phones or computers for the Soldiers to communicate back home. The Soldiers didn't have an area to shower and there was barely enough electricity to go around. What little power we had was dedicated to powering equipment deemed mission essential.

Once the First Sergeant and I addressed all of the creature comfort issues, I focused on getting better gear for our Soldiers. The first thing I tried to acquire were suppressors for some of our weapons. Thus far, a few of our engagements that we had on patrol were chance encounters. That is to say that our patrols were out moving around when we just stumbled into the Taliban. What happened next would usually be some type of close range firefight. My logic, and the logic of several the other Lieutenants that were running these missions, was that we would have more of an edge if we used suppressed weapons at the beginning of these engagements. This was shot down immediately by Saber Command. I was told by the Squadron XO that, "We weren't Special Operations and didn't need suppressors to do our jobs." I thought this was particularly amusing because, by this time, I'd already seen some of the Saber Command Soldiers at FOB Altimur walking around with suppressors on their weapons. These were Squadron support Soldiers who operated radios or fixed vehicles far away from any enemy that needed to be silently dispatched. This was clearly a case of *haves vs. have-nots*. He was making it crystal clear where we stood in the food chain. To hammer the point home, I later received a crate of special equipment that had been requested by Lieutenant Tanner a few months prior. I opened it up and discovered over one hundred yak tracks. These were metal clamps that function as snowshoes. They're designed to fit underneath combat boots to give our Soldiers traction in the snow and ice.

"Super-fucking useful." I said to myself as I looked out into the brown, arid expanse that surrounded me. "Well this is about as helpful as a solar-powered flashlight." I concluded.

I put the snow shoes in the container with the heat-ray gun and the Jaws of Life. I decided to set my sights a little lower in the hopes that I could at least get something for our guys. I settled for hand-crank washing machines and a few extra generators so that we could have some recreational power. These arrived within a few weeks and the Soldiers loved them. First Sergeant Steele was even able to get some more phones and portable shower units. Between Steele, Kramer and I, we were able to greatly improve the quality of life for our Soldiers on the COP. I was feeling particularly proud of myself one day when suddenly we received a particularly vicious attack. Sniper fire, some rockets, a recoilless rifle and some good old-fashioned machine gun fire hammered the outpost. We were having breakfast at the time when a handful of rounds tore through the top of the dining tent, just a couple of feet above our heads. I sprang to my feet, cocked my pistol and ran for cover. I was laughing at myself before long. The idea of using a 9mm pistol against an enemy who's probably shooting at me from about three hundred meters away was absolutely absurd. At the moment, the clipboard would've been just as useful. The engagement was over as abruptly as it had started and although none of our Soldiers were hurt, we had a different type of casualty. I stood there with my hands on my hips looking at the portable washing unit that had been just shot to Swiss cheese.

"Are you fucking kidding me?!?" I asked to no one in particular.

That night I set about ordering new washer units to replace the destroyed ones. They came in about a week later. We had another bad attack around that time. This time the victim was the shower units. One was blown in half by an errant rocket propelled grenade and then our Soldiers couldn't shower anymore. Shortly thereafter, the portable bathrooms had been hit and we had to find a way to replace those. It seemed as though the Taliban were equipped with creature comfort seeking rounds that were designed to seek out and destroy anything that would give us joy. Eventually, they hit our dining tent. I had begged, borrowed and stolen to get a TV for the Soldiers so they could watch movies while they ate. We had it for a solid two days before a mortar round hit the dining tent. The TV was beyond repair and a lot of our non-perishable food was peppered with shrapnel. We had to chew our food carefully for about a week or two. I remember one point looking at all the casualties of war with Kramer and Steele; twisted generators, shot-up portable bathroom units, shredded washers and other things that were too twisted and damaged to tell what they once were.

I spoke up first, "How the fuck did they miss everything else, but manage to hit this shit?"

Steele replied, "Well XO, would you rather they hit our Soldiers?"

"That's not what I'm saying. I'm glad we are looking at piles of fucked up equipment and not bodies."

"What's your point?" he asked.

"It's just kind of uncanny that they hit this stuff and *only* this stuff. God forbid they destroy the ray-gun or anything else in that conex of failure."

Kramer chimed in, "We just can't have nice things."

Chapter 19

Should Have Died.

The day was off to a good start. I had not awoken to gunfire and I even slept in a little bit. I had gotten up at roughly eight in the morning and made my way over to the chow tent. The usual fare was there; powdered eggs, re-hydrated ham, snack cakes, beef jerky, fruit and muffins. I grabbed some food and made my way back to the command hut. I wanted to get started on this month's inventory a bit early. We had fired some LAW rockets during a few patrols and I wanted to make sure those launchers were still accounted for. For whatever weird reason, disposable rocket launcher tubes were considered sensitive items and I had to ensure that Soldiers didn't ditch them in battle the moment they were fired. I popped a muffin into my mouth and chewed carefully, spitting out a couple pieces of shrapnel as I went.

When I was done with breakfast, the first cracks and pops of small arms fire began. It sounded like wooden two-by-fours being slapped together over and over again. The radios in the command hut sprang to life with contact reports from our guard towers. Captain Weaver immediately grabbed the radio and began pulling reports from the towers. We were under attack from the southwest. The machine guns in the southern and eastern towers began to open fire with sustained bursts. Within seconds, the noise was deafening. I ran into my room and threw on my armor and helmet. I gave my radio a quick check and then chambered a round into my rifle. I burst back into the command area and saw that Weaver now had a radio up to one ear and a finger in the other ear. I looked at Private Piper, the radio operator, and pointed up toward the helipad. Piper nodded and then I pointed to my radio. We didn't have to exchange words for him to understand that I was going to be on standby to distribute ammunition. Piper gave me a thumbs up and I was off toward the ammo connexes.

When I opened the door of the command hut, I was surprised to see that the volume of incoming fire had almost surpassed the output of our machine gun towers. Orange tracers flashed overhead and rounds popped and hissed by like angry wasps. Some bullets slammed into the HESCO barriers while others struck gravel and sent splinters of rock spiraling in all directions. Soldiers in all states of dress hurried to man the walls. One Soldier in full combat gear with half a face full of shaving cream nearly knocked me down as he sprinted toward the eastern wall. An explosion staggered me a little as something big hit just on the other side of the wall. A large plume of black smoke began to pall over the barricade.

I took a deep breath and began my sprint up to the ammo site. I weaved between the mortar pit and Red Platoon's tents, trying to put as much space between me and the bullets that were flying over and into the COP. The last stretch before the ammo connexes was a forty meter sprint across the helipad over open ground. I held my breath and ran as fast as I could, body armor bouncing as I went. Seconds into my sprint, enemy rounds began to land around me, slamming into the gravel and sending rocks splintering into the air. They were trying their best to get me again. I was a few meters from the ammo connexes when something throttled into my right calf. I was knocked off balance and stumbled into the gravel, just shy of the HESCO barriers surrounding the ammo connexes. I looked back in disbelief and saw a smoking piece of metal on the ground, next to my leg. In shock, I reached out to touch it. It was red-hot in my hand and I dropped it back onto the gravel with a clang. It looked like the copper jacket of a large caliber round. It was impossible to tell exactly what it had once been; there was so much metal flying through the air. I felt my calf beginning to tighten and cramp. I looked down and saw no immediate signs of injury. I quickly rubbed my hand against my leg, expecting it to return bloody. To my surprise, my hand was clean. Evidently, the chunk of shrapnel was slowed enough to simply bruise my leg and topple me over.

I hauled myself up and hobbled toward the ammo connexes, throwing the doors open. There was a gator ATV parked between the two connexes and I began loading up the vehicle with ammo. I hefted fifty caliber machine gun ammo boxes and crates of medium machine gun ammo onto the back of the ATV. I threw some grenades and rockets on for good measure. I paused to listen to the battle for a moment. All of our machine guns were rattling away at this point, spewing death into the trees and qalats all around the outpost; we were being attacked on all sides. The incoming enemy fire was not letting up either; our Soldiers were likely going to need ammo and they were going got need it soon.

It was then that my radio sputtered to life. Tower five, the tower on top of the school annex facing into the southwest, was the one that needed ammo the most. I was tuned into the force protection net which was linked all of our towers so they could cross talk with each other and the Sergeant of the Guard which oversaw them. I could hear Staff Sergeant Avery's voice over the radio and I could tell that they needed ammo. He was a tough Soldier, not one that was prone to panic, so when I heard the stress in his voice I knew it was serious. I hopped on the ATV and began making my way down toward the school annex.

Rounds flashed and popped angrily overhead and I thought to myself, "What a fucking ridiculous way to die."

There I was, driving what amounted to an electric golf cart loaded down with bullets and rockets through the middle of an open battle. The possibility of getting shot in the head while I was acting as the equivalent of a battlefield water-boy made me laugh hysterically.

"This is not what I envisioned when I signed up!" I screamed to myself like a madman.

When I got closer the school annex, I could hear over the radio that the only thing SSG Avery needed was 40 mm grenades. They seemed to have enough of everything else in the tower thanks to my stockpiling the weeks earlier. There was a small walkway next to the school annex that I had to take in order to get to tower five. This was the area of the outpost that gradually sloped downhill toward the main road that ran alongside the COP. Taking this walkway meant that I would be in plain view of the Taliban-filled wooded area immediately to our west. Whenever my little ATV came into view, I immediately came under fire. Rounds fired in anger sought me out and I swerved the ATV out of the line of fire behind the school annex. I took a look at what I was carrying; it was mainly machine gun ammo and only one box worth of grenades. I grabbed the grenades and decided to proceed on foot. There was a small gap in between the school annex and some Jersey barriers that we had erected earlier. It was wide enough for me to jog through and shielded me from a lot of the enemy fire although, if a round or two did make its way into that narrow crevice, it would've ricocheted around pretty badly. I took my chances, grabbed the ammo can and started a trot toward the narrow gap. Immediately, I came under fire again and the sound of the rounds was amplified in such a tight space. I crouched low, tucking the grenade ammo under me like a football, and ran through the small space. The sound of the enemy fire ricocheting around in such a small space was deafening. Chips of concrete and brick were chewed away and sprayed into my face. I held the grenades tight to my chest. With any luck, they'd miss the grenades. I could survive being shot, but not being blown up by the thirty two high explosive rounds pressed against my chest. I don't know how, but I made it through the narrow defile. When I emerged at the other end, I took a sharp left and began making my way toward the ladder to the top of the school annex that would lead me to tower five.

By this point, my ears were ringing and I could barely hear what was happening. I made my way up the rickety wooden ladder holding the ammo can in my one freehand. When I reached the top, I was greeted by the face of SSG Avery. He was wearing thick protective shades, but I could still see his big, toothy grin. I could make out what he was saying until I got on top of the tower and handed him the can of 40mm grenades.

Things were starting to quiet down although we were still receiving sporadic fire. I got down behind cover with SSG Avery.

He spoke up, "Hey thanks are for the grenades, XO! I really appreciate it! I just wish you hadn't come all the way up here."

"What?" I asked.

"Yeah I was trying to get your attention over the radio-net because I just found a whole bunch of grenades up here in the tower, we've got tons of ammo!"

"Oh, fuck you!" I heard myself saying. I slumped down against the tower. I laughed as tower five's machine gun hammered overhead.

Chapter 20

West Point Joins the War.

The fighting season was in full swing; there was no doubt about it now. The personal impact of that became apparent with my brush with death a few days earlier. We were being attacked every single day for weeks now so I was a little perplexed when I learned we would receive a non-combat visitor.

"A Major from West Point is going to join us for a few days." Captain Weaver said.

I vaguely remember him telling me that we were going to get a Major from West Point a few months back, but that felt like a whole lifetime ago and with all the months of sleep deprivation and stress, there was a strong possibility that I had imagined our previous conversation. Surely, I thought, whoever decided where military tourists went in Afghanistan would not send them to one of the hottest zones in the entire country, right? I pondered this off and on for the next few hours as I went about my morning routine. Eventually, like clockwork, a Blackhawk buzzed onto our landing zone and a stout, red-faced Major leapt off with a couple of large bags. "Here he is," I thought to myself, "as real as you please." Upon speaking with the Major, whose name was Smith, I learned a few basic things about him. Major Smith had come down to our outpost to gather research on his Master's thesis on leadership or some such nonsense. Apparently he taught a class at West Point about counter-insurgency and was out here with us to get a feel for what it was like on the front lines. This perplexed me as our fight had little organization to it at all, let alone anything that could be called lines.

The following morning, I was standing in the TOC sipping my way through my first pot of coffee, when Major Smith walked in through the door. I turned to face him, lowering my coffee mug a little to get a better look at him. He was clean, too clean. His uniform looked as though he starched and ironed it while humming the national anthem. His desert boots were a vibrant yellow and his rifle was shiny and black like a beetle's ass. He had a broad face and a small putting green shaped area of sandy brown hair atop his head. He took one look at me, loudly clearing his throat.

"Where's your commander, Lieutenant?" He asked, all business.

"He's still asleep, Sir." I began, "What can I do for you?" I asked.

"Can you wake him up?" he asked, ignoring my question.

"I'd rather not. He'll be up in an hour or so, but then he'll spend about twenty minutes in the shitter before he talks to anybody." I said simply.

The Major eyed me up and down for a second and considered his response. Maybe it was the shell-pocked outpost or the strung-out, dirty look of every Soldier he had seen so far this morning, but he appeared to be struggling with what to say to me next; possibly weighing the outcomes of yelling at me versus playing nice. At that moment, with my dirty hair and perpetual five o'clock shadow, I probably looked like a guy that would shoot someone and hide their body in a HESCO if properly provoked.

"We've got breakfast up in the chow tent right outside, Sir." I said as I nodded toward the door to his left. "It's pretty standard fare, but we lucked out with a good cook. Private Lang makes a mean batch of powdered eggs."

Before he could respond, I turned toward Zoomie, who was on radio duty, and said, "Zoomie, please add one O4 to our PAX count."

Zoomie looked over his shoulder at me and spit a big brown glob of dip into a Sprite bottle. A cigarette was smoldering on the edge of his workstation. We had done our best induct Zoomie into Army culture over past few months. We had gotten Zoomie on loan a few months ago from the Air Force for a six month duration in order to help us with our VSNAP satellite communications device. His real name was Jerimiah something-or-other-fucking-complicated, but since it was hard to say we named him Zoomie in honor of all the things that go *zoom* in the Air Force. He came to us as a quiet, nerdy, wisp of a boy and I and a few of my NCOs knew right then and there that we needed to toughen this kid up if he was going to survive six months with our crew out here in hell's armpit. It was hard at first, but we got him using Army vernacular by putting him on radio duty along with Private Piper. As a smart kid, Zoomie picked it up soon enough and was speaking like a Soldier in no time. We put him in the regular quarters with the rest of the Soldiers so he could soak up the rest of the culture. In a few short weeks, Zoomie was smoking, dipping and swearing up a storm. We even put him in for a few Army and Air Force combat medals from a particularly nasty Taliban attack a few days earlier. We put him in one of the guard towers and kept giving him ammunition during the entire attack. According to my Sergeants who were his handlers during the attack, he accounted for a couple of enemy fighters.

"Zoomie, when you go back to the Air Force, you don't let any of those pansy faggots tell you what to do. You're a man now." We'd say to him.

"How's that ever going to work with people that outrank me?" he'd ask. It was a good question, but one we were ready for.

"You just point to your combat badges and ask them if they ever stared down any of the men they've killed. That should settle the matter pretty well."

It shouldn't have surprised me when Zoomie asked, in regards to this new Major, "Yeah, when's this douche getting here?"

"He's behind you, Zoomie." I said, nodding in the Major's direction.

"Zoomie removed his headset and turned around slowly in his chair. "Sorry Sir; didn't know you were there."

Fortunately, the Major was halfway out the door and didn't hear what Zoomie had said. I just smiled at the monster we had created.

"You might want to look around before you say something like that in the future, eh Zoomie?" I said.

"Point taken, XO." He added.

A few minutes later, Captain Weaver made his way out of his bunk. He plopped himself down into the chair next to me, running a large hand over his face and massaging the shallow bridge of his nose with his thumb and forefinger. All I could see were his nostrils flaring with each breath under his massive hand.

Without looking, he asked, "What's up XO?"

"Well boss," I began, "we got that West Point Major at about oh-four-hundred this morning."

"Oh yeah. Where is that douche?" Weaver asked.

Zoomie chimed in, "Oh, how come he can call him that and I can't?"

"Shut the fuck up Zoomie and get back to work! Grown folks are talking." I shot back with a grin and a wink. I'd taken to being unreasonably cruel to Zoomie. Zoomie shrank back to his console and donned his headset again.

"He's probably stuffing his face at the chow tent Sir." I said.

"Alright, I'll catch up with him in a bit. I'll be in the shitter." Weaver added and began sitting up.

"Hey XO, you got any of them good baby wipes?" He asked half way out of his chair.

"For you? Anything." I smiled as I rolled in my chair, slipped an arm into my bunk and tossed him a box of deluxe baby wipes. There was a picture of an ecstatic infant on the front of the package.

"Gracias buddy." He said as he made a mock salute with the baby wipes across his brow. For a brief second during the salute, it looked like a miniature white baby was sprouting out of the side of his mocha colored face.

The rest of the day passed with surprising un-eventfulness. I made some good headway on White Platoon's monthly inventory. They were getting better at keeping accountability of their equipment and how to lay it out for me. Overall, the monthly inspections were getting a little less painful. That night, the West Point Major invited all of the available Officers to come to the chow tent so he could interview us. By this point, I had actually forgotten about the Major. He had done a fairly good job of being unobtrusive the entire day. John, Neil and I made ourselves comfortable at the wobbly wooden chow benches. The Major had set up a laptop which was facing us. West Point's school logo could barely be made out as his desktop background. I opened up a Cliff Bar and began eating. It was too dark to make out the label, but it didn't matter. I had eaten so many in the past several months that they all fucking tasted the same.

"Thanks for coming guys." He began. "I wanted to pick your brains about counterinsurgency leadership. I teach small unit tactics and I'm writing my thesis on small unit leadership in counterinsurgency warfare."

We all nodded and waited around for what he had to say next.

"So how do you think we need to do at the small unit level to win this war?" he asked bluntly.

We all looked at him squinting slightly. I think Neil was the first to speak up, "What do you mean, Sir?"

"If you could do anything, at your level, what would you do to accomplish the mission over here?" He asked, gesturing to the entirety of Afghanistan with an outstretched arm.

"Honestly Sir, we could do with some more support out here." Neil ventured.

"What do you mean?" The Major asked.

Neil continued, "Well, it's like we're the only people in the Squadron that are fighting a real war out here. Everybody else is always talking about winning the populace or separating the Taliban from the local population and that's not what we're dealing with over here. The local populace *is* the Taliban here. All we do is fight, we need more assets released to us."

"Yeah." John interjected, "It's like they want us to interface with the populace and find the areas where the people in our district support us and the Afghan government, but I tell you, that place doesn't exist. Everybody wants us gone and they try to kill us nearly every single day."

The Major looked taken aback. "Don't you think that's a bit of a defeatist attitude?" he asked. "What about working with your USAID counterparts and all of the Provincial Reconstruction Teams in the area? Don't you think that you could achieve some results that way?"

"Sir, nobody wants to build any projects in an area where the Taliban kidnaps and kills workers," I began, "We've been losing Afghan contractors and informants and pretty much everybody else who associates with us faster than we can count. We can only keep them safe if they're here on the COP and even then that's questionable." I pointed to the bullet holes in the ceiling of the tent. "We're fighting nearly every day. These aren't all just little firefights too. I can show you the contact reports where we've been surrounded and we've expended thousands of rounds of ammunition. Just the other week, a child threw a grenade at my commander while he was out on mission." I continued. "Just like John said, it's like everyone up in command is focused on what comes after the fight and we're still stuck in the damned fight. That wouldn't be a problem if command helped us, but instead, they ignore it and imply that we're still fighting because of something *we're* doing wrong on our end."

"Listen Lieutenant," he began with that special emphasis on *Lieutenant* that really meant *shithead.* "When you refuse to---"

A dull boom in the distance cut the Major off. I eyed John's MBITR radio, waiting for our own internal radio chatter. I didn't have to wait long.

"Force-pro 6, this is Bulldog 6," Captain Weaver began, "White Platoon is in contact. Let the towers know that we've got an illumination mission coming down the pipe."

John wasted no time and scooped up the radio and his pistol, "Roger that, Bulldog 6." He stormed out of the chow tent and began speaking to the towers.

Neil's radio then sprang to life, "Red 6, this is Bulldog 6." It was the Commander again. He worked fast. "Get your Platoon spun up. We may need you to go assist White Platoon. Looks like an IED."

Neil grabbed his radio as he stood up, "Roger that, Bulldog 6." He also left the chow tent, barking into his radio.

The Major looked at me and began, "Well, it's just---"

A deafening boom caused the Major to jump in his boots, he grabbed his rifle from behind his laptop and began looking around nervously.

"Sir," I began, "it's just our outgoing illumination rounds. The mortar pit is right behind us." I gestured over my shoulder with a thumb.

He looked at me and eased up a little; taking a bit of reassurance from my calm demeanor. I probably should have told him that the mortar pit was right behind us, but honestly, I wanted to see him shit his pants a little.

"Hey Sir," I continued, "I've got to get to work. It's been nice chatting with you."

I grabbed my radio and pistol and trotted back to the TOC. I could see the illumination round that we had just fired. It was falling slowly from its parachute in the night sky, casting a chemical-white glow in the distance. Listening to the radio chatter, I deduced that White Platoon had hit an IED and taken some ANA casualties. I spent the rest of the night helping coordinate fire missions and refining a lot of the reports that we had to send up to Saber Command. Our radio operators, while very smart, were not privy to all of the subtle politicking that was developing between us and Saber Command; one poorly chosen word and we were under the microscope for days. White Platoon attempted to catch the IED triggerman for a bit, but the darkness make such a pursuit futile. One of the ANA was hurt pretty badly, so we had to spin up a MEDEVAC mission. All in all it was a busy night and I don't remember seeing that West Point Major again. I ended up getting done at roughly oh-three-hundred and crashing, as I usually did, into a black, dreamless sleep.

I awoke the next morning and began making my way through my first pot of coffee. I turned to the mIRC chat on the command screen and saw that we had one helicopter visit a few hours prior. A few lines down I saw a change to our personnel headcount.

0430: CCOP Charkh PAX -1 (O4).

Zoomie was on radio duty again.

"Hey Sir, what happened to that Major?" He asked.

"Well Zoomie, it looks like our mutual friend hitched a ride so he could find someplace that was better suited to furthering his career." I said as I blew the steam off the top of my mug.

Zoomie let out a slight chuckle and went back to the radio.

"Good riddance, you fucking tourist." I muttered into my coffee.

Chapter 21

Supply Run.

June 23rd started like any other day. We were expecting a resupply from our logistics Platoon in Darkhorse Troop. By this point, the enemy knew that we needed to be resupplied about once every two weeks. Several helicopters had nearly been shot down so we were warned by Saber Command that they were going to shut down our helipad. "Get you area under control, *Lieutenant*!" Major Boyle, the Squadron XO, had screamed at me during one conversation before slamming the phone down. That's how they interacted with us. They called or radioed in and yelled at us about all the stuff we were doing wrong. "You need to get out there and get after the enemy, *Lieutenant*!" Was a common line I'd hear from him.

The Taliban continued to shoot at anything that got near our outpost so we weren't receiving air assets anymore. That meant the only way to resupply us was by ground convoy. This was equally as dangerous because the only way out of and into our outpost was by a single road. This road was always heavily booby-trapped and lined with the enemy ambushes. Imagine the Clint Eastwood flick, *The Gauntlet*, playing out every two weeks.

We developed a sort of battle rhythm where we would put out several screening Platoons. These Platoons would be tasked to keep the enemy fighters away from the road as much as possible. Then a route clearance package, or RCP for short, would go ahead of the logistics convoy and clear the route of any IEDs or booby-traps. The route clearance team took anywhere from 1 to 3 hours just to clear a few kilometers of road. Then the route clearance package would go just a little south of our outpost and turnaround on the roads there. Then, and only then, would the combat logistics patrol, or CLiP for short, proceed down into our outpost carrying precious supplies. This was the most vulnerable time of the operation, with the only thing standing between the vulnerable supply convoy and the enemy fighters being our screening Platoons. A few fighters would sometimes get through our screening Platoons and occasionally fire a wild shot the convoy. Sometimes our water would arrive with a few bullet holes in it, but nothing was ever really destroyed and, so far, the system had worked very well and all parts had played their job in a satisfactory manner.

The real pressure on my end anyway was ensuring that the combat patrol was downloaded as fast as humanly possible once it was inside our outpost. This required a NASCAR pit crew style coordination between myself, Kramer and his workers and the First Sergeant. We had gotten particularly good at it and we were very well rehearsed such to the point that the Platoon leader of the logistics Platoon, LT Ritter, complimented us a few times saying we were the fastest crew he'd ever seen. I thanked him for the compliment but the reason for my speed wasn't 100% altruistic. The more time we spent inside the outpost dicking around with pallets of rations, the more time the enemy had to try and get back on the route in place hasty IEDs, rockets or whatever they could throw out there.

This particular resupply run was just like all the others except we missed one thing. The Taliban had changed where and how they emplaced one of their traps. RCP missed it, our screening Platoons missed it and the convoy missed it; we all missed it. It was a Chinese 107mm rocket that had been buried in an embankment and angled to fire down onto the weak top armor of one of the MR AP vehicles. I was usually tuned in to both the RCP and logistic patrol radio networks to hear all their traffic as they came down. Commander Weaver spoke to our Platoons and coordinated their efforts. He had overall tactical control so I generally stayed off the radio, but I liked to listen in anyway. We all heard when the rocket detonated. We couldn't mistake the big cloud of dust to let us know that it was an explosion and that it had somewhere around the convoy. A few moments later, the logistic patrols radio network erupted to life.

The words cut the air like a knife. *Casualties, casualties we got at least two casualties coming in to you now. Get the docs ready, oh God.*

I ran down to the aid station and saw the medics and our PA getting ready. The cautious and calm pace with which the logistics patrol was advancing down the road had vanished. Now a couple of vehicles had broken off and were screaming down the road as fast as they could go. We opened up our gates and let them come as close to the aid station as the size of their vehicles would allow. What I saw next were panicked Soldiers, covered in blood, bursting into the aid station. They carried two wounded Soldiers from the Logistics Platoon. The two wounded Soldiers were hurt and they were hurt bad. Our medics and our PA, Doc Clayton, began working immediately. As I was completely useless, I got on the radio and let Captain Weaver know that the casualties were being taken care of. First Sergeant Steele was already there directing the casualty care operations. I felt so helpless, but they were being tended to buy a half dozen medical professionals far more qualified than I was.

The truth was that we still had a logistics patrol that needed to be download and sent off the COP as quickly as possible. It felt callous, but I had to get it out of there as quickly as I could otherwise there could be more casualties on the way out. The fact that we had wounded men in a partially destroyed vehicle didn't change the mission. The Taliban certainly didn't care. They kept the pressure up, firing at the screening Platoons, our outpost and generally any target that presented itself to them. I spent the next hour with SSG Kramer downloading the rest of the equipment and getting all the supply vehicles off of the COP and back out the gate as quickly as possible. I was so focused on what I was doing, I vaguely remembered medical evacuation choppers arriving to take the wounded out.

When my part was all done a few hours later, I made my way back to the command and control hut where I saw First Sergeant Steele and Captain Weaver slumped in their chairs. I looked at First Sergeant Steele and he could tell the question I was going to ask.

"We lost one of them." He said, simply. Commander Weaver was looking off at nothing in particular, trying to hold his anger in check.

"What was his name?" I asked.

"Butler, his name is Keith Butler." Captain Weaver spoke, "He was alive here. We stabilized him, but we just got word that he passed in transit to FOB Shank."

I nodded and left the command tent. I couldn't believe what I had heard. We had so many close calls up until this point and had so many people injured, but this is the first person that our Squadron had actually lost. And over what? I looked around at the supplies we'd received. Some water, food, clean laundry, ammunition lie scattered about the outpost. He had died for that. He died to bring that to us. I was so angry at myself, at everyone and no one in particular. It should've been one of us, one of the fighters that the Taliban got. He wasn't a part of this. I thought about the rounds that almost got me the previous week. Did I cheat death so somebody else could pay the bill? For a long time, I thought it should've been me that died and not some poor guy on a supply run.

Chapter 22

Unravel.

I was having a hard time in the days that followed. The death of Butler hit us all pretty hard. Even though he wasn't in our Troop, he was still within our Squadron and he was killed doing a mission for us in our territory so we felt responsible and guilty. Everyone was affected to a degree, more or less, but I think I took it especially hard. I felt very responsible since I'd ordered the resupply run in the first place. By now it was early July and we had just brokered a deal with a local Afghan construction firm in Charkh District that would provide us a steady supply of Jersey barriers from FOB Shank. The small contractor trucks would sporadically bring a few barriers at a time to our outpost. We would use the cranes to place these barriers around the outpost to make it more defensible. We were supposed to supply any type of protection we could for these convoys. We never knew when they were coming so it was only pure luck if we wound up helping them out. More often than not, they drove down to us completely unprotected. This, of course, made them prime targets for the Taliban in the area and they would hit them with everything they could muster. Morbidly enough, this was put into the contract and these guys were paid well for their services. I'm not sure who originally brokered the contract, but I think it was Steele during one of his early visits to Brigade HQ at FOB Shank.

I don't know how he got the contract to go through, but he probably worked some sort of backdoor deal with one of his connections at Brigade HQ. I didn't look too closely at it. I was simply overjoyed that we would be receiving reinforced concrete barriers so that we could put a few more inches between us and the guns of the enemy.

I was in a particularly shitty mood one morning whenever I saw smoke over the horizon outside the COP. I checked in the command hut and I saw that we didn't have any patrols in the area so it must've been some of these contractor trucks that got hit by the Taliban. "Great, I thought to myself, "That's just fewer barriers for us." Eventually a few trucks meandered their way into the outpost. I was surprised at how randomly courageous some Afghans could be. I didn't know if these truck drivers were indifferent to danger or if they didn't really understand what was happening. Were they just plain desperate for money? But here they were, plain as you like, with their tiny trucks weighed down with these huge barriers and they were trying to unload them. The workers wouldn't touch one of the trucks and Kramer couldn't get them to go near it. I took a couple of interpreters to come over and figure out what was going on. I quickly discovered that an RPG had struck the front of the truck and, miraculously, not detonated. Everyone parted for me to inspect it more closely. It looked like it wasn't going to detonate and, quite frankly, I just didn't give a shit anymore so I walked over and plucked the thing out of the front of the truck. At this, the Afghan truck drivers ran away from me. Eventually they came to realize that there was no danger and then gingerly came up and unloaded the last truck.

Kramer came up to me afterward and said, "Sir that was really risky."

"I know," I said "but why not die from that? I mean that's just as ridiculous as dying from anything else over here, right?"

"You've got a point there."

My level of *I don't give a fuck* was off the charts at this point in time. Every night I had to send up a logistical report to Saber Command to let them know what we had used that day and how much we had left. This applied to fuel, food and ammo. These communications were done over a secret-level laptop. That sounds a lot cooler than it was though. It was basically Microsoft Outlook, loaded onto a slow and shitty notebook, connected to a red Ethernet cable labeled *secret*. Very high-tech, spy stuff. After sending a report one evening, I discovered that there was another First Lieutenant Nicholas Stevens in the Army. I realized this because I kept getting his emails… from Iraq. At first, I ignored them. Then, when I realized that they weren't stopping, I politely told everyone that I was the wrong LT Stevens and that I was in Afghanistan; please stop sending me stuff. When the tide of emails refused to abate, I decided to start making decisions as though I were the Iraq LT Stevens.

This proved to be immensely entertaining because the Iraq version of me was in charge of base defense somewhere on a huge FOB in Bagdad.

"Should we install the new guard towers on the North wall?" *Go nuts.*

"Where should we house the detainees?" *I recommend asking them.*

"How many rolls of barbed wire should we put out by each gate?" *All the rolls of wire.*

"How do you want the new barricade layout to look?" *See my attached MS Paint document.*

The idea of some base in Iraq being transformed, slowly, into the *Willy Wonka Factory* buoyed my spirits a little. Even though we lost a Soldier on a combat logistics patrol, we still had to get resupplied. That meant that the resupply patrols would still go on every two weeks. Like clockwork, we received another patrol. Everyone was on edge particularly Lieutenant Ritter, who had endured the loss of Butler on the patrol two weeks ago. Ritter was on edge and I could completely understand why. I was in a particularly foul mood too. I was sick of everything over there at this point. We decided to change a few things about how we unloaded the combat logistics patrol but largely the tactics remained the same whenever the resupply patrol came in to the outpost, I began overseeing traffic control. Kramer and his workers worked to get everything downloaded as quickly as possible, but I had one Afghan truck driver that was holding things up. This particular truck driver was there to supplement the combat logistics patrol. This wasn't uncommon as these logistics Platoons usually didn't have enough Army vehicles to carry everything that outposts needed so they would hire these Afghan drivers from the local populace. These trucks with the livelihoods of these drivers and they were often embellished with good luck charms, trinkets, paintings and anything else they wanted to put on their vehicles. Oftentimes these hanging objects would jingle and clank as they moved, earning them the name, *jingle trucks.*

This particular driver had stopped in front of the ramp to the now closed heliport. He was bottlenecking the entire convoy and trying to turn his truck around 180 degrees. His 40 foot truck that was laden with water and he was executing a 20 point turn to get completely reversed. I didn't have an interpreter with me so I kept trying to tell him, through gestures and angry body language, just to go up onto the helipad and then turn around like everyone else. He refused and kept getting back in his truck and attempting to back up in the most ridiculous and inefficient fashion possible. He was costing us valuable time. This was time that the Taliban would use to hit us as hard as they could; time that could effectively cost more lives. I didn't want a repeat of the last resupply patrol. At this point I should've gotten interpreter and discovered why he was doing this, but I think I just reached some kind of boiling point. I just kept pointing at him and shouting, in English, and telling him to get the fuck up onto the helipad like everyone else. He, being an Afghan male, got out of the truck, came down and started arguing with me in his dialect, complete with wild hand waving. We must've looked absolutely ridiculous arguing with one another. Two completely physically opposite specimens; me towering over him in all my combat gear and yelling at him in English while he, a tiny brown man in a baggy rough-spun shirt leaned back to yell up at my face.

Only I didn't find it funny. I was starting to see red. I felt my hand lowering down toward the pistol strapped to my thigh. I was ready to shoot him right there in the teeth. I was going to give that little fucker discount dental surgery in front of everyone and move his goddamn truck myself.

Right when my hand brushed metal, Lieutenant Ritter walked up and said, "Hey Nick. I turned towards him as he continued, "I hope Jamaal isn't giving you a hard time. His truck, weirdly enough, only has a low gear in reverse so he has to go up this ramp backwards. That's what he's trying to do. Sorry for the delay."

"Oh." I said, a wave of realization and then shame washing over me, "Yeah sure, that's... that's no problem."

When I was I alone later that night, I thought about what happened. I don't think anyone saw my hand wrapping around my pistol and I was ashamed to think of how close I was to killing an unarmed, innocent man. It was only July and I felt myself unravel a little bit today. We weren't scheduled to leave Afghanistan until November and I wasn't quite sure if I could stay sane until then.

Chapter 23

Ten Days of Hell.

One night during the last week of July, we heard a very brief gun battle to the west of the COP. I was in the command hut with Captain Weaver and asked him if we had any patrols out at the time. He confirmed that we didn't and we were both a little puzzled. I was left wondering, "Who the hell was shooting at who?" It wasn't unheard of for the Taliban to have internecine wars and to fight amongst themselves every once in a while, but this sounded like more than just a little scuffle. I reported it in to Saber Command and didn't think much of it until a few hours later, when we started pick up some weird radio traffic from Special Operations types. These guys had just appeared from nowhere and we suspected they were talking to someone within the Brigade; we couldn't hear the other half of the conversation though. Captain Weaver and I thought that maybe these Special Forces guys were looking for one of their operatives or maybe there was some kind of secret mission going on in the area and they just had a minor firefight. We asked them if they needed help which they politely refused and we left it at that.

The following morning would prove something else was afoot in Charkh Valley. Overnight, this minor scuffle had developed into the theater-wide manhunt. As best as we could figure, two Sailors had gone missing from some kind of naval defense building outside of Kabul. It looked as though they had been kidnapped or perhaps they had simply driven off the base of their own free will. Either way, they'd left their outpost and taken a wrong turn and wound up in our backyard. I had forgotten that we were so close to Kabul and that something like this was possible. We were just over a hundred kilometers south but it felt like a whole world away. The relative calm of Kabul was in direct contrast to the frenzied fighting we'd seen every single day out here since the spring. The Shark Tank was really living up to its name and was showing no signs of slowing down. The fact that somebody would willingly come here seemed out of the question. People would find any reason not to come. In fact, just the other week, one of the female MP Soldiers had faked an overdose just to get medically evacuated from the outpost. We later learned that she had taken a whole bottle of Midol, but by that time she was already at Brigade HQ in FOB Shank complaining of *psychological issues*. Of course, she got her free ticket out and we were down one more Soldier.

Weaver and I started wondering how these two Sailors could've wound up in our backyard in the first place. We didn't get to ponder long before Saber Command stepped in. The Lieutenant Colonel Dunn, the SCO himself, got on the net and ordered Captain Weaver to investigate the suspected site where these two Sailors were ambushed. That left me in command back at the outpost while Commander Weaver went out to go find this this vehicle. We were told that the Sailors had driven in a bulletproof SUV, were armed with two assault rifles and that they were ambushed somewhere west of our outpost. Minutes later, a UAV drone was able to spot the smoking wreckage of the SUV. It was so strange because assets were pushed into our sector left and right. These were things that we had begged and pleaded for earlier and now, we were almost flooded with toys. Reconnaissance drones, armed drones, helicopters, jets, fucking everything came in to crowd our little valley. We were able to pinpoint the location of SUV within moments. Weaver took a Platoon and boarded a Chinook helicopter a few minutes later. As I watched them take to the sky, I shook my head in amazement. Now that we had a high profile operation, all the assets that had been denied to us for months were miraculously turned back on.

When Commander Weaver and the guys got to the site, they saw that the vehicle had been already been torn apart and scavenged. Within minutes, the local Afghans had taken out all the transponders, all the secret equipment and anything else that could potentially prove valuable. We were left with a stripped, burned out hull of a vehicle. The crowd of Afghans that still stood there watching the vehicle when Weaver arrived, somehow had seen absolutely nothing and gave us no leads.

What happened next was the start of a ten-day operation that was only marginally successful. I can't even say so much that I participated in it; just survived it. I averaged probably about two hours of sleep a night and I can't remember everything that happened. To me, all the days ran together and I wasn't sure what I was doing at times, a large part of this was due to sleep deprivation but also to the fact that we just didn't fucking stop. Commander

Weaver was out the entire time leading forces in the field. This left me back at the outpost managing the 300 or so additional Soldiers that were pushed into our battle space, relaying orders to all these different units, and trying to run rest and refit operations for these guys as well. Our outpost was the only supply hub for these Soldiers operating in the valley. Because of the mountain passes in the way, Saber Command couldn't communicate directly with some of the units operating in our battle-space. I became a sort of de-facto command relay station for their orders.

One of the first new units that was pushed to us was a National Guard unit from the Northwest. Saber Command worked these guys for about 30 hours straight. They used them to try and sweep the area west of our outpost. They got particularly lucky because they didn't run into any Taliban ambushes or IEDs while spending over a day in one of our worst areas. I think it was the rain that kept them safe. The Taliban didn't like to fight in anything other than clear weather. The muddy ground, much like snow, would likely slow them down and make it harder for them to evacuate their wounded and withdraw after they had sprung their ambush. The National Guard guys didn't make it entirely unscathed though. The terrain was killing them. They weren't used to the high elevation and dense, rocky terrain of the valley. Whenever they came to the outpost to rest and refit, they didn't even look like they were going to make it another hour. The Soldiers were wet and freezing cold and just trying to warm up. I got them inside tents and plywood buildings as quickly as I could. We even hooked up some of the tents to the MR AP vehicles and blasted the heaters inside to keep these guys are going into hypothermia. These National Guard Soldiers were extremely grateful that we took care of them and went back out into Charkh a few hours later. I feel like I had just nursed a puppy back to health and were sending it back out into the wilderness.

In direct contrast of these guys, we were visited by one of the Brigade's infantry Platoons. I was told that these were the guys in the documentary *Restrepo*. They were arrogant about it, too. They came into the COP and immediately started making demands of me. They needed to be quartered for the evening in the nicer facilities where my Soldiers were already staying and they wanted hot meals at three in the morning.

They weren't too happy whenever I told them, "No one gets hot meals here at three in the morning. You're going to have to make do with non-perishables or wait until breakfast. There's plenty of food in the chow tent."

A big Sergeant, obviously the leader of the group, bristled up at this and demanded that I put my cook to work for him and his men.

I simply stared him down. Maybe it was the fact I was an Officer or maybe it was the look in my eye that said, "I'm probably going to die or go to jail before this is all over. I don't care what happens to me and, most certainly, not to you." They took their quarters and rations and then left the following morning, but not without leaving a muddy mess behind like a bunch of pouty children.

At one point during the ten-day operation, I want to say day three, Saber Command found out that I had stockpiled a ridiculous amount of supplies down at the outpost.

At first I thought to myself, "Well this is it. They found out you've been squirreling away all types of supplies and ammunition and lying on your nightly reports. Time to face the music because you're going to jail."

Somehow, this wasn't the case because their next question was, "How quickly can you get some of that ready to be transported by helicopter?"

This surprised me and I said, "Well I can have water, food, ammunition and everything ready to go in less than an hour, but I don't really have anything to put it in."

Major Boyle was quickly put on the other end of the radio he chimed in, "What about body bags?"

"Well," I said, "I've got a bunch of those and fortunately we haven't had to use them."

"Do I have to think of everything, Lieutenant? Go ahead and fill those body bags up."

"Roger that, Sir." I said.

And so I began this strangely morbid task of filling body bags up with resupply material. This went on for several days, wherein at any hour of the night, we had to go and pack tailor-made body bags filled with combinations of food, water, munitions and anything else the guys in the field needed.

At about half way into to the operation, the Taliban started to fight back a little bit. At first our local Taliban and was really overwhelmed by the overnight quadrupling of US forces in the area so they laid low. Part of this, I'm sure, was their strategy to move or hide the two injured Sailors as best they could. Maybe that's giving them too much credit, in all likelihood they were simply waiting for more reinforcements before they started to pick a fight with us. They had briefly engaged the Soldiers that were out searching for the Sailors and left the COP alone. This changed at some point and it seemed that they had the manpower to engage our outpost as well. They started firing at us just with harassment fire, but they eventually brought heavier stuff to bear like recoilless rifles and RPGs. I, by this point, only had a token force guarding the outpost and every single capable Soldier, to include the ANA, were out there in the field. So, under fire and nearly alone, I cut loose with mortars and began firing heavily at enemy locations. Saber Command, of course, overheard and began squawking at me over the radio to cease-and-desist.

I picked up the hand mic and asked them, "What you expect me to do? I've got no way to hit these guys. They're out of line of sight with my guard towers and I've got no Troops to attack with. Should I divert assets searching for the Sailors to go attack these shitheads that are firing at us or should I just drop rounds on them?"

There was a hushed silence on their end of the radio.

I left the hand mic with Zoomie, "Come get me if they come up with any solutions instead of just handing me problems."

I picked up the hand mic to our mortar Platoon and spoke, "Put some white phosphorous in the mix too. I want these fuckers to burn. Get the 120mm mortar ready too. I want to send a message to these assholes."

My strategy when fighting the Taliban was to go straight to the knockout punch. I was starting to learn that the Taliban fighters here didn't really seem to respect much except for explosions. The bigger they were, the more afraid of them they were. I wanted to show them that we weren't fucking around and I certainly didn't want their attacks to escalate because they were unanswered. I guess I made the right call because after we dropped a few rounds they stopped and didn't attack the base anymore after that, focusing their efforts elsewhere in the valley.

The Squadron XO, Major Boyle, called me up later that night, yelling, "What the fuck do you think you're doing Lieutenant?!?"

"I was fighting with the only tools I had, Sir."

"Don't give me any of that bullshit! You didn't get any of those fire missions cleared through us!"

"There wasn't enough time, Sir. I acted."

"You acted wrong, Stevens. We plotted some of your fire missions and they were directly on top of civilian structures. That's in direct violation of Brigade policy. What if you had killed civilians?"

I didn't want to argue the point that hitting structures was the intent and that nearly every civilian down here was an active Taliban member or supporter. Instead I said, "Roger, Sir. Wont' happen again."

"You're goddamn right it won't, Lieutenant!" He roared, "As of now, you're forbidden to use your 120mm mortar. I'm taking it away from you, is that clear Lieutenant?"

"Crystal, Sir."

As our numbers swelled and we continued to receive more people in Charkh Valley, we eventually received a couple of Platoons from Comanche Troop to assist us. As LTC Dunn's favorite Troop, they were announced as if the SCO was unleashing some type of secret weapon. I member the radio briefing the night before that I listened in on.

The SCO began, "Well Weaver, don't worry. I'm going to send in Comanche Troop tomorrow."

There was a long pause where I think the SCO was waiting for Weaver to say, "Oh thank you, Sir! All of our troubles are over!" but instead, it was the kind of silence that implied, *and then what?*

They briefly went over the plan and I listened to them over the radio and I heard the Commander of Comanche Troop, the SCO and Captain Weaver going back and forth over where they should be inserted. The Comanche Troop Commander wanted to insert directly on top of the highest mountain near the cell phone tower, west of our outpost. This was in the middle of enemy controlled territory.

"That's probably a really bad idea." Weaver said, "There's no cover and concealment up there and, although you can see the entire valley, the entire valley can see you. The Comanche Commander wanted none of it and wouldn't listen and insisted on having the high ground.

"You know, Weaver, you guys make it sound like it is *way* worse than it is over there." I heard the SCO say.

Silence met that comment from Weaver's end.

Eventually it was settled that Comanche would come in and take the high ground. They would be dropped in a little lower in a flat area just a few hundred meters away and they would walk up the mountain. The following morning, I woke up early and was sure to get my cup of coffee and I panned the RAID camera over to where the insertion was going to take place. As sure as clockwork, they landed and began making their way up the bald, exposed mountain. About two minutes into it, machine-gun, RPG, recoilless rifle and small arms fire erupted onto Comanche Troop. Their Soldiers began a two hour long firefight. They were outside of our weapons range so there wasn't much we could do other than observe and report on what was happening. I did have one weapon that could've supported them though; the 120mm mortar which Boyle had taken from me last night. As I watched, I got a strange feeling of vindication. The SCO and his immediate circle at Squadron HQ thought that we were exaggerating events down here for months. They downplayed a lot of what was happening here and they were quick to point out all the struggles that other Troops were dealing with whenever Weaver or I brought it up. It felt like they wanted to ignore what was happening in Charkh. Here they were though, in our own backyard, seeing for themselves that this shit was as real as the day was long. It was good too that someone, other than us, was witnessing it for a change. Now that somebody else was privy to the madness that was Charkh Valley, there was a chance that we would be taken more seriously by Saber Command.

This search and rescue operation was, by far, the largest operation the Squadron had conducted. It was clearly the most high profile one because we had received units from all across Afghanistan. All of these units were pushed to Saber's direct command, to include some Special Operations assets. As the owner of the battle-space they all fell under the purview of Saber Command. This was our backyard and a lot of orders were relayed through me because our COP could communicate best to the units in the field where the action was taking place. Now because of my stunt earlier, we were not fully trusted by Saber Command. Saber Command didn't like having to relay through me and eventually created a tactical action center, or TAC, comprised of just a handful of Officers and Sergeants loyal to Saber Command which they perched on a high mountaintop in the northwest of our sector. This TAC acted as a relay between the units in Charkh Valley and

Squadron Command, a dozen kilometers away at FOB Altimur. Now they could bypass me entirely. On this relay was the Squadron XO, Major Boyle, along with Sergeant First Class Moss, who had just left Anvil Troop and gotten a new job at Squadron as one of Boyle's underlings.

Now one would expect that the Commander of an entire Cavalry Squadron, when given this type of high-profile mission with this level of responsibility, would spend nearly all of his time coordinating with, talking to and directing his subordinate leaders. I was floored at how little he spoke to his subordinate commanders. Because I had to be ready to resupply any of the dozen or so units in our sector, I monitored nearly *all* of the communications traffic during those ten days. At the end of it, I could count on one hand how many times I heard our Squadron Commander's voice over the radio. To this day, I have no idea what he was doing during that time. Major Boyle, on the other hand, continually spewed orders from the mountaintop. It was beautiful; beautiful in the way that a slow-motion train wreck is beautiful or a forest fire is beautiful. Because they were perched on top of that mountain, their radio signals went far and wide. Everyone got to hear them. It was on showcase for all these other units, too. Now everyone got to see how ridiculously fucked up Saber Command was and I relished every moment of it. I sat there, listening in, and I would get so happy whenever I would hear another order come across the net. Boyle ordered people around in circles. He didn't know the villages and sometimes he lost track of where friendly units were in the battlespace. It was a command and control nightmare and I had a front-row seat. This was a guy that would dig into me without the slightest provocation and I was listening to him drown, slowly over the radio. It eventually got so bad that he Special Forces guys in our area just picked up and fucking left. They had enough of Operation Saber Madness, picked up their ball and left the court. I was ecstatic.

This operation really accentuated the incompetence of our leadership. They absolutely awed me with their inability to run a relatively straight-forward search and rescue mission. Looking for two people, who were physically wildly different from any other human beings within the general populace, could've been a relatively easy task. The two Sailors were also, most likely, wounded and this would've made them easier to find because they would have been hard to move. This was almost a classic police-style kidnapping case. We knew that the Taliban wanted to get these Sailors out of Charkh Valley and transport them to Pakistan, where we couldn't reach them and, more importantly, where they would be used for propaganda purposes. There were only a few mountain passes out of Charkh that they could take to accomplish this. Instead of doing it in a textbook style fashion, wherein you set up chokepoints and then let the kidnappers come to you, Saber Command ordered us to pursue any lead with 100% tenacity and aggression in an attempt to flush these kidnappers out. They left the mountain passes very lightly monitored and defended.

We were putting immense pressure on the Taliban kidnappers and this, of course, forced them to continually move and relocate the wounded Sailors. If this were a chess game, it would've been like watching one player trying to take down his opponent's queen using nothing but pawns. The queen would just move out of the fucking way. This strategy kept the kidnappers and the Sailors constantly on the move and prevented them from being stabilized and treated for their wounds. Eventually, we began receiving reliable intelligence that the two Sailors were both dead. To this day, I still think that we had a hand in getting these guys killed. Say what you will about the Taliban, two things they understand very well are casualty evacuation and casualty care. Nearly every single time our patrols would engage the Taliban forces, we found no enemy dead when the shooting was over. Even on missions where I *knew* I had shot someone myself, we would find only blood spattered on the ground and drag marks in the dirt. It was like fighting ghosts. Were they not getting shot? Were they invincible? Absolutely not. As insurgents, it was vitally important to them that their wounded not fall into our hands, lest they be captured and subsequently interrogated. As a result, they got very good at getting people out of the fighting and keeping them alive. We could've used our brains a little and put the enemy's strengths to our advantage and kept these Sailors alive a little longer. Instead, we chased after them with all the planning and restraint of a dog chasing a ball onto the highway.

At the end of all this insanity, the only thing we had to show for it was the remains of two dead Sailors and a whole bunch of injured and tired Soldiers. Against all odds, we hadn't lost any of our guys and we had given the families of the missing Sailors some degree of closure. The icing on the cake was at the end of all this when we received a visit from the SCO. LTC Dunn came out to each of the three combat outposts within the Squadron. Here he was at our COP. It was one of the only times he ever came to our outpost during that entire year. One of his lackeys held up a poster board while he stood on a crate and began his speech. At the top of the poster the words *Operation Saber Rescue* were emblazoned.

"Interesting choice of words." I thought to myself. "I thought that you had to survive to be *rescued*. It should've been *Operation Saber Salvage.*"

He went over, step-by-step, the entire operation so the common Soldier could understand what they did. The tone of it all was insulting and it implied a line of reasoning that deduced these Soldiers were too stupid to understand what was going on. He pointed at areas on the map and went over everything we had done, as if we hadn't just experienced it. He couldn't keep anything straight though. He got the names wrong on nearly all the villages. He didn't know who was where and at what time. He told us we did a great job blocking certain passes even though our Soldiers didn't do any of the blocking operations. Captain Weaver had to step in and whisper corrections into his ear periodically. He had no idea what he was talking about and the Soldiers of Bulldog Troop knew it. I was the only person smiling because this was just too painful for it not to be funny. I looked around and saw the other Soldiers did not share my amusement. They were all haggard looking and stood cross-armed, ready for the SCO to finish speaking and leave. Were it not for the threat of death by firing Squad, I think some of the Soldiers would've lynched him right then and there. I'm glad they didn't though. I would've had a hard time determining if that was right or wrong.

Chapter 24

On Your Own, Kid

With all the excitement going on, I had forgotten that Captain Weaver had not had his R&R leave yet. My commander was no exception to the leave policies and his day was coming up. He would likely spend nearly an entire month away from the outpost. He would have to spend a week trying to get out of Afghanistan and nearly a week on the back-end trying to get back to our outpost. I had always been Captain Weaver's second in command so it was natural that I would take over while he was away. In the days leading up to his departure, Captain Weaver came to me and let me know what was going on. He laid out his plan for a few air-mobile missions to a few enemy held towns to our north. The SCO had recently developed a hard-on for these types of missions and doing them seemed like a way to keep him happy and off my back while Weaver was away. We didn't expect much fighting there because the enemy had been at our doorstep for the past several months. The Taliban wouldn't expect us to show up in their backfield with as many US Soldiers and ANA as two Chinook helicopters could carry. Those plans looked good to me because they would get us out to a few towns where we might uncover some caches or vital intelligence. At the very least, it would show the enemy that we were indeed capable of reaching any part of the valley with impunity.

Weaver then went to show me his patrol schedule matrix for our four Platoons. It was a busy, but still manageable schedule that gave the Platoons enough downtime while still getting a lot of patrol time in the valley. I was fairly happy with this because it meant that we would be keeping a presence in and around the outpost to keep the enemy pushed back a little bit. I had been working on our combat logistic patrols and resupply missions with Darkhorse Troop and I saw where those days fell on the matrix. We also had to fit in when and where we would be switching out Soldiers on a few observation posts that the Troop manned. It all seemed to be well thought out and like it would work well.

In the days leading up to Weaver's departure, I sat in all of his meetings and radio call-ins to see exactly where we were in regard to our progress and what the general tone was within the

Squadron. Saber Command seemed pleased with what we had put forward and they were treating everything as business as usual. The only real big operation on the horizon was the Afghan National Elections on September 18th, but the Commander was going to be back well before then. He let me know the general concept of the plan, but since it was so far out we didn't get into any real detail.

One of the last nights before Captain Weaver left, our Afghan counterparts on the COP celebrated Eid. The way I understood it was that Eid marks the end of Ramadan, where the fasting is broken. Eid is usually a big celebration with lots of food. Since these celebrations work off of the Luna Calendar, we didn't keep track of the day. Captain Weaver was invited to attend the Eid celebration on the COP, but had to pack and prepare for his departure. He sent me in his place.

"You sure you don't want to go?" I asked.

"Nah, I've got to finish this shit."

"There's going to be lots of food. It smells good."

"Just tell them I'm sorry I can't make it and bring me back a plate." He said, finally.

I had a really good time with our Afghan friends. We ate a lot of food and our interpreters had somehow gotten a bootleg copy of the movie *Air Force One* and we were watching it in a dusty tent, drinking chai tea. When I departed, I left with two plates of food for the Commander and myself. Only when I gave him his did I realize what I had done.

He looked at it briefly before addressing me, "You racist motherfucker."

"What?" I asked, incredulously.

"Really XO? I'm a black man. Look at what you're holding."

I looked down at the plate of fried chicken and fresh fruit. There was a big slice of watermelon hanging off the edge of the paper plate. The grape soda was so cold, it was sweating in my hand, "Oh." I said sheepishly, "I ate the same thing. It's what they had. I can... I can go get something else, Sir."

His arms were crossed now and he was giving me a stone silent look. He kept it up for about five seconds before cracking a smile, "Just kidding, XO! That looks good as hell. Hand it over!" With that, we both sat down and gorged ourselves on the best fried chicken I've ever eaten before or since.

When Captain Weaver finally departed, I set about implementing the plan that he and I had put together. Every day, I had to compile and send up our patrol schedule matrix along with my commander's assessment of what was happening in the valley. Within two days, I began hearing objections from Saber Command about my plan. I remember one phone conversation in particular with Major Boyle.

"Nick, I just want you to know that Weaver is a little scared" he began, "he's not thinking about the mission and the SCO and I feel like he's not getting after it."

"Roger." I said nervously. I didn't like where this was going.

"This patrol schedule that you've submitted to me is just a bunch of busy work." he went on, "And I don't think it's doing you guys any good down there. You've got patrols just going around to places that you've been to before. I'm going to change it up. I want you to go to places you've neglected."

What he meant was places that were enemy held strongholds and we were going to go there. "That son of a bitch," I thought to myself, "He waited for Captain Weaver to leave to pull this with me."

Later that night, I received a revised patrol matrix for Bulldog Troop from Major Boyle. I took one look at it in my heart sank. They had us going to the worst areas in the entire valley. It's like they remembered nothing from the ten days of hell we all just went through looking for those Sailors. Or worse yet, maybe they did remember and they just wanted to punish us. The following morning, I was thinking about how to approach Major Boyle or Lieutenant Colonel Dunn in order to revise the patrol schedule or even flat-out asking them why they wanted us to do what basically amounted to movement to contact missions deep in hostile territory with little or no support. I was trained as a fighter, nearly all of my Soldiers were fighters and I had no problem walking into a fight, but I wanted everyone else on that same page with me. These patrols were listed as reconnaissance patrols, which meant they wouldn't get any artillery assets or gunship support or anything of the sort until Troops got into contact. That meant that it would take minutes to get those assets on board and by then the Taliban would be withdrawing after having inflicted a vicious close range ambush on us. If we were going to walk into the hives of enemy activity, I wanted to have the assets to support me, ready to go.

The more I thought about it, the more I began to suspect they were doing this on purpose. If they had called these *movement to contact* missions or *attack* missions, which they really were, then they would have to give me artillery and gunship support. Support which I would almost certainly use. They didn't want that to happen because it meant questions from Brigade. *Why is this Troop fighting so much? Why did they have to drop so many bombs?* It was much easier for them to keep us quiet and not have to explain anything than it was to explain why Afghan civilians died or why entire buildings got leveled. They wanted to keep that quiet; to keep us down here, quietly getting hit in the face every single day. I didn't get to think about this very much though. Suddenly, there was a titanic explosion outside the outpost. I jumped up and grabbed the RAID camera controls and swung it over to see a huge cloud of smoke coming from the western cell phone tower a few kilometers away from the outpost. This was the same hillside that Comanche Troop had occupied a few weeks ago. We didn't have any patrols out at the time so it was some type of sabotage or accident that did this. Even though they were about 12 km away, they'd heard it at Squadron HQ and they started asking us what was happening. I let them know that the western cell phone tower had just exploded and that a big chunk of it appeared to be missing right now. I told him that we had no patrols out and I asked them if there were any friendly forces in the area. After a few minutes they responded and said there were no friendlies in the area. I knew they wouldn't leave it at that though.

After a few minutes, Major Boyle got on the radio and said, "Bulldog, this is Saber Five. I want you to go over there and do a battle damage assessment of that explosion."

I paused for a moment to take in the full idiocy of this order. This was not a battle, first of all, it was just an explosion. The Taliban had very limited resources and when they blew something up, they did it for a very specific reason. The most likely reason that I could come up with was that the cell phone guys had not paid up their protection money to the Taliban and they blew up their tower to teach them a lesson. The second most likely explanation was that it was a trap and they knew we would come look at it and they were going to ambush us. This was highly likely because it was on top of a completely exposed mountain that was visible to the most hostile areas of Charkh Valley.

I chose my words as carefully as I could before I depressed the hand mic and spoke to Major Boyle, "Sir I'm about 95% sure this is a trap of some type. Without any type of bomb forensics equipment we're not going to find out who did this or why. We are going to walk up there take a look around for a couple minutes and then get shot at by everyone in the valley."

His response was almost immediate, "Are you refusing a direct order, *Lieutenant*?" His emphasis on the word Lieutenant made it sound like a four letter word again. It was something I was becoming entirely too used to this point. I wanted to tell him *yes, I am refusing a direct order*. What he was doing was stupid and borderline criminal, but it wasn't unlawful. It was a lawful order so I had to carry it out.

There's no law against stupid orders so within minutes we were getting Platoons ready to go walk into a trap. I brought in all three Platoon leaders and spoke to them letting them know what they were in for.

"We're getting ready to walk into a fight. We all know the cell phone tower just exploded and Saber Command, in their infinite wisdom, wants us to go out there and look at it more closely." I said.

Woods looked at the RAID camera monitor and asked, "We're looking at it right now, aren't we?"

"Yes, I guess we are," I said, "but this isn't enough. We have to go look at it more closely-er." They all chuckled at this I was glad to see that there is a glimmer of morale still left. That, in spite of everything, we could still laugh at the ridiculous bullshit we had to endure.

"So we all have to eat this shit sandwich," I said, "so who wants to take the first bite? Make it a big one. It's best not to nibble."

John, to his credit, spoke up and said, "I'll go. We will take the lead."

"Okay," I said, "so you have two Platoons supporting you." I looked at Woods and Lynch they both nodded and knew what they had to do.

I explained that Lynch and Woods would set up first and provide over-watch onto the hill as best they could. I wanted them to cover from two different angles and to get in really good positions and try to watch the areas that would fire onto the mountain itself.

I looked at Harper and said, "Now, I want you to understand, this is your chicken and you can fuck it however you want, but I would recommend that you only take half your Platoon up that mountain. The other half stays in support while you take a quick look around. We check this block for Squadron and, if you don't find anything, we hurry the fuck back."

John looked at me and said, "I was thinking the same thing."

I asked if there were any questions at this point. There were none and that was that. The Platoon leaders left and began prepping their men. I sat by the radios and prepared whatever assets I could and then waited with my coffee, nervously, as was my ritual for the past few weeks anytime a patrol left our outpost.

I developed a particularly impressive talent by this point for being right about things. Unfortunately, it only applied if it was regarding something horrible. It was a kind of pessimistic clairvoyance that was only activated through despair and sadness. I watched for the half hour or so it took our Platoons to get in place and then, as sure as the sun coming up, Blue Platoon was engaged on top of the mountain. It was the usual fare though; machine guns, recoilless rifles, some heavier antiaircraft fire, rocket propelled grenades and the like. The other Platoons were very well prepared and selected some fairly good positions to support Blue Platoon. They opened up with suppressing fire on the enemy positions that they could reach and enabled Blue Platoon to get down from the mountain fairly quickly. From there it was a well-executed fighting withdrawal back to the outpost. Coordinating with our mortars to obscure areas with smoke rounds, each Platoon would fall back covering the other. They suppressed entire tree lines with machine gun fire, grenades and anything else within their arsenal. As we normally did, we handed the Taliban a sound beating but were unable to confirm any kills because of the thick vegetation and constricting terrain. We knew we had felled at least half a dozen enemy, but we could only find blood stains and drag marks as evidence of our success. It always felt like we were fighting ghosts and today was no different. We didn't even bother to assault their positions we just fired at them and fell back, our mission done.

Whenever the Platoons made their way back in the outpost and refitted, I brought the Lieutenants back and asked Harper, "Did you find anything?"

"Not a goddamn thing, XO." he said.

"Fucking fancy that, eh?" I said

I radioed it up to Saber Command and let them know that we didn't see anything up there other than what the RAID camera already told us that morning. I didn't receive a single *thank you* nor a *good job*, nothing. That lack of response pissed me off more than words can ever explain. I called in all the Platoon leaders and Platoon Sergeants and thanked them personally for doing an amazing job on this mission. I may have had shitty leadership, but I was going to be goddamned if my subordinates were going to get shitty leadership in return.

Chapter 25

Let's Not Kill the Enemy.

If I had any one particular sin while I was in the Army, it would be that I thought too much about what we did. I spent a lot of time in my own head thinking about the ramifications of what we were doing, what it really meant. I often asked myself if there was a better way to do the mission that we were currently doing or even if what we were doing mattered. I think it was good in the long term to ask these questions because, quite frankly, not a lot of people were asking them. Occasionally I would meet people who were very black-and-white in their decision-making. These were usually the people who thought they were doing the Lord's work here in Afghanistan. These were the people that would say *kill all of them* and meant it. This, of course, went against everything I was brought up to believe and I railed against this mentality. After a while though, I found their position to be a little bit enviable. For them, everything was distilled down to a binary choice of right and wrong. Ones or zeroes, yes or no, whereas I spent most of my time dealing with gray areas. If we gave blankets and food to this family would they help the Americans in the future or would those supplies wind up in the hands of the enemy? If we provided aid to this village will we have enough supplies for our Soldiers later? Do we allow the injured child onto the outpost because he's bleeding all over the place or do we let them die outside the gates because we don't have enough medical supplies? What if he's a suicide bomber? Do we do the mission, even if it makes no sense and is irresponsibly dangerous? I agonized over these decisions meanwhile, others put things in the *right* or *wrong* bin and moved on.

The one area where I didn't exercise a lot of deliberation was when dealing with the enemy. When I first got to Afghanistan, I wondered a few times at COP BBK if, when I had to kill someone, was it going to be justified. When I took someone's life was it going to keep them from harming or killing others? Was going to keep people safe if I took this one bad person out of the equation? By this point, I had given orders that resulted in the deaths of dozens of people and I didn't think about it deeply anymore. I had become more binary in my decisions about the enemy. Once identified, the enemy had one purpose to me; to be defeated. The real sticky part was identifying them. In fact the enemy was so evasive and hard to corner, that when we did have a rare opportunity to really put it to them, I relished it. It was such a cat and mouse game in the vineyards and valleys of Charkh that when we finally did get the upper hand and cornered the enemy, we did our best to grab them by the collar and hammer them in the face until they were dead.

This level of controlled aggression was not shared by Saber Command. Perhaps it was something having to do with the all the attention and scrutiny they received from Brigade during that 10 day rescue operation, but they had grown even more cautious than they were before. They did everything that they could to shut down any type of indirect fires mission, helicopter gun runs, you name it. This was all done under the pretense of limiting collateral damage. "Our maps show that proposed mortar strike target is within 500m of a civilian structure." I'd hear them say over the radio. Meanwhile I'd be on the ground looking at the area, and there would be nothing there. Just some mud brick walls or a fence would be enough for Command to call off the strike. They just didn't want to accept any risk, but it was okay for us to accept risk all day long. They were safe in their big FOB, far away from any of the real fighting.

There was one incident where our observation post to the north spotted an enemy. This observation post had been put in place after the rescue operation, as per Saber Command's orders, to observe the routes into and out of our district. We told them that it couldn't actually see down south, along the route, to where the enemy was emplacing IEDs. It really just looked up toward the North area of our sector where there was no real fighting. They ordered that the observation post stay in its current location anyway. After a day or so, I discovered that its true purpose was actually to act as a relay station where they could listen in to our radio traffic and bypass the mountains that surrounded our outpost. So our own observation post became an annoyance that we had to contend with. Another little big brother mechanism where they could look in see what we were doing at all times and, in addition to that, we had to keep it manned. We had to stretch our already strained manpower even more.

I was surprised and overjoyed whenever we positively

identified an enemy from the observation post one evening. This thing would actually do what it was supposed to and not just be a phone-tap into our radio network. Our scouts on top the observation post did their jobs very well and utilized an LRAS3 (Long Range Advanced Scout Surveillance System) to pinpoint the enemy location and they even positively identified weapons on these individuals at night with thermal imaging. All of this was relayed up to Saber Command and we requested to fire our own mortars at the enemy. This, of course, was shot down by Saber Command who said "…there were crops in the area that we could potentially damage." That's right, fucking *crops*. So there we were, watching helplessly as these enemy fighters excavated and moved weapons caches in the middle of a field and there was nothing we could do about it.

I wish I could say this was an isolated event, but the general attitude from Saber Command was, "Hey, let's let the enemy live." At one point while I was temporarily in command of the COP, we came under a pretty intense attack. It was the standard attack pattern. It originated from our south and west, with the enemy supporting fire elements at the fortress a few hundred feet south of our outpost. Heavy machine guns and RPGs opened up from the side and began hammering our southern wall. Cleverly, the Taliban used this to mask their newest weapon in their arsenal; an anti-aircraft gun. After a bit, we could tell that it was coming in from about a kilometer away and aimed at our vehicles and tents. They had acquired some new high explosive dual-purpose rounds and some incendiary rounds which left scorching holes in some of our MR AP vehicles. We weren't using the vehicles though. It was just irritating to watch them get shot up because it meant more paperwork for me and more risk for my Soldiers. I would have to annotate which vehicles had been blown up, which ones were currently on fire and which ones were riddled with holes. This meant we would be forced by Command to bring down a logistics patrol to replace these vehicles. The same thing would happen if we lost our Jaws of Life or our heat-ray. If someone, way up on the food chain, decided that we were going to have X, Y and Z equipment then, by God, we were going to move mountains to have it.

When this attack was over, I reported it up to Command like I had done countless times before. We weren't sure where the enemy was so there is no point in leading a counterattack into the vineyards at dusk. As I was wrapping everything up, the enemy did something that they had never done before. Instead of throwing their weapons down or hiding them, they congregated in an area several kilometers south of our location. This was an area where they had never gathered before and I was shocked to find them on the RAID camera. They were all crowded around a technical truck with an antiaircraft cannon on the back. There were about eight enemy fighters armed with RPGs, machine guns and other heavy weaponry milling about in this compound with no civilians in sight. They had gotten bold and I was going to make them pay. After doing some quick map work, I was able to get an eight digit grid location and found that they were out of the reach of my mortars. I needed artillery from Command. I called up to Saber Command and filled them in. Once again, because my fire request target was the middle of a compound, it was turned down. We had the opportunity to knock out at least eight fighters plus their heavy weaponry with just a word. All we had to do was launch a few artillery rounds and we could kill them right there, but Command wouldn't accept the risk. I spent the next hour or so trying to reason with anyone at Saber Command. I eventually got a hold of Sergeant First Class Moss, the former Platoon Sergeant from Anvil Troop, who had recently been promoted into the operations center at Saber Command. I begged and pleaded with him just to let us do our jobs and kill the enemy. I leveraged our friendship, our time together in Anvil Troop where we had pranked each other. Nothing worked. It was like talking to a brick wall and our time together in Anvil Troop felt like a lifetime ago. Defeated, I sat there and watched those fighters mill about for a few minutes more. Eventually, they hid their weapons and melted back into the civilian population.

I stayed up the rest of that night in my bunk, staring at the ceiling and wondering what our purpose was over here. It clearly wasn't to kill the enemy; that much was certain. We weren't here to really help the Afghan people because we turned away most that needed our help. It just seemed like we were counting the days and doing busy work while we held a spot of land in Afghanistan.

Maybe that was it? Maybe that's all we were supposed to do? What if we were there simply because we were told to be there? Was it as simple as that? My mind went back to the shopkeeper in Baraki Barak that I'd spoken with at the beginning of the deployment. His question still squirmed around in my brain. *What are you doing here?* That was eight months ago and still I couldn't answer him.

Chapter 26

Accusations.

I never got used to having Commander Weaver out on leave, but I was becoming more comfortable commanding our Troop and the Outpost. When the Commander was here, I had spent too much time focusing on the endless administrative and logistical burdens of running a Troop and not enough time focusing on how to command one. This worked great when the Commander was here. He felt almost no logistical or administrative burden and was left to do what he did best, command. Now that he was gone, I felt I was learning a lot, perhaps too much, about command on the fly. Our PA was on leave too, so we had another PA sent out by Brigade to replace him. This replacement PA was a Major and deferred to me, a lowly First Lieutenant, in the same manner as Blue Platoon's leader, Captain Harper. It felt a little ludicrous, but I was the guy in charge somehow. Despite Saber Command holding back nearly all of our mortar, artillery and aircraft assets, we had been putting a dent into the Taliban. Our Platoons out on patrol were doing exceptionally well and our COP defenses against nearly all of the Taliban attacks had gone in our favor. I had been very aggressive with the enemy and I often received intelligence reports that the Taliban went so far as to abduct young boys from the villagers to replace their losses. "Good." I thought to myself. "Let them show the people of Charkh how shitty their little terrorist group is." When our human intelligence guy, BJ, would peer down from his informant notes at our nightly COP leadership meetings to let me know that the enemy was put on their heels, I got a feeling of pride and accomplishment that I hadn't felt in a while. I was doing something. I was making those sucker-punching, sneaky insurgent fighters pay for fucking with us. And they were paying steeply.

Like all the other times in my life, I should have immediately become suspicious when things felt good. My feeling of brief satisfaction came to an abrupt end one August morning while we were providing support for a counter IED route clearance package, or CIED RCP, for short. The RCP was here to do their monthly sweep of the route into and out of Charkh District. The RCP was a Brigade asset and they would travel all around the Brigade's huge battle-space constantly looking for IEDs. Today, it was Charkh's turn to get the IED sweep. The RCP came down the main road with all of their counter-IED and mine detection equipment while we provided a screen line of Soldiers. The CIED RCP were engineers by trade so they weren't dedicated fighters. To make matters worse, they had to monitor complex equipment to see if they were driving over IEDs or not. This kept them very preoccupied. One piece of equipment looked like a construction grader and it housed one solider. It was basically a giant x-ray machine that was focused on the ground below it. The Soldier would look down at the x-ray and would have to determine if the hazy image directly underneath him was a bomb or not. I was told that they had one of the highest mortality rates in the Army. With the RCP's attention almost entirely focused on not blowing the fuck up, it was easier for the Taliban to get close and attack. That's where we came in. We were there to cover alleys and other ambush hot-spots in an effort to give the RCP some breathing room. We also served as a quick reaction force just in case the RCP guys got swamped by the enemy.

One of the benefits of being near our outpost when doing this type of mission, was the coverage provided by our 60 and 120mm mortars. It had already become evident that our Command wasn't going to do a goddamn thing to help out in a firefight. All of that big artillery and those fighter jets back on the FOBs might as well have been on the moon for all the help they would provide. That being said, the 60 and 120mm mortars were the only show in town and thus were worth their weight in gold. All of this was going through my head when I heard the first shots fired. I could hear the muted cracks of rifle fire in the distance as I sipped my coffee in the control room. As per usual, this was most likely my eighth or ninth cup. It really became hard to tell.

The radio squawked to life, "This is Rook 4, we are taking fire!" The panic was dripping out of the radio amplifier.

I placed my cup on the table and rubbed my thumb and forefinger on my nose. "So this is how it's going to be." I thought to myself. They didn't even use any of the radio protocols for firefights. I had no idea what type of enemy it was, what direction they were attacking from, how many there were, if they rode dinosaurs or if they had plasma weaponry. I needed more info to make decisions than just *we gettin' shot at, boss.* "They're not fighters, Nick. They don't know how to report this stuff; help them through this." I heard myself thinking.

I picked up the headset and began speaking, "Hey Rook 4, this is Bulldog 5. I understand all, but I need a location to the enemy if I'm going to assist you."

It took a few moments, but from there I got a grid location of their unit and the attacking Taliban. They were further north than I expected. Our mortars could reach the enemy, but it would take time for our Platoons to reach them on foot. It took some more time, but I was able to pull out exactly what the enemy composition was. It seemed they were under attack by about four to six fighters, one of which had an RPG and the rest were packing small arms. It didn't sound like anything they couldn't handle, but the RPG made me worry a little bit. The last thing I needed was one of their vehicles knocked out on the main route. That meant a lengthy recovery operation wherein we had to provide a screening force and we would be out there for hours like sitting ducks.

Rook 4 became increasingly upset as the firefight dragged on, "We need fire support out here!"

What happened next surprised me. Rook 4 called for an immediate suppression fire mission. This was one of the only ones that I'd heard called during the entire deployment to Afghanistan. Immediate suppression is a type of emergency fire mission where there is no real back and forth between the requester and the person providing the fire support. They just give you a grid location and you have to fire on it in less than a few seconds. It's quick and effective, but can also be very dangerous. As a Scout, I understood this. Doctrinally, we were trained to operate far behind enemy lines. This often left us physically isolated and outnumbered in enemy territory. We were trained to rely heavily on artillery and aircraft support to remain undetected. A long range Scout patrol would only give up their location and fire upon the enemy when there was no other option. Stealth was one of our biggest assets and we did our best to maintain it by killing the enemy with other peoples' guns. As a result of our training, every Scout on COP Charkh was intimately familiar with immediate suppression fire missions and what they meant. Route Clearance Engineers were likely not as familiar with these fire missions or what they entailed and that worried me.

I broke protocol and read the grid back to Rook 4 to confirm. I was supposed to just fire upon that given grid location, but I had a bad feeling. I was worried, that with all the chaos, they had given me a grid that would put the mortar rounds right on top of their own heads. Rook 4 confirmed the fire mission grid location with me. I looked at the map and plotted the grid and, of course, it was within 100 meters of where they were.

I picked up the hand mic and spoke again to Rook 4, "That fire mission grid location is about 100 meters from where you're at right now. You are danger close. I need you to acknowledge."

"We need fire support now! Rook 4 screamed.

I read back the grid one more time and asked, "This is where you want our mortars to fire?"

The reply was immediate, "Fucking drop it now!"

This whole time the mortar Platoon, Ghostbusters Platoon, had been listening in on the radio conversation. GB Platoon was a phenomenal mortar Platoon. They already had their mortars laid on the grid with rounds hanging above the tubes, ready to go. I turned to Lucas, my Fire Support Officer, and gave the order to proceed with the fire mission. With a word from Lucas, the mortars had put rounds in the air. I waited and held my breath. I had broken protocol at least three times to slow this fire mission down and make it as safe as possible. I was not supposed to do that. This was an emergency fire support mission. The moment I heard *immediate suppression* come across the radio, I was supposed to have mortar rounds on the way within seconds; no questions asked. I still had a bad feeling about this one though, despite my caution.

A few moments later I could hear Rook Four yelling, "Cease-fire, cease-fire!" across the radio and a chill went up my spine.

I turned to Lucas ordered him to cease-fire. Rook Four continued, "The rounds are too close to us!"

My fear quickly hardened into anger. I knew immediately where this was going. They were going to accuse us of friendly fire and dropping mortar rounds directly on top of them. I began documenting all the paperwork and all of the transmissions that took place between myself and Rook Four. After the fighting calmed down, the counter IED Platoon was outside of our gate and ready to turn around. They were stone-silent on the radio. They hadn't sustained any casualties from the fight, but it was clear they believed we tried to kill them. I was even questioning whether or not it was our mortars that landed near them. Our patrols had reported that the Taliban in the area had acquired some mortars and were throwing them in the mix during a few of our most recent firefights. Hell with the way they were reacting over the radio, I began to doubt if the RCP guys knew what mortar impacts even looked like. It could've been the RPGs impacting near them. Regardless, I called in the mortars and Lucas and we went over what had just happened.

"There is no fucking way our rounds went anywhere other than where they told us to send them." the mortar Platoon Sergeant, Sergeant First Class Lin, said.

"I know, but you know what they're going to do, don't you? I liked this particular Platoon Sergeant. He was a sharp guy and a pleasure to work with. He also had no room for bullshit.

"I fucking know, Sir. They're going to say we dropped rounds on them. We've fired over a hundred fire missions thus far and all, *all*, of them have landed exactly where they were supposed to. You know that and I know that."

"I do." I confirmed. "So that's why I want you to go and make sure all of your shit is in order." "They're going to come inspect all of our stuff and try and put this on us. You know they fucking hate us at Squadron and Brigade doesn't know we exist, right?"

"Well that's no fucking secret, Sir." He smiled, "I'll get on the rest of that right now."

I turned to Rollins and he spoke without me prompting, "This is fucking incredible. You went out of your way to confirm with them. At least twice, I heard you confirm that's where they wanted those rounds dropped. I've worked with a lot of mortars and Ghostbusters are the best in the Brigade. There's no way those rounds went anywhere other than where we sent them."

"I know." I said, "If Squadron can find anything to sink us though, they will."

Within an hour, I received a phone call from LTC Dunn. "Nick," he began, "until I figure out what happened, all your mortars are shut down. You cannot fire any of them under any circumstances. Do you understand?"

"Roger that, Sir." I replied. I could already tell he was furious and this wasn't a conversation. I wasn't going to try to explain myself now. That's what guilty people did and I wasn't guilty. I knew there'd be a full investigation and I'd let all of our documentation and equipment do the talking.

When he slammed the phone down in my ear, it marked the beginning of a weeklong witch-hunt against us wherein Squadron and Brigade did everything that they could find us liable for a mortar round that fell near the Route Clearance Platoon. One of the gunners within the RCP Platoon was utilizing a helmet camera at the time and saw the impact of the mortar. It was explained to me that this mortar was caught on film and it had landed about 50 feet from his location. I was questioned thoroughly by Brigade and Squadron inspectors who flew down to our outpost. My most memorable interaction was with a Major from Brigade.

"Why did you drop mortars on our Soldiers?" came one of the first questions. He came out swinging with that question. It was a Nancy Grace-style accusation aimed at provoking an emotional response from me.

"I didn't drop mortars on our Soldiers. I responded to an immediate suppression fire mission." I said, not taking his bait. "Additionally, the Taliban in this area utilizes mortars against us. They been doing it for weeks. Maybe that's what was firing at the RCP Platoon? I can show you the intelligence reports."

"That's unlikely, Lieutenant." the inspector countered. "What we saw on film indicates that a mortar impacted near the RCP Platoon. The RCP Platoon was able to recover the tail fin from the mortar impact site. It was a US 60mm mortar tail fin. Care to explain that, *Lieutenant*?" And there it was; their smoking gun. Mortar tail fins were used to stabilize the mortar round, in flight, and often survived the round's impact. He folded his arms and looked me over, smugly.

I had done my homework though. "We've fired exactly four hundred and ninety three 60mm mortar rounds thus far in this deployment. Roughly ninety of those have been in the area where that RCP Platoon was. You probably can't walk a hundred feet out here *without* finding one of our mortar tail fins on the ground. They probably had four or five tail fins to choose from when they plucked it off the ground and brought it back to Brigade."

The inspector clearly didn't like my attitude. He was brought here to find out what happened and to be impartial about it, but I could tell that he wanted to sink me and I was making it hard for him. "What about the helmet cam? How can you explain that?" He asked.

"As I said before, the Taliban has been firing mortars at us for weeks now. They have 60mm mortar rounds, just like us. Two weeks ago, we were patrolling and found an improvised IED. It was three 60mm mortar rounds tied together. These rounds even had US Army lot numbers on them. We took pictures of it. Funny thing, too. When we ran those lot numbers, we discovered that those rounds weren't ours here at the COP. They had come from somewhere else within Brigade. Maybe they walked off of FOB Shank and found their way here? Maybe they---"

"We're not here talking about IEDs!" he interrupted, clearly pissed at my sideways accusation. "I want to know what happened and you're going to tell me." He leaned in and I repeated the same story over and over again.

While I was getting the shakedown, Ghostbusters Platoon received their own kind of inquisition. Theirs was a technical inspection wherein some Brigade level mortar chief came down and inspected every nut and bolt in the mortars' possession. They were trying to find some kind of technical flaw within the mortar equipment that would've accounted for one round to go right on top of the RCP Platoon. My Major and this other mortar inspector were finished and awaiting their helicopter back to Brigade HQ. Before the two Brigade inspectors could leave though, we came under attack from the Taliban. It was a particularly vicious mortar barrage. Fortunately we were able to get everyone into cover in time. About an hour later, our investigators were on their way. A few moments later, SFC Lin trotted up to me with a big grin on his face.

"Was your investigation as exciting as mine? He asked.

"Hardly," I said, "we just kept talking about the same thing. I felt like a broken record with that guy."

"Well," he said, "you'd be happy to know that we passed our inspection with flying colors." He paused to chuckle a little bit.

"What's so funny?"

"Whenever that mortar barrage came in, our investigator from Brigade nearly shit her pants. We rushed her into the bunker during the barrage and she was shaking and crying the whole time. She was still a sniveling wreck when we put her on the helicopter out of here. It was hilarious."

I laughed, "Well, I guess not everyone can handle the Shark Tank."

Chapter 27

Children, Bombs and Shitters.

The following days ground by slowly. We hadn't heard back from Squadron or Brigade about their findings so our mortars were still shut off and the eye of suspicion was still fixed upon our entire Troop. I was doing the best I could, managing one crisis to the next and attempting to maintain the ridiculous patrol schedule Saber Command had forced down my throat.

One morning I was awoken by Jesse, one of the interpreters, banging on my door. "Sir," he said "there's something you need to know about."

I held the door open, "There's a lot of things I need to know about, Jesse. Can it wait?" I asked.

The look on his face made it clear that this was something very important. By this point in the deployment, I just slept in my uniform with my boots on. I was ready in seconds and walked outside to see what was going on. The sun had just come up and, within moments, I discovered that some of our Afghan National Army counterparts on the outpost had found an IED. What's more, is they had found it just outside the outpost. It was in the schoolyard, just a few hundred feet away from our side gate. Apparently the Taliban had bribed, threatened or coerced some poor boy into taking a backpack full of explosives into the school bathroom which was located in the schoolyard, separate from the school itself. From what I could piece together, it seemed as though the Taliban were targeting our ANA Soldiers as no one other than our ANA Soldiers and the school children used those bathrooms. Apparently their plan was to kill a few of our ANA Soldiers when they used the facilities. It would've worked too, but the bombs didn't go off like they were supposed to. Instead, one very lucky ANA Soldier went to go take a morning piss, looked around the corner and saw an improvised IED protruding from a child-sized backpack and did what any sane person would do. He ran out, dick in hand, screaming *bomb, bomb!*

When I had gotten the full story, I realized that I had to respond by the book to this one. I had to call EOD to come out here and take care of it. Any kind of EOD, explosive ordnance disposal, mission was an hours-long ordeal. There were only a handful of people within theater that were technically qualified to deal with explosive ordnance. If you actually called up an EOD report, you had to be ready to spend the next several hours of life where you were, sitting on your hands. In most combat operations, what we would do if we saw explosive ordnance, be it an IED, undetonated RPGs or whatever, is we would just shoot it, report up an IED detonation and keep on going. It was ten times faster. We would do this so we wouldn't have to stick around and wait for hours on end for the Army to take care of it properly. In this instance though, I didn't have such a luxury. The IED was crammed inside of a small structure and any attempt to move it may blow up anyone who touched it not to mention it could endanger the children that were there in school, just a few dozen feet away. In short, it was a bit of a sticky situation. I had to call this one in to Saber Command to get EOD on its way. There was no other reasonable way around it.

The initial report that I sent up was that the IED was placed outside of our perimeter, in the school bathroom facility. This, of course, mutated into *the Taliban got an IED onto Bulldog Troop's outpost, what a bunch of dirt bags.* I had to counter this rumor for months after the fact. The IED wasn't on the COP. It was outside of the perimeter. In the hours that we were waiting for the EOD team to show up, I took one of the Platoons and cordoned off the school. We wanted to keep the kids behind the walls of the school and away from the IED in case it went off unexpectedly. Even though these were children, I had seen bomb makers who were sixteen and, a few months ago, a child had thrown a hand grenade at Commander Weaver while he was on patrol. I knew what children were capable of over here. I also knew that the children themselves weren't the enemy. They were put in terrible situations and filled with fear and hate by people who wanted us dead. These people wouldn't think twice about using children to achieve that goal. More likely than not, a kid in that school had to drop off this backpack full of explosives because his parents were being held somewhere at gunpoint by the Taliban.

When the Air Force EOD team finally showed up, they used a small robot to drag the IED out of the bathroom and into middle of the courtyard where they had prepared a hole in which to detonate the improvised IED. They were very professional and safely detonated the ordnance and then that was that. Or so I thought.

"Get your men out there and search those kids. Find whoever carried those explosives." The order came from Saber Command across the radio.

It truly pained me to do this, but I had to. There was a slim chance that they were right and we could potentially trace this all the way back to the bomb-maker. I brought the children out into the courtyard and searched them all. We did a full body search and then we swiped their hands for bomb making residue. We did the entire school, several hundred students, in less than a couple of hours. We didn't come up with anything which was unsurprising because the child courier was likely not the bomb maker and therefore, wouldn't have residue on his hands. There was a good chance he wasn't even told what was in the backpack. We swept the entire school and came up with nothing. I questioned several of the faculty members and a lot of the children, but came up with nothing solid.

When everything was searched, I released the children and put everyone back to their normal duties. I went back to the command hut, compiled my reports and sent everything up to Saber Command. I thought about what happened that day for a while. When we were swabbing all the kids' hands, they seemed completely indifferent to what was happening. The expression on their faces read *well my life is this shitty. This might as well happen.* It was that resignation that really stabbed a knife in my heart. These were children who were exposed to nothing but violence and the threat of violence for most of their lives. There were a few, whenever they brought their hands up to get swabbed, who could only produce one limb. It was dusk and I decided to do a perimeter sweep with the RAID camera. Something caught my eye just across the street from our main gate. This was an empty lot where our Afghan workers often dumped a lot of our trash. I panned the camera over and saw some children moving about, holding some bits of Styrofoam that they'd pilfered out of the trash pile. They were playing with them. I zoomed the camera in and noticed that they'd shaped and whittled the Styrofoam down to look like weapons. One of the kids had gone so far as to make a mock RPG. He was even holding it over his shoulder. They were playing war and fortifying their trash fort. In their mock war though, they were pointing their weapons at our outpost. We were the bad guys.

Chapter 28

Democracy is Hard.

The hardest fighting I saw in the Army was September 18th, 2010; Afghan National Election Day. I should have known that day was going to go to absolute shit; all the signs had been there for the better part of a week. The general atmospherics in and around Combat Outpost Charkh had degenerated to the point where they gave off the pervasive *shit's going to go down* vibe. There were no civilians within eight hundred meters of our outpost; gone, zip, nil, nada. This was saying a lot since most Afghans in Charkh district lived on top of one another in a bid to get close to the rivers and streams and to maximize their agricultural space. Saber Command was getting nervous about the elections too. This was another big, high visibility operation and the brass would be putting them under the microscope. Saber Command, if anything, was being consistent with their behavior. As with previous large-scale operations, they got more and more jumpy as the start date approached. They re-analyzed and second-guessed every aspect of the operation, even some of the more granular components. Maybe they thought of themselves as being thorough, but it came across as jittery indecisiveness. At Saber Command's behest, I had to change my plan to guard the polling sites no less than five times in the weeks prior to Election Day.

That was a huge issue unto itself; the polling sites. Bulldog Troop was tasked with covering three of these things and they were determined by a 3rd party non-governmental organization based on population metrics that were gathered three years ago. In a nice, air conditioned office where someone wasn't actively trying to kill them every day, someone concluded that Charkh's polling sites would be placed in the most populated areas; thereby increasing the number of voter turnout. This would be completely logical in an area where the general populace didn't despise the Americans and their Afghan puppet government. The idea didn't hold as much water here though. By having our polling sites placed in the middle of the population centers within Charkh, it forced me to stretch my forces between three separate hives of enemy activity. To help put this into perspective, the map of Charkh, when charting friendly versus enemy territory, basically looked like a dot of safe happy "green zone" around the outpost as far as our guard towers could see and then an entire district of angry red bad guy territory everywhere else. At times, it felt like every man, woman, child, dog and fucking rock was itching to kill us.

Suffice it to say that I was not pleased when I had to devise a plan that would cover three separate polling sites. I begged and pleaded with Saber Command and, in a moment of fleeting clarity, they allowed me to pare it down to two polling sites. One site was immediately south of our outpost and, although it was well into enemy territory, it was close enough that we could support it with our own mortars and reserves if need be. The other polling site was to the north where it could draw a direct line of sight to our mountain-top observation post. We would have some difficulty here, but if the situation up there went pear-shaped fast, we could call on help from our sister Troop to the north, Anvil Troop. It wasn't a perfect situation, but it was do-able.

In the week leading up to the operation, we continued to receive human intelligence, or HUMINT, reports from our informants that the Taliban were gearing up to hit us with everything they had. We all knew this was coming too. The general attitude of the civilians in and around the district was, "let's get the fuck away from these Americans. I don't want to get my shit blown up too." With absolutely no civilians within a hefty radius around the outpost, it was eerily quiet and felt like the calm before the storm. I sent out a few patrols to try and sniff out any caches around the outpost. I was sure that the enemy would be stocking up and burying munitions in preparation for the massive attack they were planning. The patrols turned up nothing and I focused my attention to making sure that my Platoon leaders were ready for this operation. Harper, Woods, Lynch, Baker and I went over the plan several times to make sure that everything was in place. I was proud of our Platoon leaders. They did a real good job with this. I let them know straight up that we were in for a big fight on this one and that everybody was going to have to get in the scrap. They met the challenge head-on, with their usual enthusiasm and creativity; often offering up minor tweaks and suggestions.

The night before the operation, I received a call. I was seated in the command hut, compiling a supply report when the phone rang.

"Nick, this is Saber 6." There was no mistaking the voice of Lieutenant Colonel Dunn over the phone.

"Yes, Sir?" I inquired simply.

"I was looking over the plan for tomorrow and I wanted to make a slight change." He began, "We're going to have to take three of your Platoons and move them to Baraki Barak for tomorrow. They'll be under direct command from us for the duration of the operation."

I was floored. He was taking away all of my combat power. I couldn't do my mission now. He and his underlings had made several changes to the plan already, but this... this took the cake.

"Understood, Sir. Might I ask why?" I asked, trying to keep calm.

"Baraki Barak is going to have a lot more voters than Charkh. We need to cover those polling sites more than yours. The Anvil Troop Commander and I will be coordinating everything in Baraki Barak. We need your scout Platoons help give us the manpower we need to cover additional polling sites I want to open."

"Sir, I can only give you two of my Platoons and still have any hope of achieving my mission." I responded.

At the time, I had the Military Police Platoon was providing security for the outpost and half of White Platoon was on the northern observation post. The other half of White Platoon was going to help bolster the defenses on the COP.

"Bullshit." he started. "You have four combat Platoons out there, Nick and I need three of them."

"Sir, I've got three and a half Platoons and I need at least one and a half to defend this place tomorrow. We're going to get hit and we're going to get hit hard." I implored.

"Three and a half? Where the hell is half of one of your Platoons, Lieutenant?" He placed special emphasis on the word *Lieutenant*, like it left a bad taste in his mouth.

"Manning the OP that you ordered Sir." I replied.

"Oh, right." He had forgotten about the observation post that we'd been manning for weeks, against our will. "Well, keep the MPs and half of that Platoon and I'll take the other two. Is that understood, Lieutenant?" He asked.

"Clear, Sir." I replied. He wasn't even aware of how many Soldiers I had or where they were.

"Who are your full Platoons?" He inquired.

"That would be John and Bob. Blue and Red Platoons respectively, Sir." I responded.

"Get them on this line in half an hour. Captain Whitney will brief them. Also, we'll fly out about fifty Afghan National Army Soldiers to help you defend your outpost." He said.

I could feel a certain tone of generosity in his voice when he mentioned the ANA augmentation. He thought he was doing me a favor. Truth was, that five ANA Soldiers weren't worth one US Soldier. It took two of my Soldiers to handle each ANA Soldier; one to watch the ANA Soldier to make sure that he didn't do anything reckless or stupid and the other to actually be a Soldier. I was going to have fifty additional liabilities running around tomorrow. LTC Dunn would have known this if he had seen them in action.

"Understood Sir. Will we still be receiving any targets for fires or any air support?" I asked in a vain effort to retain any of the assets that had been promised to me previously.

"We'll be diverting those assets to the main effort up north in Baraki Barak. Plus, you still have your own organic 60mm mortar. I'm turning it back on for you." He replied.

"Understood, Sir."

"Saber 6 out." He concluded and the line went dead on his end.

   With that, I put the phone back on the receiver and shifted my thoughts to our probable deaths the following day. Would I be shot in the face? Would it be quick? Or would I get it in the gut and linger around for a bit?

"Jesus, that fucking sucks." It was Lucas. I hadn't noticed that he was seated next to me. He was staring ahead into the plywood wall of the command hut just as I was.

He turned to me in his beat-up, black swivel chair, "What do you want to do, Nick?"

I turned and faced the nearly albino radio operator, Piper, and said, "Piper, go run and get all of the Platoon leaders. They need to be here in ten minutes."

Piper nodded and donned his headlamp, jumping out from the command hut and into the darkness like some spindly ghost.

   All four Platoon leaders were in the command hut within a few minutes. They were all in different states of dress. They all had pen and paper and a look that let me know that they were ready to receive the nonsense I was about to vomit all over them. I gestured everyone over to the planning room on the opposite end of the command hut for some extra space. Each of the Platoon leaders took their places on the wall mounted benches surrounding the room. I placed both of my arms on the map table in the center of the room, looking over each person in the room before I spoke.

"Guys," I began, "we were just handed another shit sandwich and we're all going to have to take a bite."

I pointed to the phone in the adjacent room with Private Piper and the radios. "In twenty minutes, that phone is going to ring. It's going to be Saber Command's new pet, Captain Whitney. He's going to tell us the details of the new plan for tomorrow; namely how he's going to use you two." I pointed to Bob and John. "The gist is that you'll be in Anvil Troop's territory to the north."

The men looked shocked. I let it sink in for a moment before continuing, "You'll be working with Anvil Troop and Lieutenant Colonel Dunn to assist where the actual voting will be taking place, Baraki Barak. The rest of us will be defending here. There won't be any polling sites in Charkh that are defended by US forces."

"Fucking ridiculous." John said to no one in particular, as he angrily shifted his weight on the wooden bench seat.

"You need us here." Woods began, "How could they take us to another sector like this?"

"How are we going to defend this place with two Platoon now out of the equation? Without Platoons out in our sector, the Taliban are just going to focus on this place. They'll come right up to the fucking walls." Baker pointed out, leaning forward to the edge of the bench.

He was right. "Good points, all around." I replied, "We'll be defending this place with the MPs, headquarters and half of White Platoon, plus an additional fifty ANA Soldiers from Forward Operating Base Altimur."

"So that's what, fifty of us and over one hundred ANA fucks?" SFC Larson, Baker's Platoon Sergeant, asked.

"Fifty two of us and roughly one hundred ANA fucks and their 82mm mortar." Rollins interjected from his radio station.

"Oh, they brought a toy?" I asked. This was a new development.

"Yup. I just got word over the fires channel. Those extra ANA guys have their own mortar and they're being flown out here right now."

Rollins answered.

"Well, just make sure they don't shoot it straight up in the air. Otherwise, we'll welcome the additional firepower." I said. Everyone laughed nervously. After what we had seen from the ANA this past year, it wasn't entirely out of the question.

We spent the next several minutes going over the changes to the defensive preparations. The MPs would provide the majority of the manpower for the defenses with White Platoon running ammo to the walls and replacing any casualties. The ANA would help shore up the walls and the extra fifty would be placed in and around the old U-shaped school annex and the school itself since it had been vacant for days. The ANA's 82mm mortar would be set up in the school courtyard where it could direct fire into southwest where the bulk of the enemy would congregate. Those HQ Soldiers who didn't have a direct role would serve as ammo and casualty bearers for the MPs. Lucas and I would be working off of a skeleton crew in the command hut to maximize manpower on the defenses.

All in all, it was a fairly shitty plan, but it was all that we could do. We didn't have enough manpower to do anything but defend. With the ANA outnumbering US Soldiers two to one, command and control would have been near impossible during any type of maneuvering, especially a counter-attack. I shuddered at the thought of trying to rein the ANA in during the impending shit-storm that was to be tomorrow's battle. The phone rang, right on schedule, and Captain Whitney began briefing Bob and John on the plan for Baraki Barak. I listened in and tried my best to objectively see the bigger picture that Saber was seeing. It all came down to one extra polling site. John's Platoon would have the extra polling site in the south of Baraki Barak and Bob's Platoon would be doing mule work; running from polling site to polling site and generally helping out as needed. It was hard to not feel bitter about Saber's plan. Baraki Barak already had the majority of the Squadron's assets for the Election Day and now they were taking over half of my fighting force just to be sure about one more polling site tomorrow. I would have been fine with all of this if there wasn't the very real possibility that we could be overrun by the Taliban tomorrow.

"You guys got all that?" I asked John and Bob.

"We're good, Nick. We'll call you up on the way out." John said.

"Call us if you need us and we'll come down here. Fuck Saber." Woods chimed in.

"We'll be fine. Just focus on what you guys have got to do." I said with not a lot of conviction. With that, the two Platoon leaders left and began prepping their Platoons for their new missions up north.

I ran my dirty hands through my long, greasy hair. I turned to First Sergeant Steele, "We'll have stand-to at 0530."

"Better make it 0500 Sir. I don't like the way this one feels." He replied.

I nodded to him. He was absolutely right; nothing about this felt good at all.

"What about our resident ANA commander, Haled?" He asked. We had just come back from our helicopter mission toward the north of the valley the previous week. This was the mission where Haled had almost shot me and where Saber Command canceled my airstrike. I was doing my best not to remember it.

"Oh yeah, I almost forgot. Send somebody to let that useless fuck know that his Taliban cousins are going to try to kill us all tomorrow. If he wants to continue living so he can do whatever the fuck it is he does, he should put all his boys on the wall." I replied.

First Sergeant Steele smiled and grabbed his rifle and head lamp, "Well maybe not using those *exact* words, Sir."

Steele then set off to each of the Platoon areas to speak with the Platoon Sergeants. It was already 0200 and I decided I would try to get some sleep. I walked into my sleeping area, which was nothing more than a large closet sized-enclosure within the command hut. I shut the door and began cleaning my rifle and 9mm pistol. I had fired my pistol only once at the enemy during an attack a few weeks ago. It was not a very effective weapon, but there was a very slim chance I may have to use it tomorrow if things got bad enough. I ejected the magazine and checked the rounds inside. I had two hollow point rounds. I don't know where I got them from; they were just in the ammo holding area when I first took over as XO, so I kept them. I placed one of them as my third round. I figured that, if I had to draw my pistol, things were pretty bad and I'd be under a lot of pressure. I'd probably miss with my first and second rounds. The third would find its mark though and I wanted to make sure it killed who it hit. The final hollow point was put at the bottom of the magazine. That one was for me. We had all come to an unspoken agreement throughout the course of this deployment that we were not going to be captured alive. Go down fighting or sort yourself out; those were our options.

When I got in my cot, I fell into a completely dreamless sleep. I awoke with Zoomie, our Air Force satellite technician, banging on the sheet of plywood that served as my door. I hauled myself out of the cot and donned my armor. I had slept in my uniform with my boots again on so there was no need to change. I grabbed a wisp toothbrush and seated myself in front of the command console behind Zoomie. To my immediate left, Lucas was manning the radios that were directly connected to our mortar team. His command console was keyed in to all of the artillery and mortar fires chatter from our outpost and all surrounding outposts in the Brigade. To my right, Zoomie was seated behind the radio consoles, the four foot by four foot mIRC chat screen scrolled in front of him; a constant stream of data reports, statuses, queries and answers bubbled up from the bottom on the screen and rolled incessantly toward the top. Behind me, First Sergeant Steele was conversing with one of the Platoon Sergeants, putting the final touches on our defensive plan. The force protection Officer, Lieutenant Baker, was seated in front of the RAID camera console, scanning vigilantly out and around the outpost. It was already 0445 and the entire COP was up. All of my Soldiers knew the gravity of the situation. I honestly felt that this stand-to would have happened even if I hadn't given the order. I pounded a cup of black coffee and then began reading the mIRC chat on the big screen and scanning the area outside the COP with the RAID camera myself. I flipped the camera console between black-hot and white-hot infrared and found nothing but a couple of cats fucking in a field. I panned over to the ANA compound and found that they were, much to my surprise, mostly all awake and in position. The additional fifty ANA had set up right where I wanted in the school courtyard. They even had their eighty two millimeter mortar set up; self-preservation was one hell of a motivator, even for the ANA. I grabbed a radio hand mic and did a quick communications check with all ten of the guard towers. I then switched over to all the command channels and gave them all a check too. A quick scan of the FBCB2 feed to the left of Zoomie's console showed that most of Squadron's chess pieces were in position, or at least, getting there according to their little blue icons that lagged across the screen. Everything appeared to be in working order.

For the past several days we had received reports from a few informants that the Taliban were going to attack us *Apache* style. This meant, as far as we could tell, that they were going to strike at first light from the east with the sun at their backs. Large Taliban attacks usually involved the word Apache in an effort to scare us. This was really more of a curiosity to me as I couldn't figure out exactly why they picked the Apaches to be their avatar of fear. Maybe it was because they identified with the Apache resistance in the Wild West. Honestly, I was surprised they even knew who the Apaches are. For a faction that made non-religious reading illegal, the Taliban were surprisingly well-read on the subject. Too bad they didn't keep reading that chapter in American History where the Apache resistance was eventually and inevitably crushed like a walnut under a sledgehammer. They might've looked for a different way to scare us.

I didn't get to contemplate this for too long. At first light, tower five came across the radio with one word, "Incoming." I could hear the dull boom of enemy mortar rounds being fired in the distance. We had about eight seconds before they impacted the COP. Everyone in the command hut repeated the call for incoming and we all threw ourselves down onto the ground in the prone. The firm wooden floor of the command hut was not as yielding as open ground and my grenades and extra magazines pushed my body armor crushingly tight against my chest. I had to take shallow breaths while I awaited the impact of the enemy barrage. A few seconds later, six mortar rounds exploded around the COP. I think one or two impacted inside the outpost, but it was hard to tell. Then the small arms fire began; rattling and popping into and over the outpost. Heavy thuds sounded in-between the long coughs of automatic fire; most likely that DShK heavy machine gun that had eluded us the past few weeks. The thunderous boom of RPGs and recoilless rifles joined the din. All of our towers were cross-talking over the radio, attempting to pinpoint the origins of the enemy fire. I pushed myself up off the floor and looked around the command hut. Everyone was unhurt and all the systems appeared to still be functional.

Zoomie scrambled back into his chair and looked at me for a contact report to push up to Saber Command. Over the past few months, they had developed a hard-on for reporting. To what end, I wasn't sure. Their rigorous reporting structure served to do nothing but make the reports slower and more meticulous. They surely didn't speed up decisions or get us support assets any faster.

I began, "Zoomie, tell Saber we're under contact from small arms fire, mortars, rocket propelled grenades, recoilless rifle," another heavy thud sounded between the bursts of machine gun fire, "and at least one DShK. Unknown number of enemy, estimated twenty plus. More to follow."

It was too early to attempt to pull information from the towers or the Platoons on the wall; they were still trying to identify targets. Lieutenant Baker must have come to this realization too because he abruptly got up and left the command hut. The command hut door was open for a brief moment and I saw Lieutenant Baker sprinting toward the nearest guard tower. I grabbed the RAID camera command console and slewed the camera over to the east. About four hundred meters east of the COP, I could see two fighters blazing away with their AK-47s from an embankment. This was unusual because our local chapter of the Taliban preferred to attack us from the cover and concealment of the vineyards and orchards surrounding our outpost. Attacking from the open like this was just brazen. Lucas was seated next to me and saw the same thing. He grabbed his hand mic and started talking to our mortar team who, in turn, began to lay our mortar onto nearest target reference point to the enemy.

"Where do you have the tube laid right now?" I asked Lucas.

"Right here." He said as he pointed to a building in the top right frame of the RAID camera feed.

"Good," I replied, "Shift left fifty meters, add ten and then give me two high explosive, proximity fuse."

Lucas nodded curtly and relayed the fire command to the mortar team. Within seconds, I could hear our outgoing rounds. I watched the RAID camera feed, anticipating where the rounds would strike. The entire screen filled up with dust and smoke as the rounds impacted right on top of the enemy fighters. I had to pan out to see the explosion.

"Good hit" I said, "fire for effect."

Lucas nodded and relayed the message over his hand mic. More booms sounded outside the command hut as our mortar team launched more high explosive death at the enemy. Every time our mortar fired, dust was conjured up front he floor of the command hut. The small wooden building began to have a smoky haze to it. First Sergeant Steele propped the door open in an effort to let out some of the smoke and dust. The sound of the battle outside raged through the open door. I watched the screen for a few moments more, looking for any movement. If these motherfuckers were finally going to show themselves to me, I was going to make them pay in blood. Nothing happened for a few tense seconds and then a man peeked around the corner a few meters behind the now almost certainly dead fighters. He was surprisingly well fed for an Afghan and was chattering into a cell phone. I couldn't see any weapons on him, but I was almost positive that he was helping coordinate the attack. We hadn't seen any civilians in days; this guy was probably middle management in the Taliban organizational structure.

"Add 30 and give me two more." I said to Lucas.

Seconds later, two more thunderous booms from our mortar outside, more dust and dirt in the air of the command hut, more inky-black explosion impacts in the RAID camera feed. When the smoke cleared, I could see that mister Afghan cell phone was now twitching in the dirt.

"Guilty by association." I said to myself.

As much as I would have enjoyed to watch him continue to spasm and die, other matters drew my attention. The towers appeared to have finally pinpointed where the enemy fire was coming from; the answer was not good.

"X Ray this is Force-pro 6, every tower has major contact. We're talking four to six enemy per!" came the shouting of Lieutenant Baker over the radio.

I didn't need a mathematics degree to know that we were under attack from every direction by at least forty enemy fighters; and those were the ones we could see.

"Roger that Force-pro 6," I began, depressing the push to talk button on the hand mic, "Get these towers to suppress and destroy what they can and get me grid locations to what they need fires on!"

I didn't wait for his acknowledgement because more fighters had strayed in front of my RAID camera. I spotted three fighters in a loose formation, firing from a road embankment about two hundred meters east of the outpost. The heavy slap of one of our Mk-19 automatic grenade launchers resounded just outside of the command hut. Three seconds later, I watched the three fighters get shredded by a volley of forty millimeter high explosive rounds. We had added that Mk-19 emplacement a few days earlier. It was low and hard to spot from outside the outpost. I assumed that those particular Taliban fighters didn't get the memo on our defensive upgrade.

Lieutenant Baker began giving us the targets and fire requests from each tower. There were enough to keep our mortars very busy. The enemy fire was unrelenting. If anything, it had picked up. It seemed that they were throwing everything they had at us. Some Soldiers on the wall were reporting Taliban fighters just a few meters outside the walls. This was a full-on attack and if there was a breach in our walls, it was sure to be swiftly filled with Taliban fighters. Our mortar team fired non-stop, alternating between high explosive and white phosphorous rounds. They were using a technique wherein they would fire a white phosphorous round onto the enemy quickly followed by a high explosive round. The high explosive round would then scatter or spread the white-hot burning phosphorous in a wider area. We affectionately called this technique *shake and bake*.

The phone rang. I picked it up and heard the exasperated voice of Lieutenant Colonel Dunn on the other end. "Nick, what are you doing?!? I need you to get your goddamn mortars under control!!!" He shouted at me.

"Roger that, Sir" I began, "but we've got between forty and sixty enemy out here hitting us with everything they have."

"A lot of your fire missions have been near civilian structures. I don't want you hitting houses and killing civilians." He said.

I looked back onto the RAID camera feed and saw several Afghan houses smoking. In one building, fire licked out of the windows and into the air. Automatic weapons fire chattered and rattled in the background. "Sir, all of the civilians have left the area days ago. It's only us and the enemy out---"

He cut me off, "Get your goddamn mortars under control or I'm shutting them down!" and then slammed the phone in my ear.

It was ludicrous. Here he was, completely safe and away

from the fighting and he was the one losing his composure with me. Meanwhile, I was coordinating a defense against the fiercest enemy attack we'd seen so far. For a brief second, I wished my mortars could reach his position; just to put a few high explosive rounds right into his command hut at FOB Altimur. Saber Command hadn't been under any type of fire other than a few random rockets the entire year. At least then, those assholes would know what it was like to be on the shitty end of things. It was clear that he hadn't been reading any of my reports or listening to any of my assessments regarding the complete lack of civilians in and around the outpost. He appeared to be completely indifferent if we lived or died just as long as he didn't have to explain why there were dead Afghan civilians to Brigade.

"Shit, what should we do?" Asked Lucas as he held his hand mic away from his ear. He had heard enough of my conversation with Saber 6 to know that we were in a bind.

Just then, the ANA's eighty two millimeter mortar coughed out its first outgoing round. I panned the RAID camera over to our augment ANA. They were firing rounds out toward enemy concentrations in the southwest. It suddenly clicked; we could keep firing our mortars. While I was the XO, I had acted alone and fudged the books, squirreling away dozens of extra mortar rounds. These extra rounds were completely off the ammunition logs. As long as that ANA mortar was firing, we could keep firing our mortars and blame any collateral damage on the ANA. After all, they were firing indiscriminately into the valley anyway. As if to support my line of thinking, an eighty two millimeter white phosphorous round crashed down onto a mosque minaret, setting it ablaze. It was a dirty tactic, but it would work.

I looked at Lucas and said, "Keep the sixty millimeter rounds coming. Don't report them up and I'll take the heat if they find out." Lucas gave me a nod and went back to his radio.

After an hour or so into the battle, the enemy began to concentrate their forces into the fortress complex directly to the east of the outpost. The mud brick building had a distinctly medieval design and its multi-story fortified walls faced our own walls and towers. Its domineering silhouette earned it the moniker *fortress* early on in the deployment. Dozens of enemy fighters crowded into the fortress. Heavy DShK rounds poured from the fortress into our outpost. They were using incendiary rounds as some of our vehicles were covered in dark scorch marks and, in one area, some discarded tents had caught fire. Our own fifty caliber machine guns and automatic grenade launchers answered in kind, showering the fortress in hot, fragmenting steel. The enemy appeared undaunted and it looked like even our massed firepower would not dislodge them. We needed some extra help.

"Lucas," I began "We need some howitzers on the fortress. Get a fire mission spun up. I need those cannons firing on that fortress ASAP. Mark it danger close too. Commander's initials NAS."

"Roger that." Was Lucas's only reply as he turned back toward his radio station.

I was fairly confident that the fire mission was going to be stopped by Saber Command, but I wasn't going to be faulted for lack of trying of my part. I scanned the mIRC chat and saw that they hadn't communicated to anyone about our firefight; no additional assets were being prepped to assist us. I turned my attention to the FBCB2 to see where John and Bob were. It looked like John was toward the south of Baraki Barak, just north of our Charkh OP. Bob was stretched somewhere east to west along the middle of Baraki Barak. It looked like he was providing security for a longer convoy of vehicles. The thought of recalling them crossed my mind, but they were too far away to call them if I needed them. Outside, the explosions and gunfire maintained their tempo with no signs of abating. I had given my Soldiers permission to fire our man portable anti-tank rockets in hopes of dislodging the enemy from the fortress.

The battle raged on for hours. I had sent up several requests to Saber Command for artillery or gunship support, but it all fell on deaf ears so we continued to fight on our own. The ANA continued to fire mortar rounds indiscriminately into Charkh district, masking the more accurate fire of our own mortar. All of the towers had to be resupplied with ammunition at least twice. Every Soldier fired on the enemy that day. Both ammo containers were wide open and Soldiers were furiously resupplying the walls and towers. Eventually the RAID camera was taken out by enemy fire, reducing our mortar fire capability. It wasn't until dusk that the attack began to abate. Our machine gun towers had been perforated by countless enemy rounds and our Soldiers had expended several loads of ammunition. I put in a request for ammunition resupply to Saber Command just to keep up appearances. Over the past few months I had stocked the outpost with enough ammo to start World War Three and there was no danger of running out. I just didn't want Saber Command to become suspicious as to why I hadn't requested any additional munitions after I had expended over twice of what I was supposed to have on hand. Several buildings in Charkh District were on fire or had completely collapsed. Smoke was everywhere and the battle was in its last throes. I stepped outside the command hut and joined the Soldiers on the eastern wall. As I looked over the battlements, I could see the damage that the Taliban had inflicted on us. The Charkh district center had taken a few direct RPG or recoilless rifle hits, pulverizing several room on the upper floors. Several of our vehicles had been scorched and blackened by incendiary fire. Several smoking craters in the outpost told of the enemy mortar barrage. Each of our Soldiers looked haggard. Their faces were drawn and gaunt. They had been fighting for the better part of twelve hours. Miraculously, no one had suffered any major injuries. There were some minor shrapnel and grazing gunfire wounds, but nothing life threatening.

The enemy activity had finally calmed down to just a few snipers that were trying to pick us off. Their aim, although terrible, was enough to keep us occupied. Lucas and the mortars played a whack-a-mole game, trying to flush out the remaining snipers. The towers would relay the grid coordinates where they thought the sniper fire was originating from. The mortars would then shell the area and we would wait to see if the sniper fire would resume. For the first time all day, I finally felt like we could breathe a little. Suddenly, the phone rang. With all of the day's insanity, I was amazed that the phones hadn't been knocked out too. Sheepishly I picked up the phone.

"Nick, this is Saber 6." Lieutenant Colonel Dunn's voice came across the phone.

"Yes, Sir?" I asked. I had almost forgotten about the world outside of our outpost.

"I've got an Excalibur round loaded and ready to go. I need to know the exact location of that sniper and we can fire on him." He said.

"Sir" I said trying to hide my frustration "it's a sniper. If we knew where he was, we would have killed him already."

Excalibur was a single, super precise, artillery shell. It needed a pinpoint location in order to be fired. We had only a vague idea of where this sniper was so Saber was about as likely to get a precise location of this sniper as they were to get Jimmy Hoffa's last known location.

"You need to get your shit together, Lieutenant." again, the special emphasis on the word *Lieutenant* "and figure out where the enemy is!" With that he slammed the phone down in my ear.

I put the phone back on the receiver and started to laugh quietly to myself. I had run the entire emotional gamut now. I had been terrified, angry, furious and regretful in a span of just a few hours. I had depleted all of these emotional reserves and the only thing I had left was a little sliver of dark humor. Here we were; we had just fended off a twelve hour long, complex enemy attack with less than half of our normal force. All the odds were stacked against us and we not only held the outpost, but soundly defeated the enemy attack. We had suffered no serious casualties. It was a stunning victory by all accounts and Saber Command still thought we were a bunch of fuck ups. What's more is that Lieutenant Colonel Dunn had ignored all of my pleas for fire and support and had chosen, hours later, to give me a single super precise round that would have the overall tactical effect of a fart in a hurricane. It felt as if they were trying to kill us. They had taken away enough of my force the night before to keep me from conducting any type of counter-attack against the enemy. They gave me a bunch of extra ANA to babysit and they didn't even do anything about my ammunition request. Thank god I had spent months loading this outpost to the gills with extra ammo and weapons or we might have been overrun. In a way, I felt that Saber wanted some of us to die. After all, I had never heard of a combat unit in the Army receiving a valorous unit award without taking several KIAs. Maybe I was so paranoid and angry that I couldn't see the forest from the trees, but I knew in my heart that's what Dunn wanted. To put the pretty feather that was a valorous unit award in his hat and pad out his resume. Guys like him were always looking at that next step, that next career rung. The thought made me sick to my stomach.

That evening, all enemy activity had stopped. Due to our technological advantage with night-vision devices, we owned the night. The Taliban wouldn't dare fight us. They had made that mistake once a few months earlier. The Taliban, despite being a bunch of amateur level guerrilla fighters, were quick learners who seldom made the same mistake twice. I brought in all of my Platoon leaders and Platoon Sergeants. I told them that they were all heroes. This wasn't pandering, they were heroes that day. I told them what I saw and what they did. It truly was a monumental accomplishment. We finally compiled all of our ammunition expenditures and enemy kills. In total we had fired over one hundred twenty five mortar shells, the ANA had fired eighty mortar shells, each Soldier; both US and ANA, had expended about five magazines worth of rifle ammo, we had expended thousands of machine gun rounds and hundreds of grenades, dozens of rockets. We had broken or severely jammed two machine guns. By all estimates, we had killed or wounded roughly sixty enemy fighters and sent the survivors packing, tail between their legs.

I compiled all of this in a report and sent it up to Saber Command via mIRC chat. Saber Command was eager to see the statistics from each of their outposts. A few minutes after sending the report, the phone rang.

"Nick, this is Saber 5." It was Major Boyle, Lieutenant Colonel Dunn's XO and right hand man. "Colonel Dunn's busy right now, but I wanted to talk to you about your report that you just sent up."

"Yes Sir." I said, already anticipating the next comment.

"There's no way you guys killed sixty enemy fighters. It was probably more like twenty, tops. It sounds like you just let your Soldiers run amok all day. You need to refine this report and send it back up. I need it in the next ten minutes." He said.

I had never felt the urge to kill another human being as strongly as I did in that moment. Holding that phone, I envisioned pulping his skull between my two bare hands.

"Do you understand me, Lieutenant?" he asked.

"Y-yes Sir." I somehow mustered the composure to respond and then hung up the phone.

With that, I began re-typing the report. *Estimated enemy KIA: 20.* I hit send on the report and the Charkh Election Day Battle became nothing more than a foot-note; a small attack handled by a skeleton crew while the real mission took place elsewhere. No *thank you* no *good job* from Saber Command or Brigade Command ever came to me or my men. In the months and years that followed, no one from higher command ever spoke to me about that day ever again. It was like it wasn't real. For me and the Soldiers that experienced it, it most certainly was. The Soldiers there that day fought like lions and no one can ever take that away from them.

Chapter 29

You Need to Get After It.

Later that evening, I learned that Commander Weaver was on his way back to the COP. He'd gotten delayed at FOB Altimur, but would be here sometime tonight or early in the morning. I was overjoyed. It wasn't until then that I realized how tired I was. While I was only at it for about a month, I had been playing commander while still doing my job as XO and it had worn me down. I was probably averaging about three hours of sleep a day and, by the end of it, I felt like I had aged decades.

It was late and I was still up, compiling some of my logistics reports that I'd fallen behind on when the phone rang. It was Major Boyle again. I guess he felt like there was more he needed to say to me. Eventually, our conversation touched upon the strained relationship between Bulldog Troop and Saber Command.

"I hesitate every time you guys call for support on the net." He said, flat out.

I had to let the words sink in for a second. "Come again, Sir?" I heard myself ask.

"You guys always just cry wolf with stuff." Boyle stated, bluntly. "Every time you send a report up, it's exaggerated. Nobody up here believes the bullshit you're trying to spin." He added.

I did my best to hold my anger in check. "Sir," I began, "we're surrounded by enemy all the time out here. We constantly patrol and do our best to keep them pushed back, but they just keep hitting us once the patrols come back inside the COP."

"Bullshit. You guys just aren't getting after it. If you'd pursue the enemy while you were out on patrol instead of letting them get away after every firefight, maybe you wouldn't have to ask us for help cleaning up your mess."

And there it was. He had put it back on us again, somehow. He was actually implying that supporting us was not his job, nor the job of Saber Command in general. Moreover, he was implying that all the misery that we endured was due to some incompetency on our part. His solution though? To *get after it*. To basically do what we were doing, but only harder. I'm not sure which was worse; the idea that he was stupid enough to believe that this giant cluster-fuck of a valley could be pacified with some extra elbow grease or the idea that I was stupid enough to buy into his line of thinking. It was infuriating. If he had been in the room with me and not a dozen kilometers away, I would have emptied my pistol into his face. We were getting after it. We were putting the work in. Commander Weaver had already put in as much, if not more, time out in Charkh with the patrols than either of the other two Troop Commanders. We were constantly patrolling out in Charkh, doing our best to root out nests of enemy activity. We worked day and night, attempting to find weapons caches, to find enemy leaders, to do anything that kept the Taliban on the back foot and off of our front door on the COP. The dense vegetation, twisted urban terrain and hugely pro-Taliban populace ensured that our patrols in Charkh found little other than prepared enemy ambushes. After they had sprung their ambush and outpaced the pursuit of our heavily armed and armored Soldiers, the Taliban would simply hide and bide their time until we returned to the COP. Once there, they would hit us with everything they had. Going out there and patrolling harder with no additional personnel or assets was about as effective as trying to defeat a rainstorm by going outside and punching the rain into submission. Boyle's version of *getting after it* amounted to nothing more than pure lunacy.

"Roger that, Sir." I heard myself say automatically. I wasn't there anymore. I had checked out and I was watching myself in the third person.

"Good. We won't speak of this to anyone else then, Nick." He hung up the phone.

After the conversation was over I just sat there, numb. I was too tired to stay angry. I wasn't sure what to think. Was all of our difficulty down here just due to their perception of us? Did they really think that we were exaggerating what was happening down here? I thought about it more and more and came to the conclusion that it couldn't be the case. I wasn't crazy and what I was experiencing was real. There really was a fight down here. Other units had come into the valley and seen it for themselves.

As I sat there wondering about what had happened for the past few months in relation to Brigade and Squadron, I realized that we, in Bulldog Troop, were being targeted. It was the end of 2010 and the time for blowing shit up and dropping bombs everywhere in Afghanistan was over. There'd been a shuffle in the upper echelons of Army leadership and now General McChrystal was in charge. His *tactical directive* and a few other orders that he'd given explicitly implied that we were to win this war through hearts and minds. The years of blowing stuff up indiscriminately and fighting the enemy in open warfare were behind us. The Wild West was tame and now it was time to build. Overall this was a good strategy and it made perfect sense for this phase of the war in Afghanistan.

Charkh, however, was not ready for this. It was still an enemy stronghold and had to be treated as such. This was not an area that was ready for a hearts and minds campaign. It needed to be cleared of the enemy, with fire and sword first. We, Bulldog Troop, were there on the ground and we saw this. We recognized that we needed to fight and asked for the tools to do so. We never got them. Instead we were marginalized, minimized and sidelined at every opportunity by Saber Command. At first, I thought this had to do with some bad blood between Saber Command and Commander Weaver, but as time went on, I began to suspect there was more to it than that. It became clear while I was acting commander of the Troop that Saber Command didn't want to acknowledge that there was a real fight down here. I quickly got slapped back in line if I said or did anything to the contrary. Today's post-battle report that Boyle made me alter was proof of that. *Why* though? Why would they be afraid of acknowledging a major fight down here? And then it dawned on me. They *couldn't* admit that we were fighting. If they did, they would have to support us. If they supported us, that meant approving fire missions and airstrikes. It meant sending additional supplies, special equipment and reinforcements. It meant going against the grain and getting scrutiny.

Brigade would find out and they would ask questions.

Brigade would want to know why there was a heavy fight in this one area and nowhere else. Why, in the entire swathe of land that Saber covered, was this one small unit fighting and going *against* the directives put forth by General McChrystal? Saber Command wouldn't have a good answer for that. Brigade, of course, would not be interested in the backstory of Charkh being such a dangerous area, but rather they would want to know how Saber Command was going to fix it. That's where the rub came, they didn't know how to fix it. If our Squadron put all of its combat power in Charkh and we practically did during that 10 day search and rescue operation, it wouldn't do a damn thing. Charkh Valley, nearly forty five thousand people, was sympathetic to the enemy and no matter how we spun it or what we did, there needed to be an all-out war down here before we could do anything else. That would be too much work though, too much risk. Maybe it just wasn't possible to do even if the Officers above me wanted to really duke it out with the Taliban here in Charkh. I don't know if any of these thoughts or ideas ever went past Saber Command and were discussed at Brigade. Maybe they were, maybe they weren't. I do suspect that Saber Command thought about this, they discussed it and made a decision because their attitude toward and their treatment of us was uniform and coordinated. They had constructed a game, shared the rulebook amongst themselves and, by God, they were playing it well. That game was *hide the monkey*. If you can't see the monkey, then there is no monkey. If you hide the problem, then there is no problem. There wasn't an enormous enemy presence in Charkh Valley, just an unprofessional Troop that exaggerated its problems.

For the first time in months, I understood what was happening with the kind of clarity that brought everything into sobering focus. At that moment, understanding was the most unsettling thing I'd done in a long time.

Chapter 30

Gun Run.

When Commander Weaver came back, I explained everything I had uncovered to him. It took a couple of hours to recount everything that had happened and what it meant. He sat patiently and let me finish.

When I was all done, I asked him, "Well, what do you think about all this?"

"I know." He said simply.

"What, Sir?"

"I know all about this. I'm sorry you got to see it while I was away."

"Why didn't you tell me?" I asked.

"I thought it was because of me and my relationship with the SCO and XO. I didn't think they'd do it with you."

"Well, they're more fucked up and twisted than you give them credit for."

He laughed at that, "Again, Nick, I'm sorry you got to see that. I looked at it as my burden to bear and I've done my absolute best to shield you guys from it."

He was right. He did shield us from the worst of it. I wouldn't have put the puzzle together had I not been the acting commander. "I get it, Sir. I will admit though, knowing why all this is happening sure as shit doesn't make me feel better."

"You can see why I kept it to myself then, eh?'

"Yeah." I said. I was still processing all of it. It was a lot to take in over the course of just a few days.

"Let's keep it between us then. It's not going to help anyone and there sure as fuck isn't anything we can do about it." He said.

"Absolutely." I agreed, "It's only going to make shit worse if it becomes common knowledge."

"Yup." He said, "Well, we've got other things on our plate right now, XO. You'll be happy to know that we've got some visitors coming." He smiled a conspiratorial smile at me and I groaned.

I could count on one hand how many times anyone from Saber Command actually came down to our outpost throughout my time there. They were on their way though. The SCO and the CSM were both headed out to COP Charkh along with some of the leadership from the unit that would become our replacements in the coming months. The next morning, the SCO and CSM touched down on our HLZ with a handful of people wearing the new multi-cam camouflage uniforms. These people were the advance party of the 10th Mountain Regiment that was going to relieve us here in Afghanistan. These were the high-ranking Officers that would run the Battalion HQ that would eventually replace Saber Command. They arrived by helicopter and did a very brief tour of the COP before heading back up to the HLZ to wait for their pick-up. Their visit was bizarrely short and they barely spoke to us, but I was happy. The sooner they were off the COP, the happier I was. I tried my best to avoid them because, quite frankly, I didn't feel like dealing with their shit that day, but Commander Weaver wanted me to run up to the HLZ and relay a message to them while they waited for their helicopter.

We had been receiving harassing fire from the Taliban throughout the day and I think that's why the SCO was cutting his visit short. He seemed to have a natural aversion to combat. Previously when he would attempt to visit us by ground convoy, he would turn around and cancel his visit at the slightest hint of enemy opposition. This was no different, it seemed. He was just going to be fleeing in helicopter format instead of on a vehicle.

That day we had F-16s circling around Charkh Valley on standby. To me, they were just noise in with the background because, throughout our entire time here in Charkh, we couldn't get them to do anything other than *show of force* missions, wherein they would fly really low and pop flares over the enemy. This did very little in grand scheme of things. Since normally we were trying to get these planes to drop bombs and do gun-runs on targets they couldn't see, we had to request the close air support mission through Saber Command where it would be stopped cold. However, today was different. This particular F-16 pilot was able to positively ID one of the Taliban fighters blazing away at his aircraft entirely on his own. Not only was this Taliban fighter dumb enough to fire directly at an F-16, but he kept doing it. This, according to the rules of engagement for fighter pilots, allowed him to completely circumvent any and all of the usual channels he had to go through in order to fire. It basically amounted to self-defense where, if the pilot could ID the enemy engaging him, he was free to engage at his own discretion.

All of this was going through my head as I was walking up to LTC Dunn. He had just finished saying something to one of the 10th Mountain guys when this F-16 came around, low and slow, on an attack run. The SCO saw that I was smiling like a madman at something behind him and he turned around to see what it was. The F-16 screamed over the COP and opened up with its 20mm chain gun right over our heads. The tree-line southwest of the COP was ripped apart by high explosive shells. It was absolutely beautiful.

The SCO looked at me and his face had gone grey. I grinned at him like the Cheshire cat. In that brief moment, he *knew* that I was on to him. I knew that this F-16 engaging enemies on its own out here terrified him. He immediately brushed past me and ran down to the command hut.

I could hear the Soldiers cheering as the F-16 swung around for another pass. "Get some, motherfucker!" I heard myself yelling.

Chapter 31

Un-friendly Fire.

One of my toughest days at COP Charkh started fairly uneventfully. We had just received some small arms fire from the West. The towers couldn't get a good look in that area due to all the foliage. We sent out a patrol with the hopes of finding or at least flushing where the people harassing us. Blue Platoon was on force protection cycle and White Platoon was on QRF and refit so we sent out Red Platoon. I need to do a mortar ammunition count that day so I was up by the helipad counting mortar rounds at the time. I brought a radio with me along with all of my armor and weapons just in case something went down. We kept the ammo holding area away from the living areas and toward the edge of the outpost in case it got hit by a lucky enemy round. Over twenty thousand pounds worth of explosives would've left a sizable crater if it went up one day. This made practical sense, but it left me alone at the edge of the outpost every time I went to go check on the ammunition. It was unlikely, but I always brought my equipment with me in case I needed to fight. If it was a major enemy attack and I thought I was going to be overrun, I would fight back as many of them as I could and then throw a grenade into one of the ammo holding areas and go out in a blaze of glory. To me, this was just standard operating procedure. I, for one, didn't want to be on CNN getting my head chopped off. If it ever came down to it, we were going to make them kill us or we were going to take ourselves out. Being an Officer, I was no different and had to exemplify this mentality if I wanted my men to follow it as well.

I was contemplating all this when I heard a single shot rang out about half a kilometer away. By this time, the enemy that was shooting at us earlier had stopped a full thirty minutes ago. The fact that it was one round was a bit strange, especially since it sounded very much like one of our rifles. I waited for a moment or two for the next few shots but they never came. Instead my radio squawked to life and I could hear the towers talking back and forth, trying to raise Red Platoon. The first reports were hazy, but it became clear after a few moments what had happened. One of our medics had been shot. It was Doc Marsh with Red Platoon. One of our Soldiers had sprained his ankle and they were putting him on a stretcher. One of the ANA Soldiers was leaning over to help and his rifle went off, hitting Doc Marsh at point blank range, in a gap between his armor plates. Within moments, Red Platoon was at the rear gate carrying Doc Marsh on the stretcher. What followed was a blur. We got him to the aid station as quickly as we could. Doc Clayton and the other medics patched him up and stabilized him as best we could. When the medevac chopper came and whisked Doc Marsh away, we were all nervous.

I thought it was all over, but I was wrong. Not all of the danger had passed. When I came back from the aid station, I saw that Commander Weaver was furious. I hadn't seen him like this before. Weaver was with the ANA Soldier who had just accidentally shot our man. The ANA Commander, Haled, was there too and Weaver was shouting into both of their faces. His pistol was out and in his hand.

I ran up to Commander Weaver and starting speaking, "Boss, he's not worth it. Don't do it. These guys are fuck-ups and is totally their fault, but we're no better than the enemy if we just kill this guy."

Commander Weaver looked at me for a moment, processing what I said. I felt like the biggest hypocrite in the world. Two months ago, I was ready to kill an Afghan truck driver for something far less than this. That was an unarmed man who had done nothing wrong. Here Commander Weaver would've been at least partially justified in shooting this guy. Because of their constant negligence and inability to learn anything whatsoever, they'd shot one of our Soldiers and there was a chance he wasn't going to make it. The ANA were constantly fucking up, too. Just the other week, one of them shot himself in the foot because they were constantly placing their rifle barrels on top of their boots whenever they were standing around. A few weeks before that, one had gotten shot during a firefight and his comrades forgot about him for an hour. A few months before that, one had gotten the top of his head blown off by an IED because they refused to wear their helmets. It shouldn't have come as a surprise that they were going to do something like this. I guess we just made it so far without anything like this happening that we thought we were out of the woods.

It was Commander Weaver who spoke next. He was seething as he faced the ANA Soldier and Commander Haled, "You're lucky my XO is here. God help you if this shit happens again." With that, he holstered his pistol.

"Let's go." He said to me and we walked back inside the command hut.

After we had sent up all the reports and things calmed down, it was just Commander Weaver and I in the command hut. He was staring at no one in particular, just the wall really and said, "You know I wasn't going to shoot that guy, right XO?"

"I know." I said. "But I got scared because of something I did a few months ago."

"Really?" he asked. "What was that?"

"It's pretty fucking crazy." I said.

"Let's hear it then."

"During the resupply patrol after Butler got hit," Commander Weaver visibly tensed up whenever I said Butler's name, "we were trying to hurry and there was this Afghan driver that was holding everything up. He wouldn't move his truck the way I wanted so we started arguing. Before long, I was so angry that I was going to shoot him right then and there. Lieutenant Ritter just happened to walk up right at that moment. He saved that guy's life. Mine too, probably."

"Wow, really XO?" Commander Weaver asked me. "You're one of the most levelheaded guys out here."

"Yeah well we all have our breaking points, I guess." I said, "I just wanted to be absolutely sure you hadn't reached yours today.

He thought about this for a moment got up put his hand on my shoulder and said, "Good looking out, XO. I'm glad you're here with me." And in that moment I was so grateful to have such a good Commander.

Chapter 32

Close Calls.

The next day, we were under mortar attack from the Taliban. The towers announced incoming over the radios and we all took cover in the command hut. I dove to the ground... well, not really the ground. The wooden command hut building was about three feet above the ground. It felt absurd. The Taliban were using point detonation mortar ammunition; meaning, the rounds would strike the ground and then detonate. The elevated wooden floor would do very little to slow down let alone detonate the projectile. If one hit the command hut I was cowering in, it would explode right under me and laying down would probably make my injuries worse. Rotten egg smell filled the air. The Taliban must've been using some old mortar ammo for it to smell this bad. Another thunderous crash announced one more mortar impact. The lights dimmed, dust rattled, radios squawked and even more rotten egg smell filled the air.

That was the strongest memory of Afghanistan; the smells. Livestock smell, dirt smell, blood and offal smell were all smeared together like some awful olfactory finger painting. If God were here, he'd probably question why he made this corner of the world smell so bad. My nose burned and I hauled myself up. My armor was heavier than usual. The straps bit into my shoulders and I felt parts of my body creak that no twenty-six-year-old should feel. The radio was barking and bleating now. It was probably Saber Command shouting some nonsense at us again. Their default reaction to us being in combat was to panic despite the fact that they were a dozen kilometers away and in no immediate danger. Now that Commander Weaver was back, I was relishing the fact that I didn't have to deal with Saber by myself 24/7.

Captain Weaver was at the radio talking to the guard towers that initially radioed the incoming mortar fire warning. "Where the fuck did it come from tower five?" Weaver bellowed into a hand mic.

I grabbed my M4. It was then, of all the weird times that I could've thought about this, that I realized that I never gave it a woman's name like I was supposed to. I liked to call it my *shootin' iron* so I guess that counted for something. The name seemed old-fashioned and made me sound like a crazy prospector from the 1800s whenever I said it out loud. I did stuff like this a lot to keep myself entertained. A few months ago, when one of the desk phones in the command hut became damaged and began to sound like it was dying every time it rang, I kept it instead of throwing it out. I named it *Wheezy*.

I opened the door of our wooden hut to see how bad the damage was; *shootin' iron* in hand. I knew there were probably more mortars on the way, but they were like lightning strikes; loud, random and always unlikely to hit the same spot twice.

"Where the fuck are you going Nick?" Weaver had noticed the cracked door and his second in command all geared up and ready to go.

"I got to check the damage outside. We could have injured out there."

"Roger that." Captain Weaver said.

"What is your situation?" Saber Command shrilled out across the radio.

Captain Weaver and his command hut had its share of problems so I continued outside to see the damage. I swung the door fully open and the sun blinded me for a second. I guess I had spent more time inside the command hut today than I usually did. When my eyes adjusted, I saw Soldiers manning the walls and some were running to bunkers. Sergeants were shouting orders to the men... organized chaos. I looked around the command hut to search for the mortar impact sites. I didn't have to search for too long. Ugly black smoke coiled up from irregular wounds in the earth. I found the first one a few yards from the command hut. The mobile kitchen was peppered with shrapnel. A mortar shell had landed nearby and turned the olive green trailer into Swiss cheese.

This was typical Taliban behavior; destroying things that gave joy to others. In their own country, they had outlawed alcohol, most forms of education, kite flying, music and I think smiling was on the list before we invaded in 2001. I had been in Afghanistan ten months. That's ten months without alcohol, sex or any creature comforts to look forward to other than the meals that Private Lang made in this kitchen. Now those meals were most likely a thing of the past; the kitchen and all of its wonderful equipment had just been destroyed by a lucky shot from a 30 year old Cold War era mortar. No more eggs. No more hash browns. No more bacon. All destroyed by something as random as a lightning bolt.

Wait... the cook. Private Lang was probably in there. It was near lunch time. God, there was no sound. He should have been running out of the kitchen swearing up a storm by now. He was probably unconscious or worse.

I sprinted to what remained of the olive trailer and ripped what was left of the door open. Pots and pans littered the floor. Lang was nowhere in sight. Just smoke and more rotten egg gunpowder smell.

"Where the fuck is he?" I swore to no one in particular.

The next mortar round landed right next to me. I don't remember being thrown to the ground, but I came to a few minutes later with smoke swirling all around me. I rolled over onto my side and hacked and coughed up a thick gobbet of grey spittle. That awful sulfur smell surrounded me. I swore at all the gods of Olympus and probably created some new profanity. I could hear none of it unfortunately because my ears were ringing so loudly. I pushed myself up and half ran, half-staggered into a nearby bunker. Lieutenant Rollins came in crashing in after me. He took one look at me and pointed to my leg. He said something, but I had no idea what it was. I patted myself down and didn't feel anything out of place, but when I looked down my leg I noticed a red spot. I touched it and it was very sore, but it didn't feel like anything was broken nor was it bleeding too badly. Rounds kept crashing outside. Rollins made a motion to get up. We were halfway out of the bunker when another round detonated nearby. We sat back down in the bunker and waited it out. A few more rounds crashed onto the outpost after that. That was a total of about twelve to fifteen rounds. It was only a few minutes long, but it felt like the attack lasted forever.

When Lucas and I finally staggered out of the bunker, we saw smoke billowing up from all over the outpost. It seemed that about seven or eight rounds hit right in the center of the outpost. It was clear that they are aiming for the command hut or the mortar pit. My radio barked to life and someone said we had wounded all over the COP.

Just then SSGs Kramer and Ingram pulled up to a sliding stop in their Gator ATV. Ingram looked at me and asked, "Are you okay, XO?" he sounded like he was a mile away.

"I'm fine," I said, steadying myself against the bunker wall, "let's look for the wounded." and I hopped on the back of the Gator ATV.

That's when things started to get fuzzy for me. I didn't know it at the time, but my brain started to swell from the concussive force of the blast. An 82mm mortar round had impacted about ten feet from where I was standing and, for whatever reason, I wasn't dead. Maybe it was a defective round or maybe the low sandbag wall around the mobile kitchen unit had absorbed a lot of the shrapnel. Whatever it was, I was lucky that I wasn't torn to shreds by shrapnel. I did get a good bit of the blast though. I was knocked out for a few minutes and began to feel the effects. I must've blacked out with Kramer and Ingram because I came to in the aid station hut some time later. Several of our mortar-men from Ghostbusters had been hit along with several other guys from the line Platoons. I felt a little silly whenever the medics got to me and pulled out the piece of splintered rock that was sticking out of my leg. A lot of the other Soldiers were hurt a lot more than I was. To top it all off, I didn't see Private Lang anywhere. One of the injured Soldiers seated next to me told me that Lang was fine. I suddenly felt very silly for nearly getting killed trying to save somebody who wasn't even in danger.

After my leg was bandaged up, I went back to the command

hut where Commander Weaver was putting together the reports to Saber Command. He had already sent up the casualty reports and we'd gotten a couple of guys that needed further treatment medevaced off of the COP.

"I'm not feeling so hot." I said to Captain Weaver as I made my way toward my bunk.

"Yeah, you don't look too good XO. Are you okay?" He asked.

"Yeah I think so, my head is just hurting like crazy." My brain felt like it was trying to crawl out of my ears.

"Wait a minute, did you get hit?" Command Weaver asked.

"Kind of, I think. I got knocked out and I remember meeting up with Kramer and Ingram and the next thing I know I'm in the aid station."

"Holy shit," Commander Weaver grabbed the radio and spoke to the medics, "Get one of the medics in here."

A few seconds later Sergeant Edwards, one of our medics, trotted into the room. He started asking me all sorts of questions; about what happened, what day it was, if I could count backwards from 10, etc. All of these were memory-type questions geared at determining how bad my head was banged up. I remember not doing particularly well and I tried as hard as I could, but still got a low score. SGT Edwards recommended to the Commander that I be medically evacuated.

"Oh, no way. I'm not even hurt. I'm not getting on a helicopter." I said.

Well," Commander Weaver began, "if you're not going to take the ticket out of here, you're going to take the night off at least."

"That's a splendid idea." I said. I took two steps toward my bunk and then passed out, fully clothed and about three quarters inside the door.

Unfortunately, I didn't stay asleep. I spent most of the night nursing a splitting headache. Edwards had apparently tossed some pain killers into my bunk next to my unconscious body. I groped for them and stuffed a few into my mouth, but it didn't do much to stop the jackhammer inside my skull. Morning finally came and I was startled to hear the sounds of a helicopter coming towards our outpost. I thought my brain was still swelling, because this had to be a hallucination. Our HLZ had been shut down for months for anything other than medical evacuations and emergency landings. Our area was too hot to have regular helicopter traffic. Saber Command was worried about helicopters getting shot down in our backyard and rightly so. The last few medevac helicopters that had come to the COP left with a few extra aerodynamic holes.

I staggered out of my bunk and swung the RAID camera around to see a Russian model helicopter attempting to touch down on our HLZ. This was the same helicopter landing zone where I was nearly shot during every attack. It was also the same HLZ where the ammo containers were and now there was a helicopter parking on it. This was like painting a giant red target over everything for the Taliban. I knew this was going to end badly.

Fortunately, the Taliban weren't shooting at us yet. Maybe they were waiting for the helicopter to shut its engines off or maybe they were just as surprised as we were to see this helicopter appear from nowhere.

I jogged toward the HLZ and found SSG Kramer attempting to wave it off.

"GET THE FUCK OUT OF HERE!" He screamed. He bent over, scooped up a rock and winged it at the helicopter's fuselage like he was trying to scare off a big, stupid bird.

His attempts to ward off the helicopter didn't work and it landed, forcing both of us back, away from its rotors.

The pilot was gesturing for us to come over to him. We both

trotted over and began screaming at him to leave. We were frantically trying to tell him that he was in mortal danger and that he needed to go back wherever he came from. He said something back, but we couldn't understand him over the sound of the engine.

"WHAT?!?" I yelled over the din, attempting to tease out what he was saying. This was a horrible mistake on my part. He held up a finger in a gesture that said *wait a minute, friend. Let me take care of something so we can communicate better.* He then reached down and shut off the engine.

"NOOOO! What are you doing?!?" Kramer asked the pilot.

"What?" the pilot asked, his Russian accent thick and unmistakable, "Now we can hear each other."

"Cut your engines back on! CUT YOUR FUCKING ENGINES BACK ON!" I screamed in near panic. By cutting his engines off, he had just delayed his departure from our HLZ by minutes.

"What's wrong?" he asked, clearly startled by our reaction. "This is Shank, yes?"

"No! You're in Charkh, you stupid bastard!" Kramer replied.

Confusion and then fear filled this pilot's face when he realized what he had done and where he was. People knew about Charkh in a bad way. He had taken a wrong turn and instead of taking the family to Disney Land, wound up in Compton. I imagined when pilots, be they military or civilian contractor, came to this part of Afghanistan and were briefed on its different areas, they were shown a map. On this map, the word Charkh was crossed out and replaced with *Mordor* or *Here There be Dragons* or something similarly ominous. He had flown directly here, into the heart of the storm, and there was a chance that he might not make it out. He didn't get to contemplate that long because the Taliban, although fashionably late, began to attack.

"GET THE FUCK OUT OF HERE NOW!" Kramer screamed.

The pilot nodded and needed no further prompting. He frantically switched his engine back on and began the agonizingly slow start-up process. Kramer and I were unarmored and armed only with pistols so we ran to the concrete bunkers that lined the HLZ, leaving the pilot to his fate. Although we couldn't see, we could certainly hear everything. The Taliban was throwing everything they had at us in an attempt to knock out this helicopter. Our towers managed to keep the Taliban pinned down though and soon enough, the helicopter was on its way. Once it was clear to the Taliban that they weren't getting their prize, they packed it up for the day. Kramer and I emerged from the bunker and watched the little helicopter go over the horizon.

"Jesus. That was a close call." I said.

"Speaking of close calls, XO. How's the head feeling?" Kramer grinned, stretching the scars on his face.

Chapter 33

They've Seen Enough Blood Today.

With the business of the wayward helicopter out of the way, I was able to focus on my job. We had to get the inventory in order for the 10th Mountain guys that were taking over for us. I started working on the inventory again that night with Commander Weaver. My headaches were gone, but it was hard for me to focus on numbers. They just seemed to run together on the inventory pages. Serial number checks that would take just a few minutes were now taking me hours to complete. Commander Weaver saw this and was helping me. It was good having him back. I forgot what it was like before I had to take over. At best, I was a substitute teacher the barely held things together while he was away. At worst, I was a loose cannon who just made things worse here in Charkh.

The Taliban had finally dialed us in with their mortar. My lingering head problems attested to that, but I wasn't expecting them to mortar us as much as they did in the days that followed. The day after that initial mortar barrage, they tried it again. It seemed what they were going for was a counter battery of sorts because they hit our mortar pit, spot on. The barrage began in the morning. I had just walked down from the mortar pit and into the command hut when the first rounds fell. When the rounds stopped, I ran back up to see Ghostbusters Platoon, our mortars, bleeding on the ground. There was a small fire where some of the cheese charges (small booster charges for our mortar rounds) had gone off, but thank God, none of Ghostbusters' ammo stockpiles had exploded. That heavy egg smell was in the air again. Most of the mortar Soldiers were out of the mortar pit itself which led me to believe that they had been able to dive over the edges of it whenever the barrage came in. They were worried, just like me, that their ammo stockpile would go up. One of them had to go over the side directly into a pile of razor wire. He was all tangled there, moaning. The less injured ones were trying to help some of the others and I couldn't tell who is who anymore. They were all dirty and bloody in the smoke. Someone arrived with a stretcher and I remember running casualties back and forth to the medic hut and running back and doing it again. Each time we picked up someone new and put them on the stretcher, I got to see another one of my Soldiers that I couldn't protect. This whole thing was terrible. We were getting hit so much toward the end of the deployment. I couldn't help but think this was because of how hard I tried to pursue the enemy when I was in charge. It was the Taliban's turn and they were making me pay.

We had already started to receive some of the 10th Mountain replacements by this point. We had their Chaplain on site and we even had a new Air Force Sergeant that had replaced Zoomie the previous week. We simply called him *New Zoomie*. After we had gotten the medevac helicopters filled up with our wounded and sent them on our way, I made my way back to the command hut. I was dirty, tired and bloody. I was running the numbers in my head we only had one mortar Soldier left. That was it, an entire Platoon reduced to one man. We had so many guys hurt within headquarters Platoon that we could barely function anymore

First Sergeant Steele was there now too, recovering from wounds. He had gotten wounded during the attack yesterday. They told me he was still conscious when we loaded him up onto the MEDEVAC helicopter.

"Make sure they put my fucking eye-pro on my head! Tape those fuckers on! I don't want to lose them when they wheel my bloody ass in front of the Command Sergeant Major!!!" he'd screamed at us when he realized he was being evacuated to Brigade Headquarters and would likely encounter the CSM.

First Sergeant Steele was gone, the commander was still here, I was still here, Staff Sergeant Spears had left months ago for back surgery, but we still had Rollins. All but one of our mortars were gone. My maintenance section was all but gone, too. We had less than half of our headquarters Soldiers to include the Officers. The Platoons had fared better than HQ though. They spent a good part of their time out on patrol. Several of the Soldiers told me that they felt safer out there than on the COP. The numbers agreed with that sentiment.

The following day, we received a whole new mortar barrage. This one was kind enough to announce itself with a whistle beforehand though. One of the first incoming rounds must've been defective or had a bent tail fin because these things usually don't whistle before they hit like they do in movies. The rounds had landed just outside the command hut on the other side of the concrete barriers that surrounded us. I poked my head out and saw that New Zoomie was halfway under a vinyl and plastic trailer. He was bleeding pretty badly, but he was alive and conscious. Next to him, an unconscious Soldier was sprawled out in the open. He was unconscious or worse. I made my way over to New Zoomie and gestured for him to come to me. He was having none of it though. He was curled up in a ball screaming *no, no!* I kept trying to reason with him. He was sheltering under a vinyl and plastic building that offered no protection. I had to get him out from under there. Rounds were still impacting on the COP and I lost my patience. I reached under the trailer and grabbed his pant leg and started tugging him toward me. He let out a shriek and kicked my hand away. I got flat on the ground and saw that he had scurried toward the center of the trailer. He had gotten to where I couldn't reach him. He wasn't wearing armor and I was. I was too bulky to fit under the trailer.

I looked at him and yelled, "I don't have time for your shit, New Zoomie! Either follow me to the bunker or die here!"

New Zoomie starting edging toward me, "That's it! Keep coming!" I yelled.

Another mortar round landed a few dozen feet behind me. New Zoomie flinched and scurried back under the trailer. Disgusted, I got up and turned my attention to the unconscious Soldier. Staff Sergeant Ingram was there with me and we began to drag the Soldier toward the bunker. Ingram and I got him inside the bunker. We didn't recognize him though. He must've been one of the 10th Mountain guys. Ingram must've spotted another injured Soldier because he stood outside of the bunker for a moment. Right then, another mortar impacted on the opposite side of the bunker. Although Ingram was spared from the shrapnel, the concussive blast radiated through the barrier and knocked him off his feet. He was up immediately although wobbly and woozy and we had to pull him back into the bunker.

A few moments later, Kramer arrived with another injured Soldier. I wasn't sure who it was, but they were crowding over him and trying to apply pressure to badly bleeding wound. I was tending to my unconscious Soldier, but I had to keep an eye on Ingram. He was acting loopy and kept trying to wander out of the bunker during the attack. As the barrage let up, more medics made their way to our bunker. It was then that I discovered who Kramer had dragged into the bunker. It was the new Chaplain. He had been in Afghanistan for less than twenty four hours and already he was already seriously hurt. When I emerged from the bunker, one of the first people I saw was our Chaplain, Captain Lowe. I wasn't even aware that he was on the COP. It made sense though. If the incoming 10th Mountain Chaplain was here, that meant they were traveling together and Lowe was showing him around to the different outposts.

Everyone had a job when the fighting stopped. Medics, obviously, were busy dealing with the wounded. Sergeants and Officers were accounting for their men and sending reports up. Even I had to figure out what ammunition we expended and if there was a change to our logistical and material situation. Everyone was buzzing around with purpose. Not Chaplain Lowe though. He was slowly walking around the bunker and pouring water onto the ground. This was strange and I approached to find out what he was doing. When I got closer, I could see that he was rinsing the blood out of the gravel. He was going from one bloody puddle to the next, washing them away.

He must've felt me there, watching him. He stopped, turned to face me and spoke, "I'm doing it for the Soldiers. They've seen enough blood today. They don't need to see any more."

Chapter 34

The Road Home.

In the days that followed, we received a huge influx of 10th Mountain Soldiers. They were not ready for Charkh. Some of them were so fat they could barely walk from one end of the outpost to the other without breaking a sweat or becoming winded. Part of this was due to the elevation change from the US to here, but a large part of it was just purely being fat and out of shape. They were confident about Charkh though. They seemed to think that they were going to turn this place around once we were gone. *We'll fix what you guys couldn't.* Their Commander, Commander Weaver's replacement, was equally arrogant. I don't remember his name, but I do remember him mouthing off to Commander Weaver and I one evening when we were going over the enemy situation here in Charkh Valley.

"We'll show these Taliban guys what Infantrymen can do." He said.

I couldn't hold my tongue any longer and said, "Their bullets aren't going to care what your job title is." The new commander bristled up at this and was about to lay into me when other Commander Weaver intervened and explained that I'd been through a lot these past few days. I was quietly excused.

Whenever a new unit comes in to replace an existing unit in a combat zone, they do this thing called left-seat/ right-seat rides. The idea is the incoming unit gets to shadow the outgoing unit and, after one week, this role is reversed a little bit. The outgoing unit then stays on in an advisory role for another week and follows the new unit around, helping them out as needed. This is a two week transition and it's done at most levels. The combat Platoons do it and I had to do it on a logistics level. The XO that was going to replace me was there at the COP as well. I don't member anything special about him other than the fact that he seemed overly eager to please his command and didn't really seem to understand that you needed to be a criminal to survive as an XO here. I tried to let him know that there was a certain way to get things done and you had to stockpile munitions and food if you're going to survive out here. He didn't seem to understand. He was very straight-edge with everything and I knew this would cause problems for him down the road. This became blatantly obvious to me whenever they ran out of food within a month. I kept telling him that his Soldiers were burning through our food supplies and that he needed to over-order if he was going to keep up with or get ahead of consumption. He ignored me and each night, I would watch fat Soldiers stack their plates up with three Soldiers' worth of food. Sometimes they would get corrected and pare it back down to a two Soldier helping. I had stockpiled enough food for two months on that outpost and I couldn't believe what was happening. When they finally ran out of food, the XO approached me and asked for my advice. I think I said something along the lines of build a time machine, use it to go back a few weeks and listen to me in the first goddamn place.

The combat Platoons didn't have it any easier. What few of us remained at this point had to deal with these new guys out on patrol. They knew that Charkh saw the most combat and a lot of their Soldiers were keen to earn their Combat Infantryman Badges. In order to get these as Infantrymen, they had to return fire with the enemy. So any time there was one probing shot fired in their general direction, the entire formation would get down and fire everything they had at the enemy. It was ridiculous to watch. At one point, they left some of our guys out on patrol. We were at the second portion of our transition and we really only had a skeleton crew left. Most of our Soldiers had left in little groups via the resupply convoys. We only had a few key positions left to act as advisors to the new guys. Two of our men from White Platoon were out with one of the patrols and they just left them out there. The new guys had returned from their patrol and announced that they had everyone. It was only when one of our radio operators noticed that the personnel count was off, that we realized something was wrong. Commander Weaver and I were furious at this and sent them back out to recover our guys. After that, we had a heart to heart with the new Commander and his subordinate leaders. Leaving Soldiers outside the wire was a cardinal sin and losing accountability of people is a huge no-no in the Army even in *training*. In war, it's unforgivable. We told him that the shit was absolutely real out here and you had to take it seriously or it would kill you. We tried to give them every tidbit of information to help them, but they seemed set on doing it their own way. Long story short, they didn't want to listen to us. I and the rest of the Bulldog guys wished the new guys good luck and we washed our hands of the situation.

When my time came to leave combat outpost Charkh, I didn't really know how to feel. I was tired sure, but I was surprised to feel *sad* that I was leaving. As fucked up as it was, this was my home and I was turning my back on it. A lot of our work felt undone, too. I left so many projects half-finished. Now, I had passed the torch over to somebody else and they may turn around and scrap everything I was working on. We had been getting pounded daily by the Taliban those last few days in October. We had received random mortar fire throughout the year, but they really stepped it up toward the end. Those last few weeks were hell. We had more casualties during that time than we did during the entire deployment. Of our one hundred and forty Soldiers on the COP, over one hundred of them were wounded at some point during the deployment. Some were minor injuries, shrapnel peppering and concussions like me, but other Soldiers were in critical condition. Some Soldiers had lost limbs. I was leaving all of that now and I wasn't sure how I felt about it.

Whenever a unit leaves its outpost in Afghanistan, it does so in phases. The entire unit doesn't depart at the same time. Small groups of Soldiers filter their way off of the COPs and back to the larger FOBs and congregate there before moving on. We left COP Charkh in groups of six to eight. I was toward the beginning of the pack. With Commander Weaver back, he needed to make sure the incoming Commander got all the help he could. My responsibility fell back to the property side. Our property had been packed up a few weeks ago and I was charged with following it to its final destination. I left for Brigade HQ at FOB Shank, a place I'd only been to a couple of times throughout the entire deployment, and arrived with about eight or so other Soldiers. Soldiers transitioning into or out of Afghanistan traveled with only their rifles and one magazine of ammo. We arrived late one night and shuffled toward our temporary housing area. We all felt weird without all of our combat gear and ammo. I felt almost naked with just my rifle and one magazine. I'd gotten so used to walking around, fully kitted-out with body armor, grenades, and my helmet and sidearm that anything else felt *off.* I couldn't understand how anyone could walk around in a war zone with just a rifle and one thirty round magazine and a bunch of optimism.

I placed my gear on a cot after letting the other Soldiers pick the best seating areas in the tent. I tried to do little things like this all the time. It made no difference to me whatsoever what cot I slept on or where I stood in the chow line, but it meant a lot to these young Soldiers. Where he slept that night or how close he was to his buddy could mean the world. Soldiers were strange like that. When you took away nearly all their possessions and reduced it all down to a footlocker and what they had on their person, they placed value on things that would seem crazy to outsiders. No sooner than I got my bearings, then I was greeted by the smiling face of Lieutenant Woods. His arm was in a cast, but he seemed completely undeterred by that fact. He seemed generally happy and his million-dollar wound had gotten him out of Charkh a few days ahead of schedule. He got hit by an RPG. The blast had broken his arm while out on patrol about a week ago. We sent him off to FOB Shank to receive treatment where he sort of became the Bulldog Troop official greeter. And what a great one too; Woods was one of the few genuinely good Officers I had worked with. Not that he was a tactical genius or possessed insane heroism on the battlefield, he was just a good person who put his Soldiers first. Rare to come by over here.

When I eventually got my bearings around Shank, I began to have second thoughts about the whole armament issue out here. Nearly everyone walking around seemed as happy and peaceful as Hindu cows. This giant FOB was in the middle of nowhere. It wasn't part of the strategy to interface with the Afghan populace. No, this place was different. It was away from the populace because it was supposed to be safe. It's where the brass stayed. It's where plans were made and was also where reporters, journalists and the outside world come down from Kabul to get a feeling of the *real* Afghanistan. The only thing that could touch FOB Shank were a few poorly aimed rockets from the surrounding mountainside. These would impact about once a month or so and there really wasn't anything they could do about them. They were as random as lightning strikes and about as fatal. I'd only heard of one Soldier being killed by those rocket attacks throughout the entire year. I realized that this place was so far removed from what was actually happening that it didn't matter if the Soldiers here were armed to the teeth or not. The only enemy here was boredom. Although there were some real fighters here, the majority of people here were planners, logisticians, intelligence people, etc. Basically, they were the folks that were just as likely to shoot themselves in a firefight as the enemy. The decision not to hand out ammunition and grenades to everyone, although it didn't sit well with me at first, began to make more practical sense as I looked around in broad daylight and saw all the pristine, seldom-used rifles.

We were waiting for a helicopter ride out of Shank for days, but remained stranded. We eventually settled into a routine of three squares a day, hot showers, coffee shop and post-exchange privileges. Hot meals and clean laundry were a welcome change of pace, but I didn't know what to do with all the spare time. I decided to sleep as much as I could. The Soldiers that were there with me were exhausted so they really couldn't get up to much trouble at all. It was all the better because if they had wanted to burn Shank to the ground, I probably would've let them. Occasionally someone from Brigade HQ would poke his in the tent and do a quick head count to see how many of us were there. This was some Officer or Sergeant that was tasked with ensuring that people were filling up the transient tents in a sufficient number. This was done to ensure that enough of us were present to fill an aircraft on Shank's runway, should it arrive. This aircraft would in turn take us to Bagram Air Force base where we would get on a much larger aircraft and then fly out of Afghanistan entirely. The plan was that we were going to go to Kyrgyzstan and then back to Germany.

A couple of times rockets would screech overhead and impact somewhere on FOB Shank, but we really didn't care that much. If everything else hadn't killed us thus far, a random rocket wasn't going to seal our doom. We continued to wait for a ride out of Shank with nothing to do.

The hours passed into days and we eventually caught our ride off of Shank and into Bagram Air Force Base. Each bigger outpost had better creature comforts and amenities. I remember a full ice cream bar at Bagram Air Force Base. I also remember rows of computers and prepaid payphones and MWR facilities. It was crazy that thousands of people spent their entire deployments like this. We were the statistical outliers. We had fought tooth and nail just to get a few phones on our outposts so our Soldiers could call their families. I remember talking to my wife maybe once a month because of the tempo of my job and the long lines for the phones. If I had been deployed here at Bagram, it wouldn't have been like a deployment at all. There was free Wi-Fi, there was a Burger King, a library and even a coffee shop. Other than the occasional rocket strike or failed enemy infiltration, there wasn't much danger here at all. It felt like a college campus where everybody had rifles instead of backpacks.

We spent a few days at Bagram before my small group of Soldiers caught a flight to Manas, Kyrgyzstan. If Bagram Air Force Base was something to marvel at, then Manas was like the Taj Mahal. This place had every creature comfort imaginable. There was a small movie theater, long-distance phones with no waiting lines, restaurants and even a small, but very heavily monitored bar. We weren't allowed to have alcohol for obvious reasons, but the Soldiers that were stationed there Manas were allowed to have up to two beers a day. They were given a rations punch card and they could enjoy alcohol in reasonable quantities. I hated them so goddamn much. As a borderline alcoholic who had been denied alcohol for the better part of the year, I was ready to kill for a drink. By my reckoning, I had killed for that drink several times over. I was just waiting on the drinks to show up. Our command made it clear that we were not allowed to have alcohol yet so I had to wait a little longer. My time at Manas passed relatively uneventfully except for one run-in I had with a group of Marines that it just returned from Helmand Province. I wasn't sure what unit they were a part of, but they all carried the long M-16 muskets that were issued to Marine Corps frontline Troops.

I was walking with a small group of Soldiers to the laundry facility, when three Marines decided to make fun of our uniforms. "I wish my uniform had cute little badges on it, like that." The Marines chuckled at that. Because we were such a gigantic force, the Army decided that its Soldiers should display their badges, qualifications and identifiers on their uniforms nearly all the time in an attempt to differentiate its myriad Soldiers. The Marines, on the other hand, were disdainful of this practice and its members were mandated to adorn their uniforms with simply their names, rank and *US Marines*. The last part, according to the Marines, was enough to make up for any badges.

This guy had clearly not seen that I was an Officer and that he was about to have his face melted off though. I wheeled toward the Marines. They quickly realized their mistake when I pointed to the rank at the center of my chest and spoke. "Oh, cool little badges like this Officer rank? Or maybe you were talking about this Ranger tab here or the combat one? Perhaps it was this Parachutist badge or this Air Assault one? I've got so many, it's hard to keep track of them all, Marine."

"Sorry, Sir." The Marine who slung the comment was at parade rest, attempting to salvage the situation, but I continued anyway.

"I don't give a fuck what you are, motherfucker," I said. All three were stone-still as I continued, "I just spent a whole year, that's twice as long as one of your bullshit Marine deployments, watching my boys fight, kill and bleed on some godforsaken rock in one of the shittiest parts of Afghanistan. The last thing I need is a trio of limp-dick faggots making cute remarks."

He bristled at the word *faggots*. I could tell he wanted to hit me. God, I wanted him to. I wanted any excuse to rip his throat out. All the hate and anger and frustration that I'd felt for years, bubbled up to the surface.

He was deciding whether or not to stay at parade rest or take a swing at me when I leaned in to his ear and hissed, "Do it. Give me a reason. Give me a fucking reason."

I leaned back out and took stock of him. Discipline had won out and he was stuck in place at parade rest. His eyes were fixed straight ahead. It was obvious that he wasn't going to hit me. When I realized that he was saner than I was, I let him go, "Get the fuck out of my sight." With that, the three Marines trotted away.

Apart from that incident, the rest of my redeployment went pretty uneventfully. We eventually caught a flight to Frankfurt, Germany out of Manas. Somehow, none of the Soldiers lost or damaged any equipment, so my job was pretty easy. We touched down in Frankfurt and then piled onto some buses that began the trek back to our home base in Schweinfurt, Germany. These were the same buses that we took out of Schweinfurt a year ago. The driver even looked the same. I looked around the bus and noted all the empty seats. Stew was right all those months ago. There would be plenty of seats on the way back. The whole experience had a surreal quality to it. It all felt like just a complete dream.

When the bus pulled in to our home base at Conn Barracks in Schweinfurt, I didn't know what to think. We parked at the gym and we all filed out and were taken through the back entrance of the facility. I didn't know what was happening, but we were told to wear the cleanest uniforms that morning and we did as we were told. From what I could tell, we were going to see our families that night. I could hear an announcer speaking as I followed those in front of me into the gym. I could already hear the crowd on the other side. I thought it would just be a small setting and someone would say a few words behind a podium and release us to our families, but it was a much bigger production. I walked through a smoke machine and there were lighting effects like we were some goddamn high school football team. There were even home-made banners everywhere. They had no idea what the fuck we did over there. This was the closest thing they could liken it to; some weird parody of a pep rally. They wanted it to feel like we had just won the big game. It wasn't like that at all though. We had killed people. Innocent people died, children died, animals were torn apart and for what exactly? What the fuck did we do over there other than just survive? I'd tried to do what I thought was right over there, but so little of it made sense. I was so angry and I had so many questions. None of this felt *real*. All of this was running through my head whenever I got blindsided by my wife. She nearly knocked me over, she hugged me so hard. I hugged her back, but it was a reactionary gesture. She thought she was hugging the person that left her a year ago, but she was hugging someone else; a stranger. I was not that same person because the old me had died, half a world away.

Chapter 35

Seamless Transitions

It was obvious from the first night back that I wasn't the same. I was jumpy, hypervigilant; always looking over my shoulder. I didn't realize how bad it had become because it kept us alive for so long. It came out when I was in the car with my wife. I still didn't want to drive any more than I had to because cars were too open and things moved too fast. As we were rounding the corner to our house at night, I very briefly saw my German neighbor shoveling snow. It was dark outside and I couldn't see the person very well because they were wearing dark clothing. I just saw what looked like snow lifting up off the ground on its own power. I lurched across my passenger seat and grabbed the wheel, steering the car away from that side of the road. It was just automatic. I thought something was exploding. I'd almost put the car in the ditch and my wife looked at me and I thought, for a moment, she understood at least part of what happened to me.

The Army takes great pride in its reintegration program. The gist is that Soldiers returning from war are taken through a several weeks long process designed to reintegrate us back into society and earmark those that need further assistance. A good part of this is administrative; making sure that people's finances are in order, their children are back in school, etc. More recently though, there has been an increasing emphasis on psychological screening. They paired us up with counselors to ensure that when we went home, we didn't strangle our wives and children. Seeing as how we didn't have most of our equipment back from Afghanistan yet, there wasn't a lot for us to do. We did have our personal weapons because they traveled with us, but the rest of our stuff was floating over the Atlantic and wouldn't be back for a few more weeks. The only thing we could do, apart from catch up on administrative work, was brush up on our marksmanship at the range. I was there with my Soldiers and we were shooting little targets whenever I got the call to go and see my counselor. I had forgotten that I was actually scheduled to see the counselor because I'd spent so much time making sure that everyone else went. When I got to the medical facility, I was greeted by the counselor. She took me into her office which was filled with strange Alaskan and Native American pieces. Everything had that weird dream catcher vibe to it.

"What are your qualifications?" I asked.

"I'm a licensed counselor."

"So not a psychologist, then?"

"No, I have a Masters in counseling." She said.

I knew little bit about the distinction because my degree was in psychology and I knew that counselors were limited in the tests they could conduct and the treatments they could provide. She went down the standard battery of questions *have you thought about killing yourself? Do you think about hurting others?*

I paused at the last one and said, "Yeah, of course I think about hurting other people."

She looked a little troubled at that and I explained, "It's my job. My job is to hurt other people. I lead Soldiers and direct them to kill other human beings. Just a few minutes ago we were practicing marksmanship and shooting at little pieces of paper. Do you know what shapes were on these little pieces of paper?"

She said, "I'm not sure."

"Little human shapes," I said. "They're shaped like people."

A few weeks later, we were all brought into a big auditorium for the culmination of our reintegration training. About half of the Squadron's Soldiers were seated at different tables within the ballroom and I took my seat with a few Soldiers from Bulldog Troop. One of the counselors that I'd recognized from our initial check-in led the event. She passed the microphone to a spokesperson at each table and then asked a lot of probing and open-ended questions. The exercise was designed to let us blow off steam and work through some of our problems about Afghanistan. I was angry and I didn't feel like doing the exercise. The previous tables were led down a talk track of *what would you do if you could do anything?* Type questions that were designed to let Soldiers vent. The previous table had said something along the lines of *win the lottery*. When she came to my table, she immediately homed in on me. She waved the microphone in my face and I politely tried to refuse. She shoved the mic into my chest and I thought to myself *OK bitch, you asked for this.*

She fielded her first question, "If you could have anything that you wanted, what would it be?"

"To go home tonight to a house filled with billions of dollars." I said. Why win the lottery when you can skip the middle-man altogether?

She asked, "And what then?"

"I would take all the money and spend it."

"On what?"

"I would build a giant wall around Afghanistan." I responded. Some of the Soldiers that knew me chuckled at this.

"Ok," she said, "and then what would you do?"

"I would build a pipeline from China to Afghanistan."

"Really? And then what will that do?"

"I would pump all of China's sewage into Afghanistan and drown them in shit." The entire room erupted in laughter at this.

She waited for things to quiet down, her face serious. She did her best to look composed as she continued with the exercise and asked, "And then what?"

"Well is everyone in Afghanistan drowned at this point?" I asked.

She looked disgusted at the question and said, "Yes, I would assume so."

"Well then," I said, "I guess I would have a Coke." The entire room was howling with laughter. The entire room, that is, except for one very angry counselor.

It wasn't all fun and games though. Our unit was having a hard time readjusting to life back home. There wasn't a lot for us to do that winter in Germany. Our unit had a rash of suicides and alcohol-related events. Domestic events also spiked. We had only officially lost one Soldier in combat, but it seemed that Afghanistan was still somehow claiming our boys. I wasn't immune either. Without any property to take care of, I spent a lot of time brooding and replaying events in my head. I thought about the events surrounding the Election Day, the 10 day rescue operation and all the times we let the enemy go. I thought about all the times we were denied assets, whenever my F-16s are pulled away. I thought about all the unnecessary danger Saber Command put us in. I couldn't help but feel that there was some level of traceable criminal neglect there. It was one thing to fight an enemy in combat. We expected that. It was another thing to feel like you were fighting your own command. That was another thing, entirely. This wasn't what units were supposed to experience while deployed, was it?

I developed an unhealthy focus on our SCO and XO. I felt that they were primarily responsible for what happened to all of us at Charkh. I knew that there were others within their circle that had a hand in it, but these two were the ringleaders. The irrational and negative opinion of our Troop within the Squadron made me suspect that this was something that was cultivated from the top-down. I remembered reading one intelligence report while I was still at Charkh and it surmised that a lot of the enemy activity in Charkh was due to our unwillingness to engage the enemy. This was put out in a morning intelligence report and was written by our own intelligence people who had never even been to our outpost or knew what it was like. They wrote what they were told to write. This was the story the rest of the Squadron was fed. Bulldog Troop could solve its problems if they would just *get after it*.

I knew other people were doing the work too, but I blamed Major Boyle and Lieutenant Colonel Dunn for producing and promoting such a toxic environment. I would spend hours a day fantasizing about the worst things that could happen to these two individuals. When I went home at night, I drank to escape my own thoughts. I was in a bad way and it was only a matter of time before something happened. That day never came though. Something happened that made everything clear to me. Our Brigade Commander, Colonel Bailey, was suddenly relieved of command in March. I had almost forgotten about the distant and cagey Colonel that had visited Charkh, all those months ago, until I saw his face plastered on the front page of *The Army Times* under a headline that read, *173rd Commander Disgraced*. The story was almost unbelievable. The commander of our Brigade was facing charges such as bigamy, embezzlement, conduct unbecoming of an Officer, to name a few. Apparently he had an illicit relationship with one of his Iraqi interpreter from a previous deployment back in 2005. He smuggled her into Europe and used his position and status as a Brigade Commander to protect her. He had even funneled money to his paramour's family. He also awarded the family contracts in Afghanistan. He maintained this secret relationship while he was married too; a huge no-no in the military. As a Colonel and commander of an entire Brigade of Soldiers, this kind of conduct was mind-blowing.

As the story about our Brigade Commander exploded all over the news, I began to understand more about what happened to us in Charkh. That night after the Election Day attack when I talked to Major Boyle, I had figured out that Saber Command was doing its best to keep the situation about Charkh quiet. Now I knew why. Saber Command couldn't take any of this up to the Brigade Commander. With all of his illicit activity, he wouldn't have cared or listened. He had his plate full covering his tracks and living his double-life. Worst case scenario, he would've made things even harder for our Squadron for being the squeaky wheel. Our Squadron leadership decided to keep that wheel quiet. There was no problem in Charkh and anybody who said otherwise was challenged, discredited and marginalized.

I realized that we were more victims of bad timing and circumstance than anything else. There wasn't some shadowy plot to get us. It was just incompetent people doing their best to hide a problem. It was a shitty, shitty situation and we were left with the bill. The discovery of all this left me feeling deflated. I couldn't prove any of this, but the pieces were all there. I just had to line them up to get the picture. I decided to get out of the Army in the months that followed. If there was any chance that I would be under leadership like that again in combat, I wanted no part of it.

In the years that followed, I was often asked about my time in the Army. For a while, I gave an ambivalent answer saying that it was the best and worst thing I ever did. I think I was still sorting through everything and trying to tease out meaning from a very murky and convoluted deployment. I tried to understand what our mission was and why we did what we did. I spent years trying to categorize everything I did into right or wrong and I found that very little fit into either bin. I wasted so much time trying to apply meaning to every little thing that happened; to assign purpose to every nuance of that deployment.

Going back and re-living all of this in order to write the book made some things clear. I think I knew early on at some level that things were not right and that we were getting the short end of things at Charkh. We were being sidelined and suppressed and I hated it. I wanted people to know what happened over there. I wanted our leaders to acknowledge what we went through. I spent so much time trying to fix this or just being angry that I didn't think of why it bothered me so much in the first place. If what happened in Charkh never got recognition, then the Soldiers that were there didn't get recognition. I couldn't have that. I wanted people to know what happened to these Soldiers and what they did. I hope that by telling my story I have, at least in part, told theirs. I saw some terrible, but also amazing things over there. I saw Soldiers that never gave up, that put others before themselves. And through it all, they rarely complained while I bitched all the time. These Soldiers were the real heroes. I was just some combat bureaucrat that will always be proud to have been there with them.

THE END.

68496206R00169

Made in the USA
Middletown, DE
16 September 2019